ENDORSEMENTS

What happens when we die? In *Near Death Experiences: 101 Short Stories That Will Help You Understand Heaven, Hell, and the Afterlife*, authors Randy Kay & Shaun Tabatt take a fresh and exciting approach to this age-old question. This book shares 101 detailed accounts from those who were at death's door—and lived to tell about it. With each turn of the page, you will find a treasure trove of insights about the afterlife that are informative, inspirational, and parallel biblical understandings. This is one superb book that you won't want to miss! *Near Death Experiences* is an outstanding book that is well-written, easy to read, and enthusiastically recommended.

JEFFREY LONG, MD
New York Times bestselling author of *Evidence of the Afterlife: The Science of Near-Death Experiences*, and *God and the Afterlife: The Groundbreaking New Evidence for God and Near-Death Experience*

Near Death Experiences: 101 Short Stories That Will Help You Understand Heaven, Hell, and the Afterlife by Randy Kay and Shaun Tabatt, chronicles amazing stories of near-death experiences, which are intended to help you better understand Heaven, hell, and the afterlife. The basis of what we believe about life after death should always be based on the Bible—but books with stories like these encourage many people because they contain real-life accounts of those who ventured beyond the veil and came back to testify of it. I encourage you to read this book, garner what is helpful from it, and lay hold of, with fresh faith, what the Bible says about Heaven, hell, and the afterlife.

RICK RENNER
Pastor, author, and broadcaster
Moscow, Russia

Near Death Experiences by Randy Kay and Shaun Tabatt invites you to explore the mysteries of the after-life and dimensions of the supernatural. I found it very hard to put the book down when I started reading. Whether consciously aware or not, you have internal questions regarding experiences and events that take place following death and about the reality of the unseen world. With an open heart, read this book containing the life-transforming testimonies of those who have experienced glimpses of the afterlife and supernatural dimensions, and allow it to open up realms of realization, hope, faith, and anticipation. The read will most likely change the way you live your life here and now.

PATRICIA KING
Author, minister, media producer and host

I am indeed excited to heartily endorse *Near Death Experiences: 101 Short Stories That Will Help You Understand Heaven, Hell, and the Afterlife* by Randy Kay and Shaun Tabatt. Their categorization describing the experiences of those, including myself, who are intimately familiar with these events provides empirical knowledge and valuable insight. I have no doubt it will fill a void of information that has not been adequately addressed for far too long.

JIM WOODFORD
Author of *Heaven, An Unexpected Journey*

Near Death Experiences is brilliantly written and shines a light on the reality of life after death. Truths about Heaven, hell, and eternity become clearer with each page. Through exhaustive research, authors Shaun Tabatt and Randy Kay describe detailed accounts of numerous NDE survivors. Credible answers to valid questions depict what actually happens after life on Earth ceases.

My story as the only survivor of perhaps aviation's most ironic airplane crash is included. With my own NDE as a foundation, I find *Near Death Experiences* accurate, enjoyable, and profound. This excellent, in-depth book not only provides insight into how each of us can live a better life now but guides the reader in making quality choices to best prepare for the afterlife.

Capt. Dale Black
Author of *Visiting Heaven*, *Flight To Heaven*, and *Life, Cancer and God*

My friends Randy Kay and Shaun Tabatt have carefully interviewed, researched, and documented both the experience of death and the experience of living after death from a bunch of folks who got their lives back.

As a preacher and teacher of the Bible, I know anyone can argue against a position of theology and philosophy, but you can't argue against personal experience from authentic people. I believe all of these accounts to be truthful, but if only one of them is, it busts the entire paradigm of a non-biblical worldview. Imagine the power of 101 of these testimonies!

These near-death experiences are full of awe and wonder, hope, and victory. This book will help you keep your passion and move you to the very edge of a healthy dose of the fear of the Lord.

Troy Brewer
Author of *Redeeming Your Timeline*

Shaun Tabatt and Randy Kay were plunged into the afterlife and near-death space through personal experience, divine appointments, and a heavenly mandate. In their previous books and broadcasts, they've done an amazing job helping us grasp God's purposes for these types of encounters. With their new book, they're taking that help to another level by creating a framework of understanding for these supernatural experiences of the "beyond." In each of the short, easy-to-read, and gripping chapters, they give us a grid for the meaning and messages of what awaits each and every one of us when our days here on earth come to an end.

ROBERT HOTCHKIN
Author of *Realms of Power*

Randy and Shaun break supernatural near-death encounters into bite-size pieces that are easy to understand. This book will stimulate one's senses for more of God. Their inspired teachings will help awaken our spiritual senses to explore the spiritual realm's beauty and its mysteries. It chronicles testimonies of people who have experienced the outer rim of the spiritual realm, Heaven, and the many lessons that NDE individuals returned with.

RABBI FELIX HALPERN
Author of *A Rabbi's Journey to Heaven*

The thing I love most about Shaun is that he always searches for truth that makes us better.

KAMAL RAVIKANT
Author of *Love Yourself Like Your Life Depends on It*

Near Death Experiences is a book filled with actual personal experiences. Reading these will fire your imagination and fill you with hope. The bottom line: We were created to live with God forever. Life now is but a preparation for our destiny: Eternity in Paradise. God has revealed to some glimpses of Glory in order to change their lives and inspire hope in others. As a Catholic priest who has experienced the Glory to come, I heartily endorse this book!

FR. CEDRIC PISEGNA
Author of *Death: The Final Surrender*

In *Near Death Experiences* we read about the most exciting life-changing encounters that impacted these people's lives forever. The thread throughout is how God met and immersed them in His supernatural love and care. Some encounters open our eyes to see that the dark kingdom is also real. But, by and large, people came back with a message of hope and love. This book gives profound insight and understanding of the supernatural realm and will answer so many of your questions about Heaven, hell, and the afterlife. I just love how these people were able to convey their encounters in comprehensible language.

You will be deeply stirred by this timely message, and you will also have a personal hunger for more of God's love. We see in all these encounters that God is real, He deeply cares for us, and He will never leave us nor forsake us. I want to honor all these people who shared their treasures with the world and made themselves vulnerable to tell about the unknown—we truly appreciate you!

My own son had such an experience 19 years ago while in a coma, and in my deepest moment of pain, I cried out to God and He took me deep into His heart, where I was baptized with God's love.

To Randy Kay and Shaun Tabatt, thank you both for your unrelenting pursuit to bring the unknown and make it known to the world with such dignity and love. This book carries the flavor of Heaven—you will be changed forever.

RETAH MCPHERSON
New York Times bestselling author of *A Message from God*

Heaven is so full, it leaks! Heavenly encounters are real, and these true-life stories will make the glory land even more tangible and real to your heart! I was moved by reading how these powerful near-death experiences left a forever imprint on the lives of those who encountered life after death. Shaun Tabatt and Randy Kay have joined together to compile these previews of coming attractions for every believer in Jesus. You will find your heart on fire for more of God and more of Heaven as you read these accounts. Get ready, my friend, *Near Death Experiences: 101 Short Stories That Will Help You Understand Heaven, Hell, and the Afterlife* will change your life, your view of eternity, and how Heaven is more real than life itself! Make sure you buy an extra copy to give to a friend!

BRIAN SIMMONS
Passion & Fire Ministries
The Passion Translation Project

Shaun Tabatt and Randy Kay's *Near Death Experiences* is a must-read for anyone searching for answers and comfort in the face of death. This book is a powerful testament to the mercy, forgiveness, and salvation available through Jesus Christ. Through the extraordinary stories of those who have undergone near-death experiences, you'll discover a new perspective on life after death that will eradicate fear and give you peace.

DARREN STOTT
Author of *Pattern Interrupt* and *Carve*

Near Death Experiences is a welcome new publication by two of the best authors studying this incredible, but not uncommon event that is being shared among more and more of us humans every day. Tabbat and Kay have collected data from hundreds of NDE survivors and have investigated countless aspects of NDEs since Raymond Moody coined the term in the 70s. The authors have compiled information from many experiences, along with consistencies, in order to establish a communication standard within the near-death experiencer community. Regardless of which type of NDE one endures, as the number of journeys reported rises, the validity of each will increase directly in proportion. It seems prudent that, as with any scientific or behavioral study, a standardized language and vocabulary can only serve to improve the consistency and objectivity of the data collected. More importantly, an objective standard will help clarify the significance of NDEs, for the survivor as well as anyone looking for their relevance in the midst of the struggles all Christians endure along their journey in this fallen world.

MARK McDONOUGH, MD
Author of *Forged Through Fire: A Reconstructive Surgeon's Story of Survival, Faith, and Healing*

With prolific excellence, Randy Kay and Shaun Tabatt have composed *Near Death Experiences: 101 Short Stories That Will Help You Understand Heaven, Hell, and the Afterlife*, giving the reader a rare glimpse behind the veil into the afterlife. These authors have masterfully compiled real-life accounts that vividly describe what really happens when a person steps out of the earthly realm and into another.

This book is urgently needed for the times in which we live. Today we are constantly bombarded with the secular viewpoint of the supernatural, often mixed with New Age ideology. People desperately need to know the truth, and this book gives firsthand accounts of what the Bible describes. There is life after death! There is a world beyond! There is a place prepared!

The testimonies revealed within the pages of this book will minister hope, bring comfort, and challenge misconceptions regarding death. Every written line ultimately displays the love of our Creator and His great mercy extended toward us. Although each story is unique, they are woven together by the outcome of these life-changing encounters.

I pray that as you read this book, the love of Jesus shines through, Heaven becomes more real to you, and your relationship with God is strengthened. If you want to know if near-death experiences are true, this book is for you!

ANDREW TOWE
Lead pastor, Ramp Church Chattanooga
Author of *Breaking the Spirit of Delilah* and *The Triple Threat Anointing*

Randy and Shaun have done a fantastic job compiling near-death experiences to bring everlasting hope to all who have recently lost loved ones, are just curious, or may themselves face the inevitable. Each story reads like a headline and, while one story can be far-fetched, a hundred testimonies cannot be wrong!

JEFF OLIVER
Publications managing editor, MorningStar Ministries

From the beginning, Shaun Tabatt and Randy Kay have recognized the importance of breaking down the real-life stories that many have questions about concerning Heaven, hell, eternal life, and much more. *Near Death Experiences: 101 Short Stories That Will Help You Understand Heaven, Hell, and the Afterlife* is a phenomenal collection of real-life encounters from those who are Christian, non-believers, atheists, and much more. These real-life stories will challenge what you may think about life beyond this world, and yet each individual has a common reality of God's glory and goodness. This collection will leave you yearning for a deeper and more committed relationship with the Father. I am grateful for the hard work and dedication Shaun and Randy have spent with their research, conversations, and contemplation of genuinely powerful stories.

RYAN JOHNSON
Author of *How to Contend for Your Miracle*

Randy Kay and Shaun Tabatt have compiled a must-read book! It's filled with real-life supernatural stories that take the reader on a suspenseful journey into eternity. The afterlife is often surrounded by mystery and at times even fear. When you read this book, your eyes will open to see God's mighty power as well as the reality of the invisible world that some have experienced firsthand!

CHAZDON STRICKLAND
Author of *Supernatural Upgrade: Keys to Walking in the Glory Realm*

A book of this quality, research, and lasting impact is long overdue. Authors Randy Kay and Shaun Tabatt have done an amazing job capturing the essence and message of near-death experiences. As a long-time pastor, I've now ministered to more than a handful of people who have experienced this very phenomenon. But it's not just the experience that is, admittedly, fascinating…it's the stunning life-changing effects that are often manifested in these people. This book will inform, encourage, and inspire. It will keep you engrossed from first to last!

Pastor Carl Gallups
Amazon Top-60 bestselling author
carlgallups.com

Randy Kay never thought in a million years that he would leave his body, see Heaven, experience the love of Jesus, and then return to his body. Who could ever imagine such a thing? Yet, like a supernatural story straight out of the Bible, Randy has been helping common people like you and me process the afterlife and also what that revelation can do for us in this world. The hope of Heaven and the Father of love who is awaiting His kids to be with Him forever one day is raising up people like Randy in this final hour to give us a glimpse of what is to come. Randy has been faithful to stewarding an assignment that he did not see coming since his NDE.

For this book, Randy is teaming up with a man who has had the privilege to investigate on his own what can happen when we learn from other people's NDEs. Shaun Tabatt is not only a good friend to me but he is also someone who seeks God with his whole heart. Randy and Shaun are giving us a practical guide on how to process things that seem so out of the norm. However, as you read this book and get to know these authors, I believe you will find yourself getting more comfortable with the God who created all of this in the first place. I've often wondered why God is releasing so many NDE stories recently and I have come to the conclusion that it is to know Him more intimately (Eph. 1:17, John 17:3). I believe you will enjoy this practical book that helps us all process such mysterious things.

CHAD NORRIS
Senior pastor, The Garden Greenville

If there was ever a doubt about the reality that we are spirit beings with souls who live in bodies, that doubt should be permanently removed by the riveting encounters described in this book. Shaun Tabatt and Randy Kay once again give us a peak behind the veil into this supernatural spiritual dimension. This book is riveting and revelatory at the same time!

ISAAC PITRE
IPM Ministries
II Kings Global Network
Isaacpitre.org

For as long as I can remember, I've been fascinated by NDEs. So, you can imagine my excitement when my good friend, Shaun Tabatt, asked me to endorse his and Randy Kay's latest literary undertaking into this supernatural realm, only experienced by a divinely chosen few.

As a kid, I vividly remember watching *Beyond and Back* in an old, rundown movie theater in downtown Chicago. It was the first time I heard the acronym, NDE, originally coined by Dr. Raymond Moody in his best-selling book, *Life After Life*. In fact, my grandfather actually had an NDE in which he died and went to Heaven. The Lord graciously allowed him to come back. My grandfather later told me that death was most peaceful, and there was absolutely no pain! He also stated that he was no longer afraid to die.

In their new book, *Near Death Experiences: 101 Short Stories That Will Help You Understand Heaven, Hell, and the Afterlife*, you will procure a glimpse beyond the veil of this reality into one that feels familiar, yet is infinitely more real than any other that you've ever undergone. Here, the authors have generously compiled 101 real-life stories, from real people, not unlike yourself, that provide a compelling case for the existence of life after death. The authors bring clarity to terms, concepts, and phrases to help others to better understand them. I love how this book provides hope for any reader who may find themselves in a seemingly hopeless situation. To be honest, I would call it "A Book of Hope"! If you have ever lost someone, then this book may give you peace, comfort, and encouragement through the supernatural experiences of others. I highly recommend it!

JOHN VEAL

Author of *Supernaturally Prophetic, Supernaturally Delivered,* and *Racism: The Church and the Nation* (coauthor)

This profound collection of supernatural stories offers a unique glimpse into the mysteries of the afterlife. As you read through its pages, you'll be immersed in events that challenge your perspective and renew your faith in Christ. Though we should always make the Word of God our sole source of Truth, particularly in matters like these, the authors' method of analyzing these accounts points us back to the Bible, demonstrates the transforming power of faith, and reveals the amazing love that awaits us in Heaven.

ALAN DIDIO

Host of Encounter Today

Pastor, The Encounter Charlotte

Near-death experiences are controversial. They aren't mentioned in the Bible, so how do Christians process stories from people who claim they've seen beyond the veil that separates us from the afterlife? Randy Kay and Shaun Tabatt present a logical framework for understanding these supernatural events wisely tempered with caution to avoid basing our theology on individual stories or details that go beyond Scripture.

DEREK and SHARON GILBERT
Gilbert House Ministries
Co-authors of *Veneration* and *Giants, Gods & Dragons*

An amazing, rich collection of stories of God sweeping us into His Presence; stories of hope, wonder, and awe. I enjoyed it very much.

SCOTT L. SMITH
Author of *True Ghost Stories & Hauntings: Real Catholic Exorcisms* and the *Cajun Zombie Chronicles*

If you want to grasp a touch of Heaven on earth, this book is meant for your hands to open. Shaun and Randy have been able to miraculously bear the weight of near-death experiences and somehow translate and reflect them onto pages you can read. These testimonies all reflect a different angle of the crystal light of Father God, and by the time you read them all, you will find your own spirit growing even more into His image than before.

GABE POIROT
Author of *Built Different: 90 Days to Becoming all God Wants You to Be*

It seems to be wired into us to inquire about what exists beyond our life. What happens after we die? Is there an afterlife? If so, what is it like? In the sea of humanity who asks these existential questions, sprinkled among us are those who have taken a tour of the beyond. They are messengers among us: people who have glimpsed the beyond and lived to tell us the tale. Often, they are sent back to share what they have experienced. What are we to take from these experiences? What do they tell us as a whole? *Near Death Experiences* explores these questions by looking at a collection of these stories and offering a shared framework of what we can expect beyond our lives. As I read, I found myself encouraged, inspired, and filled with hope at the beautiful things Jesus has for us for all eternity!

PUTTY PUTMAN
Author of *Live Like Jesus* and *Kingdom Impact*

Death is the final frontier. The one place where we feel our science will never be able to see past, no matter how good it gets. So we're left with faith. Yet faith itself needn't be blind. In *Near Death Experiences*, Shaun Tabatt and Randy Kay have done an amazing job of applying a structured approach and a scientific methodology on a collection of near-death experiences from a cross-section of individuals that may give us a glimpse of, at the very least, the event horizon of death, if not what may possibly lie beyond it. Careful to not overstep the boundaries of their approach, both authors stress that they want to "…avoid building a theology around individual stories." At the same time, their methodical approach to the near-death experience has produced what is, arguably, one of the most powerful books on hope and the afterlife that I have read for a long time.

DAVID AMERLAND
Author of *The Sniper Mind* and *Intentional*

One of the greatest mysteries to man is what happens when we die. There is no question, we will die. However, what happens and what awaits us at the moment? Is it the end? Is there an eternal place we step into of rewards or torment? In the midst of biblical truth, Shaun Tabatt and Randy Kay bring us the experiences of people who have stepped over into that eternal realm and then came back to tell us. This book is intriguing and enlightening. Let it speak to you and prepare you for your day of death, but more than that, for the rest of your life here on earth.

Robert Henderson
Bestselling author of the *Courts of Heaven* series

Shaun and Randy have hit the bulls-eye. This perfectly drafted book brings us face to face with the reality of eternity—something most people fail to think about until it is too late. These testimonies are fascinating and thought-provoking. God will use this book to awaken the Church as well as the unsaved, in order to help them prepare for the afterlife. Great job, Shaun and Randy!

PASTOR TODD SMITH
Christ Fellowship Church, Dawsonville, GA

When I was a young boy my great-aunt told me a story about something very unusual that happened to her as a teenager. One day she went swimming at the beach, and was sucked in by an undertow. Very quickly, she began drowning. She said that her entire life literally flashed before her eyes. Then, suddenly, a bright flash of brilliant light burst in front of her, drawing her deeper into the depths of its extraordinary power…until, unexpectedly, she "awoke" and found that her physically limp body had been rescued by some heroes who were brave enough to go into the water and pull her out.

The impact of this event bewildered my great-aunt her entire life. It wasn't the trauma of drowning that stuck with her as much as the supernatural aspect of seeing glimpses from the other side. There is a whole world of true reality that most people have never been aware of before, and, for that reason, I am so grateful that my friend, Shaun Tabatt, and bestselling author, Randy Kay, have written this book about near-death experiences. Through these pages, the doorway to the other side of that brilliant light is being opened.

If you have unanswered questions about Heaven or hell, you can expect to find some answers here. I love that this book contains many short stories that are easy and exciting to read. Also, I was thrilled to find the many angelic encounters that are shared in this glory-realm treasury. In my extensive work and personal ministry with angels, I have discovered that there is still so much more to learn.

This book is filled with personal testimonies, but it is also scriptural. I invite you to read *Near Death Experiences*, study its pages, and glean new wisdom as you learn more about this supernatural realm.

Joshua Mills

Bestselling author of *Power Portals* and *Seeing Angels*

Near Death Experiences is a powerful compilation of stories of the afterlife that will grip you from start to finish. The encounters in this book are a true gift to the world from the heart of Jesus. Shaun and Randy bring us HOPE from the stories of these men and women who experienced what we will all step into one day—the realm of eternity. I have enjoyed learning so much about the afterlife through this book—and I know you will too!

Cristina Baker

Author of *Hope in 60 Seconds: Encountering the God of the Impossible*

The apostle Paul was a man clearly acclimated with the revelatory realm of Heaven. His presentation of the gospel came not by the teaching of men but by the revelation of Jesus Christ. That same apostle reiterated in 2 Corinthians 4:18 that we look not at the things which are seen but those that are unseen. The things that are seen are temporal but those that are unseen are eternal. It is clear that the veil between these two realms is becoming increasingly thin as we move closer to the end of the age.

We have always been fascinated by genuine near-death encounters and out-of-body experiences as conveyed in this book and described by Paul in 2 Corinthians 12.

"And I know that this man was caught up into paradise—whether in the body or out of the body I do not know, God knows."

Such experiences that are authentically from the Holy Spirit always emphasize the glory of God and the supremacy of Christ. In this book,

Near Death Experiences, Randy Kay and Shaun Tabatt have clearly accumulated for us numerous accounts of these experiences intended to amplify our faith and position us with greater anticipation for the kingdom prepared for His beloved from the foundation of the world. They have also included stories of people that experienced hell and eternal punishment, which inspires a holy fear of God and will awaken the reader to the reality of the unseen realm and eternal destiny.

PAUL KEITH and AMY DAVIS

Randy Kay and Shaun Tabatt have accomplished something truly unique in their new book *Near Death Experiences*. They powerfully bring out the firsthand encounters of many who have visited the other side and returned to talk about it. These stories will certainly get the attention of believers in Jesus, and of greater importance, they will engage those dwelling in this fallen world who are looking for answers. I have had the privilege of being interviewed by Shaun Tabatt and must say he has a Holy Spirit talent for extracting valuable insights from those he speaks with. The results are the same with this book; both Shaun and Randy have done great work bringing light to realms seldom talked about. I pray it makes a difference to every person who reads it. Bravo, gentlemen!

JOSEPH Z
Author, broadcaster, prophetic voice
JosephZ.Com

An absolutely fascinating and thought-provoking MUST-READ! Shaun and Randy have done extensive work collecting and studying countless near-death experiences. One hundred and one of these reports are referenced through a framework that will empower the reader to have a deeper understanding of these life-altering events and their impact on how we live our lives today!

JULIE HEDENBORG
Everyday Miracles Podcast

Shaun Tabatt and Randy Kay have a gold mine of divine inspiration and proof that there is life beyond what we experience in our natural lives. Having survived my own near-death experience in 2005, I am thrilled to read the amazing testimonies of countless others who have also encountered life on the other side of physical death. Knowing Shaun and having met Randy, both of these men carry a heart of compassion for the hurting and lost. They have endeavored to bring credible life-changing stories to the forefront to eradicate the confusion and chaos surrounding faith in God in our current cultural climate. Come along on this amazing journey with them through their new book, *Near Death Experiences*, and discover the tangible evidence and faith to believe that God exists and stands at the door of every heart, beckoning all of us into His love.

REVEREND JOANNE MOODY
Author of *Minute by Minute* and *Everyday Supernatural*

Whew! This book is an absolute MUST read from page to page. I could not put the book down. *Near Death Experiences: 101 Short Stories That Will Help You Understand Heaven, Hell, and the Afterlife* is by far one of the most riveting books I have ever read. Every section of this book has been thoughtfully written to help develop vocabulary and an interpretive framework for the reader to make sense of and to effectively communicate about these afterlife experiences.

What a job well done in this comprehensive and exhaustive literary work to help readers of all walks of life imagine and understand the experiences of those who have walked on the other side of the veil—the afterlife.

DR. NAIM COLLINS
Author of *Realms of the Prophetic* and *Power Prophecy*

Many believers and even unbelievers have had near-death encounters and divine occurrences regularly in private. Oftentimes, they are too afraid to share them with anyone because people may not believe them or think they were dreaming it. *Near Death Experiences* by Randy Kay and Shaun Tabatt is a collection of 101 life-altering, extraordinary experiences by ordinary people. I have never read a book so intriguing and powerfully moving; each story shared will bring you into the unseen reality and discovery of the afterlife. The supernatural and prophetic accounts in these pages will make it hard for you to put the book down. This powerful book has truly blessed my life and answered many questions that most pastors and leaders couldn't really answer. I highly recommend this book for anyone ready to receive the spiritual truths contained in each chapter that Heaven wants to deposit in every reader.

Dr. Hakeem Collins
Lead pastor of Glory Central
Prophetic voice, international speaker and author
Author of *Unseen Warfare, Heaven Declares,*
and *Command Your Healing*

My friend Shaun Tabatt and his co-author Randy Kay have written an important book about near-death experiences; it's a book I encourage everyone to pick up and read.

On the 3rd of July 2001, I had my own near-death experience at a church service where I had been asked to come and share my testimony of how I overcame heart disease. Being considered a virtuoso guitarist, and singer/songwriter within the entertainment world, the church worship leaders had asked me to sit in and play with their praise band before I played an acoustic solo set of my original songs and shared my testimony.

The kingdom of darkness tried to take my life in the middle of praise and worship that night and I was left without a heartbeat near the end of the service. Can you imagine the sheer audacity of the demonic realm trying to kill a child of God amid a time of worshipping the Lord Jesus/Yeshua?

I am convinced that all things are possible with God. No matter what the devil tries, our God is Almighty and shall always outmaneuver him.

Pastor Caspar McCloud
Recording artist/visual artist, researcher, conference speaker
Author of *What Was I Thinking, Unmasking the Future, Spiritual Encounters with the Shroud*
TheUpperRoomFellowship.org
CasparMcCloudMusic.com

NEAR DEATH EXPERIENCES

NEAR DEATH EXPERIENCES

101 Short Stories That Will Help You Understand Heaven, Hell, and the Afterlife

RANDY KAY & SHAUN TABATT

DESTINY IMAGE® PUBLISHERS, INC.
PO Box 310, Shippensburg, PA 17257-0310
"Publishing cutting-edge prophetic resources to supernaturally empower the body of Christ"

This book and all other Destiny Image and Destiny Image Fiction books are available at Christian bookstores and distributors worldwide.

For more information on foreign distributors, call 717-532-3040.
Reach us on the Internet: www.destinyimage.com.

ISBN 13 TP: 978-0-7684-6391-0
ISBN 13 eBook: 978-0-7684-6392-7

For Worldwide Distribution, Printed in the USA
3 4 5 6 7 8 / 27 26 25 24

CONTENTS

FOREWORD. 1

INTRODUCTION 5

    The Importance of Building a Vocabulary and
    Framework for the Afterlife 9

SECTION 1   GATEWAY TO THE AFTERLIFE. 25

1   Man Stung by Five Jellyfish
    —IAN MCCORMACK. 26

2   Man Has Blood Clots that Lead to MRSA Infection and Cardiac Arrest
    —RANDY KAY. 30

3   Teenage Girl Is Crushed in Horse-Riding Accident
    —HEIDI BARR. 33

4   Medical Misdiagnosis Leads to Drug Overdose
    —RABBI FELIX HALPERN 35

5   Overmedicating Leads to Drug Overdose
    —JIM WOODFORD 37

6   Man Drinks Contaminated Water and Contracts Cholera
    —BRYAN MELVIN. 41

7   Distress over Mortal Sin Leads Man into a Profound Spiritual
    Transformative Experience
    —FR. CEDRIC PISEGNA. 44

8   Soul Death Leads Man into Encounter in Heaven
    —ALWYN MATTHEWS. 47

9   Man Hears the Voice of God Telling Him to Turn His Bike Around
    —ED LOUGHRAN. 50

10   Skateboarding Accident Puts Young Man in a Coma and Leads to a Journey to the Other Side

       —GABE POIROT 52

       Conclusion 54

SECTION 2   OUT-OF-BODY EXPERIENCE (OBE) 57

11   Pilot Shares Detailed Testimony of Out-of-Body Experience

       —JIM WOODFORD 58

12   Demon Yanks Man's Spirit from His Body and He Knows He's Destined for Hell

       —IVAN TUTTLE 61

13   Plane Slams into Building and Pilot Finds Himself Floating above Three Lifeless Bodies at a Crash Site

       —CAPTAIN DALE BLACK 64

14   Man Has Out-of-Body Experience Chasing His Ambulance from Accident Site to the ER

       —CAPTAIN DALE BLACK 67

15   Man Flatlines During Organ Transplant and Encounters Angels Singing, "Mike's Coming Home!"

       —MIKE OLSEN 70

16   Man Dies from Neurotoxin in Hospital and Enters a Realm of Complete Darkness

       —IAN MCCORMACK 73

17   Man Takes His Last Breath and Floats Through the Ceiling and Past a Swamp Cooler Toward a Bright Light

       —BRYAN MELVIN 76

18   Jewish Teen Surprised to Encounter Jesus as She Left Her Body and Floated Toward a Bright Light

       —HEIDI BARR 78

19   Man Leaves His Body and Sees Angels and Demons Warring Over His Soul

       —RANDY KAY 80

20   Teen Receives Burns Over 65 Percent of His Body and Has an NDE When He Bleeds Out During Surgery
—MARK MCDONOUGH 82

21   Mennonite Teen Snaps Neck and an Angel Tells Him, "It's Time for Judgment"
—JOE JOE MORRIS 85

22   Woman Drops Dead in Backyard and Is Pulled into a Deep, Dark, Cold Place
—KARINA FERRIGNO MARTINEZ 88

       Conclusion 92

SECTION 3   HEIGHTENED SENSES 95

23   The Heat, the Demonic Torment, Man Recounts the Horrors of His Time in Hell
—IVAN TUTTLE 96

24   When It Comes to Experiencing Colors, Earth Is Like the Walmart Version of Heaven
—GABE POIROT 98

25   Man Describes the Landscape of Heaven as Breathtaking to the Extreme
—RANDY KAY 100

26   Man Visited 52 Countries, the Most Beautiful Places, but It All Paled in Comparison to the Landscape of Heaven
—JIM WOODFORD 102

27   Near-Death Experiencers Smell Grandma's Cookies and Tapioca Pudding in Heaven
—JIM WOODFORD AND RANDY KAY 104

28   Man Goes from Five Senses to 3,000 Senses in Heaven
—ALWYN MATTHEWS 106

29   Woman Recounts How Every Blade of Grass in Heaven Sings Praises to God
—HEIDI BARR 108

30   In Heaven Your Mind Can Outperform Google
     —IVAN TUTTLE. 110

     Conclusion 112

SECTION 4   ENCOUNTERING OTHER BEINGS 115

31   Man Encounters Three Angels Ranging from 10 to 15 Feet Tall
     —JIM WOODFORD 116

32   Man Witnesses an Angel Showing Jesus the Book of His Life
     Accomplishments
     —JIM WOODFORD 118

33   Man with Lifelong Love of Horses Elated to Discover Them in Heaven
     —JIM WOODFORD 121

34   Man Receiving Double Lung Transplant Meets His Organ Donor in
     Heaven
     —MIKE OLSEN 123

35   Man Learns All About Different Types of Angels in Heaven
     —IVAN TUTTLE. 125

36   Man Encounters Jesus on the Outskirts of a Grand City
     —BRYAN MELVIN. 128

37   Man Encounters Adolph Hitler in Hell
     —BRYAN MELVIN. 130

38   Man Dead for 30 Minutes Is Ushered into the Presence of Jesus
     —RANDY KAY 132

39   Man Meets Beloved Childhood Pet in Heaven
     —RANDY KAY 135

40   Woman Meets Her Deceased Puppies Max and Tasha in Heaven
     —KARINA FERRIGNO MARTINEZ. 137

41   12-Year-Old Boy Meets Another Boy in Heaven Who Sends Him Back
     with a Message for His Parents
     —RETAH MCPHERSON. 139

42   Angels Take Woman on a Tour of Heaven and She Sees Golden Streets
      and the Tree of Life
      —KARINA FERRIGNO MARTINEZ. 142

43   Man Encounters All Three Parts of the Trinity in Heaven
      —ED LOUGHRAN. 144

44   Young Man Sees How Omnipresent God Has Been in His Life and Just
      How Much God Loves Him
      —JOE JOE MORRIS. 148

45   Man Describes How Every Part of His Being Gravitated Toward the
      Presence of Jesus in Heaven
      —ALWYN MATTHEWS. 150

46   Man Encounters Satan in Hell and Describes Him as the Most Beautiful
      Creature He'd Ever Seen
      —IVAN TUTTLE. 153

47   Man Who Lost His Mom and Little Brother in a House Fire Sees Them in
      Heaven
      —MARK MCDONOUGH 155

48   Man Sees Famous Preachers and Evangelists in Hell
      —IVAN TUTTLE. 158

49   Woman Gives Extremely Detailed Account of Jesus's Appearance in
      Heaven
      —HEIDI BARR. 160

50   Man Encounters Jesus in Heaven and Gets a Glimpse of the New
      Heavens and New Earth
      —IAN MCCORMACK. 162

51   Man Encounters a Whole Group of People Welcoming Him at the Gates
      of Heaven
      —CAPTAIN DALE BLACK 165

      Conclusion 168

SECTION 5   LIFE REVIEW. 171

52   Man Goes Through Life Review and Sees Vision of Cancer-Stricken Boy
      Who Prophesied He'd Be in Heaven One Day
      —RANDY KAY 172

53   Teenager Has Life Review in Heaven and Could Literally Feel How She
      Had Hurt Others
      —HEIDI BARR 174

54   Young Man Nervously Waits to Find Out If His Name Is Written in the
      Book of Life
      —JOE JOE MORRIS 176

55   Man's Evil Deeds Are Laid Bare During Life Review
      —BRYAN MELVIN 179

56   Man Declares, "When I Return to Heaven, They're Going to Need Three
      Angels and a Forklift to Get My Book of Life Open"
      —JIM WOODFORD 181

57   Pastor Receives a Corporate Life Review of His Church's Ministry Impact
      in Heaven
      —ALWYN MATTHEWS 183

      Conclusion 185

SECTION 6   ENCOUNTERING OTHERWORLDLY
             ("HEAVENLY" OR "HELLISH") REALMS 187

58   Man Sees Nursery with All of the Lost Children and Aborted Babies in
      Heaven
      —JIM WOODFORD 188

59   Man Sees Parents Being Reunited with Their Aborted Babies and Lost
      Children in Heaven
      —IVAN TUTTLE 190

60   Man Recounts Seeing Vast City in Heaven
      —IVAN TUTTLE 192

61   Man Experiences the Formless Void of Darkness and Chaos in Hell
      —IVAN TUTTLE 194

62   Demon Shows Man Souls Imprisoned and Tortured in Jail Cells in the Pit of Hell
      —BRYAN MELVIN 197

63   Jesus Invites Rabbi to Experience the Second Heaven
      —RABBI FELIX HALPERN 200

64   Man Finds Himself at the Border Between Heaven and Hell
      —JIM WOODFORD 203

65   Man Deceived into Thinking He Had Arrived in Heaven, but It Was Actually the Gateway to Hell
      —BRYAN MELVIN 205

66   Jesus Takes Man to a Heavenly City Filled with Mansions
      —ALWYN MATTHEWS 208

67   Man Sees a Massive Party Erupt in Heaven's Throne Room over One Lost Sinner Coming Home
      —JOE JOE MORRIS 212

68   Angels Give Man an Aerial Tour of Heaven
      —JIM WOODFORD 214

69   Man Finds Himself Face Down Before God's Throne Surrounded by a Ring of Impenetrable Fire
      —RABBI FELIX HALPERN 216

70   Man Is Instantly Translated from the Pit of Hell to the Gates of Heaven
      —IVAN TUTTLE 218

      Conclusion 220

SECTION 7   LEARNING SPECIAL KNOWLEDGE 223

71   God Shows Man that the Demons Hate It When We Play Worship Music
      —IVAN TUTTLE 224

72   Man Sees Vision of Creation in Heaven and Realizes God's Glory Is on All the Water of the Earth
      —IVAN TUTTLE 227

73   Young Man Sees People's Prayers Build a Bridge in Heaven that Allowed Him to Return to His Body Back on Earth

       —GABE POIROT 230

74   Woman Dying of Cancer Asks Young Man Who'd Returned from Heaven, "How Do You Die?"

       —RETAH MCPHERSON 233

75   Young Man Is Instantly Taught Music Theory in Heaven

       —JOE JOE MORRIS 235

76   God Sends Man Back from Heaven with the Secret that Will Change Your Prayers from Transactional to Transformational

       —RABBI FELIX HALPERN 237

       Conclusion 240

SECTION 8   RETURNING TO YOUR EARTH-BOUND BODY 241

77   Man Returns from the Dead and Tells His Wife, "Jesus Has Horses in Heaven!"

       —JIM WOODFORD 242

78   Man Scares Paramedic Half to Death When His Body Suddenly Comes Back to Life

       —IVAN TUTTLE 244

79   Young Man Comes Out of Three-Week Coma Wondering Why He's Even in the Hospital

       —GABE POIROT 248

80   Man Says the Day He Returned to His Body Was Both the Best and Worst Day of His Life

       —RANDY KAY 250

81   Man Says It Was Like There Was a Huge Board Meeting to Decide Whether or Not He Should Return from Heaven

       —MARK MCDONOUGH 252

82   Woman Says When Her Spirit Returned from Heaven It Was So Fat It Almost Didn't Fit in Her Body
—KARINA FERRIGNO MARTINEZ.................. 254

83   Man Returns from Heaven and Wakes Up in the Morgue
—IAN MCCORMACK.......................... 257

84   Woman Experiences the Worst Panic You Can Imagine When Her Spirit Returned to Her Physical Body
—HEIDI BARR......................... 260

85   Man Returns to His Body After Four Days in a Coma and Asks His Nurse, "Do You Know God?"
—CAPTAIN DALE BLACK 263

Conclusion 265

SECTION 9   POST-NDE LINGERING EFFECTS 267

86   In the Days Following His NDE, Man Is Confronted by Seven Demons Who Say They're Ready to Come Back Home
—IAN MCCORMACK.......................... 268

87   Man Continues Having Demons Harass Him Following His NDE
—IAN MCCORMACK...........................271

88   Man Encounters White-Eyed Demons Coming Out of an Idol Statue
—IAN MCCORMACK.......................... 274

89   Man Sees Angels Watching Over Him after He Returns from Heaven
—MIKE OLSEN 276

90   God Tells Man It's Time to Begin Sharing the Story of His Time in Heaven
—MIKE OLSEN 278

91   After Returning from Heaven, Man Has Endless Passion and Drive to Introduce the Lost to Jesus
—CAPTAIN DALE BLACK 281

92   Man Returns from Heaven Infused with an Entirely New Depth of Love and Empathy for Others
—RANDY KAY.................. 283

93   Man Says He's Much More Purposeful with How He Spends His Days after Time in Heaven
—GABE POIROT 285

94   Near-Death Experiencer Says He's Confident Jesus Is the One True Way to Heaven
—MARK MCDONOUGH 287

95   After 35 Years of Waiting, God Releases Man to Share About His NDE in a Book
—IVAN TUTTLE 290

96   Woman Walks in a Lifestyle of Deep Consecration after Her Time with Jesus in Heaven
—KARINA FERRIGNO MARTINEZ 293

97   Man Says, "People Like Me a Lot Better after I Died and Went to Heaven"
—ED LOUGHRAN 295

98   Young Man Healed of Anger, Depression, Celiac Disease, and Bed-Wetting after He Returns from Heaven
—JOE JOE MORRIS 297

99   Man Says He Cried for Two to Three Weeks Any Time He Said the Word "Heaven"
—ALWYN MATTHEWS 299

100   Man Has Proof God Literally Healed His Hereditary Heart Defect after He Returned from Heaven
—IVAN TUTTLE 302

101   Man Says that after Heaven, God Gave Him a Love for Other People that Completely Enraptures His Soul
—RABBI FELIX HALPERN 304

Conclusion 306

AFTERWORD   Is God Trying to Get My Attention with These Near-Death Experiences? 308

APPENDIX   Meet Our NDE Story Contributors 310

FOREWORD

I had the privilege of meeting Randy Kay when he contacted me after reading my book *Imagine Heaven*, where I compare the commonalities of near-death experiences (NDEs) to the Bible's expectation of the afterlife. After studying over 1,000 cases where a person's heart stopped or their brain waves ceased, I found Randy's account one of the most intriguing for several reasons. Randy was at first hesitant to talk about his experience, as are many who have NDEs. As a CEO, Randy knew it could damage his reputation talking about going to Heaven, meeting Jesus, and the life-altering insights he discovered. Yet he, like others you'll read about in *Near Death Experiences: 101 Short Stories That Will Help You Understand Heaven, Hell, and the Afterlife*, was willing to risk his career because he said his NDE was the most real thing he'd ever experienced. Randy also gained unique insights from Jesus that perfectly illustrate Jesus's words in John chapter 15, so I brought my son along to hear this wisdom when I first interviewed Randy.

Since the day we met Randy in a San Diego restaurant to hear his incredible story, Randy has become a good friend. Randy left his corporate life for ministry, and he has teamed up with Shaun Tabatt to interview hundreds of others who have had NDEs. I've personally interviewed many of the people you'll read about in this book. Like Randy, they are doctors, nurses, airline pilots, and pastors—respectable, trustworthy people—with nothing to gain and a lot to lose by talking about their NDEs.

Experiences like these are far more common than most people realize. The Gallup Poll found one out of every twenty-five people (millions) have had a near-death experience, where they reported various common elements of the life to come. In this book, you'll get to hear firsthand how each describes these common elements of the typical NDE experience—allowing you to compare where they overlap and how they are each unique.

After 35 years of studying the Bible and near-death experiences, I found far more reasons to believe in the God of the Bible than to disbelieve, and I also discovered amazing commonalities across NDE stories that align with the Bible—intriguing, detailed descriptions like you'll read in the following pages—all giving different angles to what started to look like a very similar picture.

During that same 35-year timeframe, I went from a career in engineering to becoming a pastor. The more I studied the Christian Scriptures, on my own and in seminary, the more intriguing and confusing reading about these near-death experiences became. Intriguing because so many of them described the picture of the afterlife found in the Scriptures; confusing because individual interpretations of their experiences could wildly vary and even at times seem at odds with the Scriptures.

After reading enough of these experiences, I started to see the difference between what people reported experiencing and the interpretation they might give to that experience based on cultural background, worldview, or life circumstances. While interpretations vary, the core experience points to what the Scriptures say. I think that's important to keep in mind as we read NDE stories. I've found even Christian NDEs sometimes contradict each other as they seek to interpret and explain their out-of-this-world experience. For that reason, I always advise people to hold all NDE stories up against what the Scriptures say, and let the Scripture interpret the NDE, and not the other way around. Having said that, NDEs together as a whole can illustrate with vivid color the picture of the life to come that the Bible paints.

Randy Kay and Shaun Tabatt have collected a myriad of fascinating stories from ordinary people who have embarked on extraordinary journeys to the realms beyond death. Each of these brief accounts serves as a brushstroke, painting a brilliant and awe-inspiring picture of what Heaven is truly like and the radical life-changing experiences of those who have stood in the presence of Jesus.

The stories contained in this book are not mere flights of fancy or fantastical tales. I believe they are God's gift to our world today, testimonies of Heaven's reality to our global village. These narratives resonate with the commonalities found in countless near-death experiences, providing a compelling tapestry of evidence that speaks to the reality of the afterlife.

The 101 narratives you'll read transcend mere curiosity; they confront misconceptions, impart healing love, offer a heavenly perspective on earthly trials, bestow hope to those grieving, and portray the dynamic activity of Heaven and its direct effect on our daily lives. These supernatural encounters provide glimpses into a reality beyond our five senses, where the experience of time and space expands, and the eternal truths of God's kingdom become tangible.

For those who have faced the deep ache of grief and the sorrow of losing loved ones, *Near Death Experiences* offers solace and hope. These stories remind us that death is not the end but rather a transition into a realm where love, joy, and a great reunion awaits us. They provide comfort, assuring us that our departed loved ones are not lost forever but are embraced in the loving arms of God.

Through the pages of this book, you are invited to embark on a journey of exploration. Keeping the Bible as your guide, you will see how these people illustrate the truths of Scripture about the afterlife. It's the opportunity to challenge your preconceived notions, to expand your understanding, and to find solace in the eternal truths that await beyond the veil.

The collection of narratives Randy and Shaun have gathered offers a breadth of perspectives and experiences, ensuring that readers from all walks of life can find resonance and insight within these pages. Through these powerful testimonies, you will gain a deeper understanding of the afterlife, a clearer vision of Heaven, and a renewed sense of purpose in this present life.

As you embark on this journey, I pray these stories will open your heart and mind to God's ever-present guidance and the hope of Heaven that awaits you. May the testimonies shared in *Near Death Experiences* lead you to a deeper connection with God and a profound transformation of your own understanding of life, death, and eternity.

John Burke
Pastor and author of The New York Times bestseller
Imagine Heaven: Near-Death Experiences, God's Promises, and the Exhilarating Future that Awaits You

INTRODUCTION

Countless people have said to me, "I wish I could have a near-death experience." Then I remind them that most of those Shaun and I interviewed clinically died after a traumatic event. Encounters like mine and others usually started from a hospital bed attached to a monitor that flatlined, or in an ambulance with paramedics attempting to resuscitate the deceased. Most afterlife accounts happened not because someone wanted to experience them, but because death forced them.

After explaining the "prerequisites" for a near-death experience or afterlife account, most say something like, "Oh, on second thought…." If you are reading this, then you will have to simply wait for that moment when you encounter an eternity in the afterlife. But invariably, you will experience the afterlife, and my prayers are that you experience an eternity in Heaven.

Some, very sadly, experienced hell. They entered this God-forsaken place because they denied Jesus as their Lord and Savior. Their accounts detail a place of torment, not because God desired that they go there, but because only a relationship with Jesus could have prevented their soul from going to this wasteland. Some afterlife survivors who went to hell experienced the false allure of evil before going there, much like the temporary allure of evil in our world today.

This world is like a "vapor" as described in the Bible (James 4:14) and as evidenced by our short lifespan in comparison to forever. The harsh reality of death lies in our future short of a sudden rapture by God, and even if that happens, the fact remains that life in this world will suddenly cease. I know this firsthand. In my forties I never considered my own death. But then in a matter of seconds after blood clots formed from septic shock throughout my bloodstream, I transitioned from my body on a hospital bed to my spiritual body hovering in an entirely unfamiliar place. I was dead—but not really. Life goes on forever.

So why, then, do so few people consider their eternity after life on this earth ends? Most of us live in a state of perpetual denial, living day to day, spending more time wondering what we will have for dinner rather than what we will be served for 99.99 percent of our life in eternity. That changes when we are awakened by a tragedy or some potentially life-threatening news.

For many of us who transitioned into the next life through death, we entered a world both familiar and otherworldly. The otherworldly part includes an ethereal realm that is more real than this world, wondrously more varied, and infinitely more expansive. This may surprise you, but for me, I long to return. Moreover, I long to be with Jesus again in a way that only living fully in Heaven can provide. My brain still cannot fathom the depth of God's Love, but my spirit mind remembers my time with Jesus in Heaven more vividly than my physical mind can remember what I ate for breakfast today.

The afterlife survivors you will read about in this book reveal something loftier than life itself. Whereas our physical minds could not comprehend it all, our spiritual minds could fathom the most important parts of life. And for those of us who entered eternity in Christ, some of us met Jesus. Knowing Jesus intimately in Heaven introduced us to the person of Love; and that, my friend, is better than anyone or anything.

All of those whom Shaun and I interviewed either entered their afterlife as believers in Jesus as their Savior, or as unbelievers who became Christians after their hellish experience. Shaun and I come from two different perspectives. As Shaun likes to say, "I didn't go to Heaven but I got the t-shirt." I so much appreciate his perspective because Shaun views the near-death experience (NDE) through the vantage point of most people who consider these experiences being part student, part skeptic, part curious seeker, and part believer. Having known Shaun now as a friend for years, I think you can remove that last part. He is a full believer in near-death experiences. Although only those of us who directly experienced the afterlife can believe NDEs from direct experience.

Which leads me to my final point: if you have not yet experienced the afterlife, you are more blessed than those of us who have been to Heaven or hell. I say this because of what Jesus said to Thomas when Jesus returned to His disciples following His resurrection. Thomas doubted that the figure who stood before him was truly Jesus, who had been crucified three days prior. So Jesus reached out His hands so that Thomas could press his fingers into the holes created by the nails that hung Jesus to the cross.

Then Jesus said to Thomas (John 20:29 NIV): "Because you have seen me, you have believed; blessed are those who have not seen and yet have believed."

Today, God has chosen to return a few of us who have died and returned to testify of Jesus, Heaven, and hell for a reason—to tell you and the world that indeed God is real and that only Jesus is the Way to God, as declared by Jesus Himself in John 14:6. The question for you now is whether you will believe.

One moon crested night I gazed at the stars wondering if I should share my own story that I hid within my heart for 14 years. Then within the stillness of my spirit I clearly heard the Holy Spirit speak to me: "Take back the narrative, My beloved. All that exists in Heaven I created, and all that is apart from Me I had established.

Tell them the truth of what I have created for them after they leave this world." I knew that "taking back the narrative" meant telling accounts that glorified Jesus as Lord.

That is the moment I knew that I must begin sharing not only my own story, but with Shaun, we would share the stories of many others who experienced the truth of the afterlife. Now the mysteries of the afterlife according to God's plan are being revealed. I pray these accounts bring you closer to Jesus. I hope they inspire you to do more of God's will on this earth. And I pray they bring you comfort after having lost your loved ones, and for the promise of your own eternal future. No longer need you fear death. Life, indeed, springs eternal.

With Love in Christ,
RANDY KAY

THE IMPORTANCE OF BUILDING A VOCABULARY AND FRAMEWORK FOR THE AFTERLIFE

We All Need the Hope of the Afterlife

When Randy and I began interviewing people about their near-death experiences on our 2 Christian Dudes podcast back in 2021, we had no idea of the extent to which these afterlife stories would consume our lives. Three books and numerous podcasts, TV shows, and livestreams later, it doesn't appear to be slowing down.

From the very beginning of our journey together, we've seen lives changed. A day doesn't go by without one or both of us receiving emails and comments on social media telling us how one of these afterlife stories had made a tangible difference in somebody's life. The typical feedback we receive contains one of the following statements:

- I now have hope and confidence that my loved one is in Heaven.

- I wasn't sure about what would happen when I die, but now I'm no longer fearful.

- I rededicated my life to following Jesus after watching this interview.

- God healed me while I watched this interview.

Like our viewers and listeners, I've been encouraged by these many afterlife stories and have had a renewed hope about what will happen after I die. However, a journey that started in August of 2022 brought me to a place where I desperately needed to hold on to the hope of Heaven that we've encountered in so many of these stories. On August 10, 2022, my wife, Lynette, collapsed at our home in South Carolina and was soon diagnosed with stage four glioblastoma. She went on to have four brain surgeries over the span of six weeks.

When the neurosurgeon tells you to be ready to say goodbye to your wife in the event of a complication every time she goes into surgery, there's a part of you that feels so crushed and no longer in control. I learned to hold on to Jesus and the hope of Heaven during those dark days in the fall of 2022 like I never have before. Lynette went on to spend a cumulative sixty days in the hospital during the latter part of 2022.

As I'm typing the updated opening to this chapter, we're back home and a little over seven months into our cancer-fighting journey. We pray every day for total healing along with pursuing everything possible medically and holistically to eradicate the tumor in my wife's head. When the dire prognosis of a brain tumor and related complications post-surgery are your reality 24/7, Heaven always feels very near.

Struggling to Find the Right Words

If you've read Randy's and my earlier books *Real Near Death Experience Stories* and *Stories of Heaven and the Afterlife*, you've already encountered my early efforts to expose our readers to the language of and a general interpretive framework for afterlife experiences. I'll be expanding on those efforts shortly in this chapter and have plans to give a much more expansive treatment of this material in a future book project.

Whether you've had your own near-death experience like Randy, are somebody who is helping others to tell their afterlife stories like me, or are somebody who does research in the NDE and afterlife space like the authors whose books are referenced throughout the footnotes in this chapter, you need an agreed-upon vocabulary and interpretive framework to make sense of and effectively communicate about these afterlife experiences.

One common sentiment you'll find expressed by near-death experiencers is frustration with the inability of our earthly language to express the fullness of what they encountered on the other side. In his bestselling book *Imagine Heaven*, John Burke helpfully states, "every individual near-death story is actually an interpretation of an experience that's beyond our finite, earthly language. That doesn't mean it's completely foreign; actually, you'll be pleasantly shocked to find Heaven vastly more 'earthy,' 'physical,' and 'real-life like' than you ever imagined, yet so beyond earth as well."[1]

This challenge of expression is compounded further when you add the difficulty of describing an experience that is completely disconnected from our existing experiences in a space- and time-bound reality. Since near-death experiences often involve the feeling of going from one place to another and back again, the best way to describe that experience is through a travel narrative. It was Dr. Raymond Moody who coined the phrase *near-death experience* back in the '70s. He clued me in to the usefulness of travel-related language to express something that is to some degree both ineffable and nonsensical.

> Since they could not describe their experiences, they narrated the experiences instead. That does not involve

a logical inconsistency since ineffability is not the same thing as inexorability. Apparently, what they could not describe, they narrated instead, or told in the form of a story.

Specifically, narratives of near-death experiences are travel narratives, or travel stories. People said they got out of their bodies, went through a tunnel into a joyful, loving world of light, and then returned to life. That format is plainly a travel narrative. However, the narrative stipulated and presupposed that the near-death experience did not take place in the time-space continuum. Furthermore, the travel narrative also stipulated that no words are adequate for describing near-death experiences.

How can travel narratives be meaningful and intelligible in relation to transcendent experiences that purportedly did not take place in time or space? Saying that an experience was not in space or time removes the necessary preconditions for a meaningful, intelligible travel narrative. Hence, familiar accounts of near-death experiences meet our previously stated criteria for nonsense travel narratives.[2]

Later in this chapter I'll break the journey of a typical NDE travel narrative into its various stages, which will guide your experience throughout the rest of this book. However, before we get to that, we need to talk about the three different types of experiences our friends have shared during our interviews.

Three Types of Afterlife Encounters

As I've been a part of numerous interviews with near-death experiencers and read countless books in this space, I've come to realize that these experiences can be arranged into three helpful categories. The blanket term that is most commonly used is near-death experience or NDE for short, which as I mentioned was originally coined by Dr. Raymond Moody in his book *Life After Life*.

There are numerous definitions for this term across the many books in the NDE space, but to date the one that has resonated with me most is that offered by Dutch cardiologist and NDE researcher Dr. Pim van Lommell. He says:

> In my definition, a near-death experience (NDE) is the (reported) recollection of all the impressions gained during a special state of consciousness, which includes some specific elements such as witnessing a tunnel, a light, a panoramic life review, deceased persons, or one's own resuscitation. This special state of consciousness can occur during a cardiac arrest, that is, during a period of clinical death, but also in the course of a serious illness or without any apparent medical indication. The experiences nearly always brings about fundamental and lasting changes in people's attitude to life and a loss of the fear of death. Because the experience is highly subjective and lacks any frame of reference, other factors, such as individual, cultural, and religious perceptions, determine the way it is described and interpreted. A child will use different words than an adult while a Christian description or interpretation will differ from that of a Buddhist or atheist.[3]

A good majority of the NDEs that we've shared in our interviews and previous books are positive "Heaven" experiences. This may partly be due to the fact that people are often hesitant to share about negative or hellish afterlife experiences. I believe this hesitance is in part due to the traumatic nature of these sorts of experiences as well as the social, emotional, and spiritual challenges that come with revealing that you didn't go to Heaven. Nancy Evans Busch and Bruce Greyson's collaborative chapter in John Hagan III MD's book *The Science of Near-Death Experiences* best captures the challenges faced by the experiencer in the following definition of the distressing near-death experience or DNDE.

> In the DNDE the "heavenly and redemptive" themes of most NDEs are replaced by a "hellish and damnation" experience.... Much time and effort is required by these individuals to work through the debilitation and negative residua of the DNDEs. Researchers have noted three types of reactions to the DNDE among those who report them. The first type of reaction is "I needed that" in which the individual seeks to make amends in their life and become a better person. The second is reductionism in which the DNDE is explained away or repudiated as a hallucination or an adverse drug reaction. The third group struggles for years trying to comprehend why the DNDE happened to them and why they cannot shake off its negative aftereffects. This reaction tends to result in the experiencer engaging in protracted self-reflection and interpreting the DNDE as a message to "turn one's life around."[4]

The final category that needs to be mentioned is the near-death-like experience that takes place even though the person does not clinically die and was not sick. I asked Dr. Pim van Lommel what you should call this sort of experience during an interview, and he suggested these experiences best fit under that heading of spiritual transformative experience or STE.

Dr. Bruce Greyson leaves room for the STE in his definition of NDE. Greyson states:

> Near-death experiences are profound psychological events with transcendental and mystical elements, typically occurring to individuals close to death or in situations of intense physical or emotional danger.[5]

In my experience, these STEs occur with individuals who are as Greyson says in "emotional danger" and I would also include spiritual danger or turmoil—somebody who is walking through what you might call a dark night of the soul. Even though those experiencing an STE are not ill and didn't clinically die, they often exhibit the travel narrative retelling and some if not all of the same stages of a typical NDE, which we'll be unpacking next.

The Typical Elements of a Near-Death Experience

You only have to read or hear a few NDE stories to realize that there are several consistent elements that are a part of these experiences. As I mentioned earlier in this chapter, I shared a list of "ten things to watch for" in the opening chapter of Randy's and my previous collaborative books *Real Near Death Experience Stories* and *Stories of Heaven and the Afterlife*. I'll present a modified list at the close of this chapter, but wanted you to see where my thoughts took me previously for context.

1. *Out-of-body experience (OBE):* The experience of your spirit rising out of your body. You are often aware of the details of what is going on around your body, even though you are not in a conscious state.

2. *Tunnel:* As a person's spirit is transitioning from the physical world to the spiritual world, people often recount seeing and being pulled into a tunnel.

3. *Bright light:* There are many occurrences of bright lights during NDEs. They tend to be an indicator of coming into the proximity of God the Father, Jesus, and sometimes angels.

4. *Torment:* Many people recount torment by demons and/or an awful experience in hell before transitioning into Heaven.

5. *Cry for help:* Many people recount crying out for help during the above-mentioned time of torment. This often results in either Jesus or angels showing up to rescue them and escort them into Heaven.

6. *Life review:* A review of the good and bad things that you did in life. Many near-death experiencers tell us they were able to experience and feel how their actions impacted others from the other person's point of view.

7. *Encountering friends or loved ones:* People often report encountering deceased friends and family members in Heaven.

8. *Encountering animals/pets:* People often report encountering a beloved deceased pet in Heaven.

9. *Saturated in love:* Love permeates everything in Heaven. Many people say they felt completely and totally immersed in love during their time in Heaven.

10. *Communicating in Heaven:* You do not need to talk in Heaven. Communication is instantaneous. The best way we have come up with to describe it is spirit to spirit or thought to thought.[6]

As I read more widely in the NDE space this past year, I realized that I definitely had some gaps in my initial attempts to classify the typical elements or stages of these experiences that I had formulated largely on the many interviews Randy I have conducted.

Each researcher tends to add their own unique spin and perspective to the conversation. Bruce Greyson identifies sixteen elements that he groups into four clusters, Michael Sabom identifies three categories, Kenneth Ring identifies five phases, Raymond Moody identifies twelve elements, and Jeffrey Long identifies twelve elements as well. All this to say, there is a wide range of opinions on the best way to classify and break down a near-death experience into its component parts.

Dr. Jeffrey Long's Near-Death Experience Research Foundation has surveyed a few thousand NDEers via their NDERF survey. I found the twelve NDE elements he lays out in his book *Evidence of the Afterlife* to be the most helpful in highlighting some of the things I may have missed in my initial list.[7] Long's list of elements is as follows:

1. Out-of-body experience (OBE): Separation of consciousness from the physical body
2. Heightened senses
3. Intense and generally positive emotions or feelings
4. Passing into or through a tunnel
5. Encountering a mystical or brilliant light
6. Encountering other beings, either mystical beings or deceased relatives or friends
7. A sense of alteration of time or space
8. Life review
9. Encountering unworldly ("heavenly") realms
10. Encountering or learning special knowledge
11. Encountering a boundary or barrier
12. A return to the body, either voluntary or involuntary

Using my original list of "ten things to watch for" as a starting point along with Dr. Long's list of twelve NDE elements, I present to you the following list of nine stages of the NDE journey that will frame our journey throughout the rest of this book.

1. Gateway to the Afterlife

While all roads don't lead to Heaven, just about any road has the potential to bring you to that brink where you cross the veil to the other side. Some of the near-death experiencers you'll meet in this first section of this book were engaged in activities that some would label as dangerous, but the majority of them were simply going about their daily business carrying out tasks and activities they've done many times before. You'll be both amazed and surprised by the great variety of experiences that ushered these men and women across the threshold into the afterlife.

2. Out-of-Body Experience (OBE)

In some ways you could describe the entire NDE and STE journey as a sort of out-of-body experience, but what we want to get at in this particular section of the book is the point at which the experiencer departs from their physical body up until they cross some sort of border or threshold to the other side. Some of the frameworks we mentioned briefly in the opening part of the book differentiate the OBE from experiences of going through a tunnel and being drawn toward a bright light. For our purposes in this book, we're putting all of those sorts of experiences under this heading of out-of-body experience.

3. Heightened Senses

Most near-death experiencers report having a heightened sensory experience when they are no longer tethered to their physical body. The typical senses we associate with our physical body such as taste, touch, smell, hearing, and sight are cranked up to a superhuman level. Experiencers report not needing to talk when they are in their spirit body. Communication is a sort of instantaneous thought-to-thought or perhaps better stated spirit-to-spirit exchange. Many also report receiving or having access to knowledge that gives them a deep understanding of the things they're encountering on the other side. Sometimes that might look like receiving a massive knowledge download in Heaven and at other times that looks like fully understanding why the people you see tormented in hell are there.

4. *Encountering Other Beings*

Near-death experiencers often share about beings they encounter on the other side during their afterlife journey. These beings can include:

- Angels, demons, and even satan
- Divine beings: Jesus, God the Father, and the Holy Spirit
- Deceased people: family, friends, strangers

The above beings are the less controversial of the bunch. Some experiencers also report encountering animals in Heaven. We've heard stories including:

- Lions
- Horses
- Deceased pets

Given the scope of who or what we're putting under the heading of beings, this is the longest section in the book.

5. Life Review

Many near-death experiencers report a time during their NDE when they see their life passing before their eyes. Some describe it as a movie of their life that is playing in their head. This can include the good things you've done in life as well as the bad things. Some people say that in the midst of the life review, they're able to sense and experience how other people were impacted by the choices and actions that are replaying in front of them. It is not uncommon for people to express feeling overwhelmed by the many things that God has forgiven them for.

6. Encountering Otherworldly ("Heavenly" or "Hellish") Realms

When NDEers cross over to the other side, not only do they meet other beings, they can also encounter entire cities, structures like houses, other buildings, roads, etc., and vast landscapes filled with all of the things we'd expect to encounter in nature, all very much like what we might encounter down here on earth.

Sometimes these things are simply a part of the scenery in Heaven or hell that don't have a significant meaning, and other times they reveal profound truths. As you read through these stories, keep an eye out for the hidden truths that might be revealed in these structures and landscapes.

7. Learning Special Knowledge

During their time on the other side of the veil, many experiencers receive special knowledge. This may come through something they saw, something they experienced, or a special impartation of knowledge or information from a being they encountered.

8. Returning to Your Earth-Bound Body

All journeys must eventually come to an end. Some NDEers know they're returning to their body very early in their experience, while others don't know up until the moment they're about to return to their body. Some people's re-entry accounts are just as dramatic as the circumstances that started the experiencer down their whole NDE journey in the first place, while others are about as exciting as waking up from a nap.

9. *Post-NDE Lingering Effects*

Whether somebody has a Heaven experience, hell experience, or the afterlife combination platter of the two, it's impossible to not be profoundly marked by it. People report having dramatic shifts in their personality, new direction in their journey of faith, and some are now fully awakened to the supernatural activity that is taking place here on the earth.

While the majority of the people we've encountered have been dramatically changed for the better, we've also met experiencers who still carry a certain amount of trauma and PTSD from some especially disturbing experiences with hell and the demonic.

A Note on the Worldview Lens Randy and Shaun Use to Process and Understand NDEs

As we get ready to step into the next phase of our journey together in this book, I want to be up front and let you, the reader, know that Randy and I are Christians who believe in the Bible. This most certainly impacts the lens we look through to process and understand what people have shared with us about their near-death experiences.

The afterlife encounters you'll experience throughout this book are each in their own right amazing and fantastical. And while they give us a glimpse of what may await each of us on the other side of the veil, so to speak, we must as John Burke wisely says, "be cautious to avoid building a theology (or view of God and eternity) around individual stories or details that go beyond the framework of Scripture or the core elements found in most NDEs."[8]

Why the Book Is Organized Around the Nine Stages of the NDE Journey

Before I close, I need to give a shoutout to Dr. Leonard Hoffman. When I interviewed him earlier this year about *The Time Line New Testament* (Destiny Image, 2022), he talked to me about how when we organize the Bible chronologically, it completely shifts what we can see and experience as we read the Scriptures.

Dr. Hoffman's perspective completely shifted the plan for this book. Originally, we had intended to organize the sections around themes like angels, throne room encounters, etc., but talking with Dr. Hoffman inspired organizing this book around the stages of the near-death experience. Each section of this book will give you the opportunity to immerse yourself in multiple firsthand accounts that illustrate a specific part of the NDE journey. Each short story is taken from one of Randy's and my interviews, so you're getting to hear the experiencer in their own words.

Our hope as you encounter the 101 short stories in this book is that you'll build a solid foundation of the nine stages of the NDE journey framework and the related key vocabulary, so you can more deeply understand NDE stories, process your own experience if you've had an NDE, and grow in your ability to dialog and share about these experiences with others.

Discussion Questions

1. What's the difference between an NDE and an STE?
2. Who is the author who originally coined the term near-death experience?
3. What's the difference between an NDE and a DNDE?

Notes

1. John Burke, *Imagine Heaven* (Baker Books, 2015), 51.

2. Raymond Moody, MD, PhD, *Making Sense of Nonsense* (Llewellyn Publications, 2010), 234-235.

3. Pim van Lommel, M.D., *Consciousness Beyond Life* (HarperOne, 2011), 7.

4. John C. Hagan III, *The Science of Near-Death Experiences* (University of Missouri, 2017), 7, 93-101.

5. B. Greyson, "Near-Death Experiences," in *Varieties of Anomalous Experiences: Examining the Scientific Evidence*, ed. E. Cardena, S.J. Lynn, S. Krippner (Washington, DC: American Psychological Association, 2000), 316.

6. Randy Kay and Shaun Tabatt, *Stories of Heaven and the Afterlife* (Destiny Image, 2022), 7, 12-14.

7. Jeffrey Long, M.D. with Paul Perry, *Evidence of the Afterlife* (HarperOne, 2010), 6-7.

8. John Burke, *Imagine Heaven* (Baker Books, 2015), 51-52.

SECTION 1

GATEWAY TO THE AFTERLIFE

While all roads don't lead to Heaven, just about any road has the potential to bring you to that brink where you cross the veil to the other side. Some of the near-death experiencers you'll meet in this first section of this book were engaged in activities that some would label as dangerous, but the majority of them were simply going about their daily business carrying out tasks and activities they've done many times before. You'll be both amazed and surprised by the great variety of experiences that ushered these men and women across the threshold into the afterlife.

1

MAN STUNG BY FIVE JELLYFISH

Meet Ian McCormack

New Zealand native Ian McCormack was in his late twenties and living a carefree surfing lifestyle in some of the most beautiful places on the planet. One fateful night in 1982 he was night diving for lobster off the island of Mauritius when he was stung by five box jellyfish, one of the most venomous creatures in the world. A sting from a single box jellyfish can kill a person in under five minutes. Getting stung by five should have been beyond lethal.

On April 19, 1982, I dropped into the ocean and could vaguely make out what I thought was a transparent cuddle fish because I had never seen a jellyfish that looked like this. It was bell-shaped with two finger-like tentacles. Had I known what it was, I would have immediately gotten out of the water, but unfortunately I had never seen a photograph of a box jellyfish. So right in front of me was potentially the deadliest creature known to man. The neurotoxin from a box jellyfish is 100 times more lethal than a cobra!

I saw it, took note of it, but continued to dive. I found the water in the tropics quite warm, so I was wearing a wetsuit with a short-sleeved vest. This meant my forearms, neck, and ankles were all exposed. The Creole divers who had lived there all their lives in the tropics had put on full wet suits with rubber hoods and booties, leaving them all encased in a layer of protective rubber. My exposed skin was going to lead to a life-threatening issue this fateful night.

Suddenly something smashed into my arm and it felt like I had been shocked by a bolt of electricity, like someone touching my arm with a branding iron under the water. Shaken by it, I could not see what hit me. Then another one hit me. This time I saw it was a jellyfish. That was when I realized I was in a soup of thousands of jellyfish that had been washed up onto the reef. Before I could get to the reef and climb up to talk to the divers, I was hit four times across my forearm. My arm was blistered as though I had been whipped across my arm. My skin was raised and looked like it was about to burst.

As I sat there dazed and staring at my arm, my friend Simone, the Creole fisherman, said, "How come you not know?" I said, "I have not known this one." He said, "Go quickly to the hospital." The trouble is, we were at least half an hour away from the hospital and were standing on an outer reef. They lowered me into the water and dragged me to the fishing boat. And as my right arm, which was partly paralyzed, was dragged up into the boat, I got hit a fifth time.

I thought, *What on earth have I done to deserve this?* That is when I had a flood of memories of the things that I had done wrong in my life. I thought, *Well, I forgot about that. Gosh, I did that too.* How many of us have short memories? Been there and done that. Well, at this stage in my life, I no longer believed in any form of God. I was an atheist. I thought that was something that my mother did and my grandmother, who was in the choir. This is for old ladies, people who need religion. For me, my scientific background at university had knocked any form of faith or belief in God out. So here I am confronted with my mortality and confronted with the fact that I could potentially die.

When you see black men turn white, it is quite unnerving. And these guys loved me. I was as close as a brother to them. When I saw them panicking, I knew that I was in serious trouble. They told me to urinate on my arm to nullify the neurotoxin. That is one way to release the tentacles that were microscopically embedded into my skin. Next, I began to apply a manual tourniquet because I had no rope. I peeled my wetsuit off because I could hardly breathe. I got changed into my sweats and a T-shirt and a young boy began taking me toward the shore. I said to Simone and the other divers, "Come with me, please." Simone said, "Ian, there is no motor. Let the boy take. He has only got a pole. He must get you to the hospital quickly." It was a fatal mistake. They should have come with me.

When we got to the beach, I stood up and tried to walk but collapsed. To my horror, the neurotoxin had paralyzed the righthand side of my body within that brief period of time. I fell headlong into the bottom of the boat, trying to brace myself on my fallen arm. The kid motioned for me to put my arm around his neck and he dragged me bodily. I do not know how he did it, but he got me up the sandy coral beach to the main road. It was 11 p.m. when we got up there, so there was not anyone around. The boy started to freak out. He could see that I was dying. He knew his brothers were still out there on the reef, so he wanted to go out and rescue them. In my limited French, I was trying to get him to call a doctor, an ambulance, a police officer, or anybody who could help. But of course, this was 1982. You could not just pull out your cell phone and make a call.

I was feeling overwhelmed, weak, and tired. I laid down on the side of the road and my eyes just automatically began to shut. Suddenly, I heard a man's voice saying, "Son, if you close your eyes, you will never wake again." It was so clear and so audible that it caused me to turn to look in the direction of the man's voice. Amazingly, there was no one there. I thought, *Where is he calling from and how on earth did I hear that?* And then I realized that no one was there. I had just heard an invisible man speak audibly to me.

I found out later that Jesus said, "My sheep hear My voice." Well, I was a black sheep, a million miles away from God, but what is amazing is that Jesus said, "I go looking for the lost sheep." He goes searching for them. And of course, at that time I did not realize I was lost. I thought I understood life. I was fairly together. I had no concept that there was a living God who could speak to mankind. So I ran the thought through: close your eyes and you will never wake again. And of course, I knew from my own physiology training as a lifeguard and from veterinary science that you cannot go to sleep with a neurotoxin. That is not sleep; it is a coma, which would lead to certain death. I believe, had I not heard His voice, which I now know to be the voice of God, I would have died on the beach.

Hearing God's voice was a turning point. I stood up, summoned whatever adrenaline I had left in me, and began looking for help.

Reflections on Ian McCormack's Experience

Ian McCormack would eventually make it off the beach and after a series of mishaps arrive at the emergency room a whole 30 minutes after he was stung by the five box jellyfish. Given the amount of time that had passed and that a person normally succumbs to a box jellyfish sting in about five minutes, Ian should have been dead six times over. Throughout his journey to the hospital, it was the voice of God that gave Ian the courage and strength to keep pushing forward against impossible circumstances.

2

MAN HAS BLOOD CLOTS THAT LEAD TO MRSA INFECTION AND CARDIAC ARREST

Meet Randy Kay

Professionally I'd had a series of mountaintop experiences, so to speak, and now found myself in the valley. I had exhausted much of my resources to the point where I was thinking, *What am I going to do?* I was virtually destitute at that point. And I remember sitting in a Christian coffee shop with my wife, Renee, and I said, "At least we have our health. God seems to have allowed all of it to evaporate with the exception of our health." And two weeks later I came back from an interview with a major healthcare company, and I had a soreness in my calf. I was about to find out that even my health would be lost.

should have known better. After all, I had led clinical teams in neurology and cardiology, but we were planning a trip to the Sierra Mountains with my family for a long, I won't say deserved, but awaited trip. So I let it go. I did not go in to the doctor until my calf had basically swollen to almost one and a half times its normal size. By then my breathing worsened to the point where I couldn't go from the kitchen to empty the trash without feeling a heaviness in my chest. I have asthma and other breathing conditions like COPD, so I just passed it off as soreness. I had been cycling before this, so I thought it was partly from that along with a strained calf muscle and my asthma.

I went to the orthopedic surgeon for some painkillers and was rushed to the emergency room. After an ultrasound, CAT scan, and a number of other tests, a D-Dimer test determined that I had six blood clots by this time because I had let it go way too long. The blood clots had traveled from my calf all the way up through my leg into my pulmonary artery, which carries blood from the right side of the heart to the lungs. My biggest fear in life was the inability to breathe. Because I had suffered from asthma and breathing problems before this, I said, "God, if You want to take me with a heart attack or whatever it is, I can probably endure that, but just let me breathe," because I knew how precious breathing was.

And at this point I couldn't breathe. My airway was completely blocked. I needed an airway device to allow me to regain the oxygen I was being deprived of. The decision to be made was whether to keep me there or transfer me to a specialist. It was a little more than half an hour away to a site that could perform the surgery, where they'd crack open my chest and remove the blood clots. But it was determined that by the time I'd arrive at the hospital, I'd be dead because of pulmonary emboli, which is the third leading cause of death. A patient at the end stage, which was my case, could die in a matter of seconds or minutes. And in fact, there was a 27-year-old surfer who had died that very day from that same thing. So, it was determined that it was kind of a wait-and-see game at that point.

And I remember thinking, *Lord, I don't want to be a vegetable. If it comes to that point, just take me.* I had young children at the time and I wanted desperately to know how they were going to be taken care of. And I had all these worries swirling in my mind. So I was waiting in the room and the doctor came in to draw blood and said, "Well, this is strange." And that's not something a patient wants to hear. At that point, he said, "I can't draw any blood from you." What had happened is they left the IV in my arm for too long. They hadn't changed it. Through the IV, I contracted MRSA, which is a drug resistant bacteria. That was now coursing throughout my body. So on top of the pulmonary embolism, I had an MRSA bacterial infection, which caused sepsis, which is endemic throughout the entire body.

This caused a state of hypercoagulability, which means I was clotting all over. That's why he couldn't draw the blood out. It was like a traffic jam in the arteries. The cars were corpuscles, red blood cells in this case, clumping together. So it was at that point that I started convulsing and everything went dark, and I died. My heart stopped for approximately 30 minutes. And that's when I met Jesus. And this is the part where even thinking about it I start to get emotional.

Reflections on Randy Kay's Experience

As Randy recounted above, the delay in dealing with the pain in his leg led to a series of medical dominoes falling, so to speak, that would ultimately usher him to the other side. Randy's medical records show that he had no heart or brain activity for approximately 30 minutes. It's fair to say that Randy was clinically dead and well beyond the acceptable timeframe at which any hope of resuscitation was possible.

Randy didn't even believe that near-death experiences were real before experiencing this health crisis. He found out that NDEs are very real and that there were life-changing encounters waiting for him on the other side.

3

TEENAGE GIRL IS CRUSHED IN HORSE-RIDING ACCIDENT

Meet Heidi Barr

At age 16, Heidi Barr experienced a freak accident when the horse she was riding stumbled off a hillside and crushed her underneath. Although she had been raised Jewish, Heidi found herself holding hands with Jesus.

When I was 16 years old, I was riding my horse bareback out at the ranch where we boarded her in Iowa where we lived. My sisters were there with me. My 14-year-old sister stayed in the car with the windows rolled up because she is allergic to horses.

After riding for about an hour, I decided to go back to the barn because I figured my sisters were getting bored. I headed back to the barn, and above the barn was what we called the Ridge Trail. It was a trail along a hill that overlooked the barn and the valley on the far side and in front of the barn. I rode to the end of the Ridge Trail, which was a dead end. The only way to get off the trail was to go back to the barn. I was sitting there enjoying the view when suddenly I heard hoofbeats behind me. I knew exactly who it was. It was a man on an out-of-control Arabian.

He was coming fast, so I just stayed on my horse because most horses when they are running out of control will run back to the barn. I assumed his horse would do that, but instead the horse with the man flapping wildly and crazily on his back came down the Ridge Trail.

I froze because I did not know what to do. I did not know if I should jump off my horse because I was afraid I would be trampled if there was an interaction between the two horses. I thought, *Okay, once this horse sees my horse standing calmly, he will stop.* But he did not. He ran right into my horse and my horse reared up. The first time she reared, I dropped the reins and just grabbed her neck. The second time she reared up, she stepped backward off the Ridge Tail and flipped over upside down onto me. We flipped off the trail and down the slope. She rolled across my body, and as she hit my chest, I knew I was dead. Every cell in my body stood stock-still.

Reflections on Heidi Barr's Experience

Of the many NDEers we've talked to, Heidi Barr is one of the few who had a near-death experience as a child. Accounts from men and women who had an experience as a child are important, especially because children don't have all the baggage adults have as they process and share these experiences.

As is often the case, Heidi was doing something she'd done many times before without any problems or issues. When her horse rolled across her body, crushing her, Heidi was immediately ushered into an out-of-body experience that we'll pick up in the next section of the book.

4

MEDICAL MISDIAGNOSIS LEADS TO DRUG OVERDOSE

Meet Rabbi Felix Halpern

Messianic Rabbi Felix Halpern died when his body became toxic after a medical misdiagnosis and the related wrong prescription.

My health has always been good, but this time the doctor misdiagnosed me with a thyroid condition. She prescribed a medication incorrectly, and I consumed seven and a half months' worth of medication in 29 days when I did not need it to begin with. Looking back, I can see that within three to four days, my body began to manifest what doctors call an inner storm. It was a tremendous amount of tension, pressure, and pain. My body felt like a furnace. I thought it was spiritual. Quite frankly, I thought it was part of the manifestation of my profound experience in Israel. I kept telling myself this was spiritual, that it couldn't be physical because I was healthy. This went on every single night for a month and half.

Everything was building up to one night in September. This was the most difficult night out of the entire month and I was feeling the symptoms of a cardiac arrest. You know: pain in the shoulder, pain in the arm, pain in the chest. Instead of telling my wife what was happening, I went downstairs at 3:00 a.m., thinking I was going to rest and believing that it would go away. Unfortunately, it did not. I got downstairs, lay down, and in short order my heart just stopped. And that was it. My soul jumped out of my body and my spirit began to rise in the room. My body was lying horizontally at that point, and from a height above I was able to see my lifeless body on the couch.

I saw a bit into the future. I saw Bonnie and my children planning my funeral, and I saw the grief and the sorrow on them. It was not even momentary. It was the only time something like that entered my being and then I became aware of a powerful angel. It felt like I was just brought into an emergency room and I was lying on an operating table and the doctors were working on me, but this angel was moving his hand over me. I had this sense that he was ministering to my soul. I did not know what that meant at that point in my life. It only had meaning 15 months later when I began to understand something. And in that place, I saw a white light, a cone-shaped cylindrical light up and to the right side of me, which I knew was Heaven. There was a brightness at the end of it.

Reflections on Rabbi Felix Halpern's Experience

Rabbi Felix's OBE is rather unique in that it goes beyond the traditional tunnel and bright light experience. The vision of the future and the angel encounter are both things I would've expected him to encounter once he had fully crossed into his Heaven experience, but in God's providence those profound moments needed to be a part of the early steps of Felix's afterlife journey.

5

OVERMEDICATING LEADS TO DRUG OVERDOSE

Meet Jim Woodford

A successful airline pilot and businessman, Jim had it all—a loving family, substantial wealth, and all of the good things that come with it. But none of this was enough to satisfy the emptiness he felt in his heart. He always hungered for something more. And then he died.

Jim Woodford had Guillain-Barré syndrome, which he compensated for by overmedicating himself to allow for a small amount of functionality. On that fateful day in his truck, he would take one pill too many and find himself in an out-of-body experience.

One evening in April, I had received a request from a company that was acting as my surveying company to go and look at a large tract of land that I was trying to sell and to make sure that the markers were in the correct place. I didn't drive much because of my medical condition, but it was all on back roads. So I got in my truck and drove to that field. It was late afternoon, early evening in springtime. And I managed to get to the field. When I drove into the field, I didn't plan it this way, but I was facing the setting sun, and I turned the truck off and sat there trying to get up the strength to make my way around this large piece of property and check the markers. I remember thinking, "Boy, I don't know if I can do this. That's a long way around."

I'd gotten into the habit of hiding medication so that my wife wouldn't see that I was overtaking it. I moved some things in the console of my truck and I saw some of the medication and a bottle of pop. And I thought, "Well, a few more. One won't hurt." Famous last words. I took them knowing full well that I had already taken far more that day than the prescription called for. And I sat back in the truck seat waiting for that warm relief that I had become accustomed to as the pain was dulled for a few hours. But as I sat there, something different started to happen. I remember the feeling of heat in my lower legs was so intense that I thought the truck must be on fire. I looked down quickly and there was no fire. And this raging heat came rushing up my legs, and then from my fingertips, inward toward my chest.

I tell people that you know when you've done something catastrophic. And by catastrophic, I mean life-ending. Suddenly my lungs started to seize; it was as though the cab of the truck was filling with water and I kept raising my head to try to breathe and I could not. And that was the moment of realization that I was dying. And remember, I wasn't agnostic, but I believe the old saying, "There are no atheists in foxholes." There are no atheists dying in trucks either. I remember raising my hand—it was shaking violently—to the setting sun, and from somewhere really deep inside of me, a place that I had never been to, came this overwhelming feeling of "not fair, not fair." I'd had engine failures. I'd landed in difficult situations. It wasn't fair. It was a feeling of remorse that I had lived by a standard that many would have thought the ultimate success, and I'd never thanked the Creator, if He existed. And so I raised my shaking hands to the setting sun, and I cried out the first three of six words. And the first three words that I cried out were, "God, forgive me."

It came, as I said, from a place inside of me I hadn't been to in a long, long time. No sooner had I gotten the words out than

I collapsed on the steering wheel and hit my head violently and I was gone. The next thing I was aware of was a tremendous pain on my forehead. I sat back up and I was in the truck looking out, and I knew time had passed because the sun was now on the horizon as it set. And then the realization flooded through me that I had no pain. The pain was gone. I finally got it right. You have to take the whole bottle.

I slid out of the truck and I walked about 15 to 20 feet away. I felt incredible. It was as though I'd taken off a heavy, wet overcoat and, with it, the pain. I felt like I was 16 again, and I was just overwhelmed and overjoyed. And I was looking out at the setting sun. I could hear the birds at springtime. I could smell the grass, and I was just overwhelmed that the medication finally worked. And then I turned and looked toward my truck.

And I was outraged. Someone was in my truck. Not only that, he had the audacity to be sleeping on my steering wheel. And so I turned to go over there and give him a good what-for. Have you ever had a dream where you're trying to run from something and it's as though your feet can't move? I realized that as hard as I tried, my feet would only move an inch or two at a time. I was stunned; I felt so good. Why couldn't I just run over there and grab this guy? I did make slow progress. And then I looked up and the realization hit me that the man in the truck leaning over the steering wheel was no stranger. It was me.

Reflections on Jim Woodford's Experience

What is fascinating about this early part of Jim's experience is that he slides out of his truck and walks 20 feet away from his truck to enjoy the sunset, but still doesn't realize that he is dead and out of his physical body. Interestingly enough, he describes not only hearing the birds sing but also smelling the grass, which is something I wouldn't have expected to be possible in his out-of-body state. It's only when he turns around and goes to investigate the man slumped over the steering wheel of his truck that he realizes something has gone terribly wrong, because it is in fact Jim who is slumped over the steering wheel of the truck.

6

MAN DRINKS CONTAMINATED WATER AND CONTRACTS CHOLERA

Meet Bryan Melvin

Bryan Melvin, a self-described militant atheist, died after contracting cholera from drinking contaminated water at a construction site.

I was an electrician working at a construction site in Tucson, Arizona. It was always hot there. On that day, the marquee on the bank across the street read 121 degrees. We always tried to get started super early in the morning so we could be done by noon or 1 p.m. at the latest. My supervisor had just gotten back from taking his family to Mexico. On the way back his car overheated, so he filled up the company thermos with pond and creek water from Mexico and brought it back in his truck.

In those days it was construction etiquette that if you ever walked by a truck and you saw a cooler, you could drink out of it because it was so hot. The first thermos I grabbed from the truck was empty. The one way in the back was full. I lifted this big five-gallon jug over my head and started drinking. Then I handed it to a coworker and I said, "Boy, this is warm." He took one little sip and spat it out. When he opened the top of the jug, it looked like Darwin soup. Have you ever seen algae-infested water? That is what I drank. It had little worm things swimming around in it that looked like flat spaghetti.

The short story is that I drank contaminated water and contracted cholera and who knows what else.

My surroundings were, simply put, that I was a strong guy who was going to do things his own way. I took the medications of Jack Daniels and Wild Turkey, thinking that would kill whatever it was I drank. I joked about it the whole night. I did not go to the hospital right away and thought I could just take care of it myself.

I had a duplex apartment with a couple of roommates and we had been making plans to go up and fly over to the Grand Canyon on the holiday weekend. I had a friend up there in Phoenix with a private plane. I fully expected to go along, but then I got sick.

The next day I went to work and suddenly it hit me fast. Let me warn you: if you ever have cholera, it comes out of both ends. I had a high fever and it felt like razor blades were cutting up my stomach and gastro-intestinal tract from the inside out. It was extremely painful. My friends still left on the Grand Canyon trip that Saturday and planned for a neighbor to check on me.

With cholera your body goes into shock from losing too many fluids. At that point, you temporarily feel great. The pain goes away. You can get up and walk around. I was telling the guys, "I am fine; it will pass. I am up and around. I am just a little tired. See you in the evening." I walked into the kitchen as they walked out of the house and got in the truck. I assured them they did not have to worry about me. I walked back into the kitchen and stood there at the window, trying to take a drink as they drove off.

Suddenly it hit me again and I collapsed on the floor like a ton of bricks, following the classic symptoms of cholera. I do not know how long I was on the floor, but I crawled back and managed to get into the bathroom before I passed out. Then I crawled into my bedroom and somehow lifted myself up on the bed. I was lying on my bed, looking at my alarm clock, and trying to pet my German Shepherd dog at the same time. That was when something happened. It was like I took my last breath.

Reflections on Bryan Melvin's Experience

Of all the things that could've taken Bryan Melvin out, he likely never figured it'd be drinking water at one of his construction sites. Like Randy Kay, whom you met earlier in this section of the book, Bryan also used poor judgment when he avoided going to the hospital, which caused him to experience a medical crisis.

7

DISTRESS OVER MORTAL SIN LEADS MAN INTO A PROFOUND SPIRITUAL TRANSFORMATIVE EXPERIENCE

Meet Fr. Cedric Pisegna

Fr. Cedric Pisegna was in college and on track for a business career, but grief and turmoil over what he describes as a mortal sin led to two spiritual transformative experiences (STEs) that would not only deepen his faith but also direct him toward lifelong service as a Catholic priest, something that had not been part of his life plan.

I was born and brought up Catholic in Massachusetts, baptized as an infant like many Catholics are and raised in the faith. But I had fallen away like most teenagers and didn't really have any inkling about priesthood and the mass. The ritual never really did anything for me, but I had it as my foundation. It was my background. I prayed once in a while but had fallen away from the faith. That's when something happened to me that totally revolutionized my life. Let me set that up by being very vulnerable and very intimate by telling you that I was dating in college at the University of Massachusetts where I was studying business. I ended up getting the woman I was dating pregnant.

I was not ready to get married. I was 19 years old and I felt stuck. We talked it over and we decided to have an abortion, much to my shame. After this I went through the worst time of my life. We broke up. I was empty, ashamed, and guilty. It felt like God was far from me. I bottomed out. I didn't know where to go or what to do. I was still in college, of course, but my parents didn't know I was going through this. I kind of retreated into my own shell. Even though I wasn't religious, I knew that I had cut myself off from God. It was awful. And then finally, because I wasn't happy, I went to the Bible, and that was a move of God just to get me to go to the Bible. I read Matthew 7:7, which is, "Asking, you shall receive, knocking, the door will be open, seeking, you'll find." And it spoke to me. Here I am, this 19-year-old teenager coming off an abortion who had no religion anymore, and God was speaking to me through the Bible. That's why I stress the Scripture so much in my ministry today.

I started praying. And what do you pray for when you're 19 years old? I prayed for wisdom, prayed for something. God was real, that I would come to know God somehow. But I noticed that nothing happened right away. In between times, I started changing my life—the way I spoke. I used to take the name of the Lord in vain quite a bit. I would say "Jesus" all the time. I didn't say G- D- or that type thing, but I would say Jesus all the time. And I realized I had to stop doing that. So I repented. I changed in other things too. I was honest with people and honest with myself. I stopped being angry. I went through the seven deadly sins. That's what led up to these experiences. They didn't just happen out of the blue. There was a precursor to that. And all the while my faith was growing. Faith is something that grows. I believed in God, but it was only as I started changing my life and made those decisions that my belief really started growing. I know this because I had these two near-death experiences about six months after I started coming to the Bible.

Leading up to my experience, I was a healthy, athletic 19-year-old young man. This was in July of 1977, so I had just turned twenty. Most people talk about having an accident or being in a hospital room and your vital signs go down to zero. What propelled me through the tunnel wasn't being sick or having been in an accident—it was my faith.

I have a very vivid memory of this. As I started to go, I remember distinctly saying, "Oh no, I believe." It was my faith that was propelling me through the tunnel. Most people go through the tunnel because they died, but it was my faith that had been growing in me. It was propelling me. And I said, "Oh no," because I knew where I was going. I was about to have an imminent experience with Almighty God. When you start to go through the tunnel, you know exactly where you're going. There was no doubt in my mind. It was very clear to me. So I started going through this—the only way to describe it is a tunnel.

I was completely healthy, and I had two near-death experiences. For me, it was a summons by God. God was summoning me to the throne.

Reflections on Fr. Cedric's Pisegna's Experience

Fr. Cedric is one of the few people Randy and I have interviewed who had spiritual transformative experience (STE). Again, that means he had an experience with most of the traditional stages of a near-death experience, but he wasn't sick and didn't clinically die.

I had originally wanted to interview Fr. Cedric to see if there was anything particularly Catholic about his experience on the other side, but his time with God was on par with the experiences of people on the Protestant side of the church.

Take note that Fr. Cedric's two experiences came on the other side of him intensely pursuing God through prayer and spending time reading the Bible. As a result of his two Heaven encounters, he would ultimately dedicate his life to serving the Catholic Church as a priest.

8

SOUL DEATH LEADS MAN
INTO ENCOUNTER IN HEAVEN

Meet Alwyn Matthews

Alwyn Matthews was pastoring a thriving church, but a series of unfortunate events would lead him down a path of despair and depression that ultimately resulted in a life-altering encounter in Heaven.

We'd planted this church, and it was such an incredible journey. Within the first three years, our church had grown exponentially, we had an incredible impact in the area, and we were seeing people saved. I think one year we averaged around 150 baptisms, and all sorts of things were happening. And then when we went through COVID, we experienced a betrayal. Some of the key members of our team began to make up stories and falsify information. And I mean, it's one thing to go through a form of betrayal, but we literally began to feel we were being canceled as a church and as a family due to bitterness and jealousy. We were under a spiritual attack, and the attack went on for months while we were navigating the birth of our third baby with no family support and things like that.

I found myself in a deep dry place. I had to preach and pastor, and I myself needed help because I was just in a dry place. I was crying out to God. I was seeking God. I was talking to my mentors. I was getting all sorts of professional help, and I would get better for a moment, but I would always find myself going into this deep dry pit. And I'm a fairly positive person, a fairly joyful person. But I was just finding it hard to even be happy. The only thing I could relate to is in Mark 14, the words of Jesus. He says, "My soul is deeply grieved to the point of death." I felt that way. I felt all the work that we had put in, all the hard work, all the sacrifice just felt destroyed to the point that I didn't have hope to live for the next day.

I don't think I would have ever contemplated ending it all. I contemplated throwing in the towel. I contemplated the purpose of my existence. When you feel like you've lost everything, lost a huge part of who you are and the people you loved have walked away, the pain is just so deep. When we needed people around us, that's when we felt no one was there. And I was just crying out to God. I'd go on a fast; I'd go on prayer retreats. I'd feel better for a moment. Some of my counselors toyed with the words *clinically depressed*. I was not officially diagnosed with that, but what I was walking in was to that point. I'm like, "I'm the senior pastor of a church. People are looking to me for spiritual nourishment." All I can say is, during that season, when it came to Sunday somehow I was able to preach a good word and people were touched and lives were changed and all sorts of things. And I would walk away even after preaching, thinking, *God, I need this thing that I'm sharing. Lord, I feel dry. I can see You're touching Your people, You're touching Your church. But I feel dry and empty.* I just kept crying out to God.

Everything changed in 2021 on the 25th of August. That day was an absolute turning point. In fact, that point in my life is so dramatic that I actually don't remember a lot from February of 2021 to August of 2021 because of just how much of a difference it's made in my life. That's the context, the backdrop of my experience. We were in a dry and dead place. I say to people now that my greatest spiritual experience did not happen when I was the most spiritual.

My greatest spiritual experience happened when I was at my lowest, and it's changed everything for me.

On the 25th of August, I was going to bed, I was about to sleep, and something in me said, "You have an appointment with God." I did not know what that meant. I just felt something was about to change. I didn't have the faintest idea that I was going to have this experience. I lay down and instantly I got pulled out of my body, but I was still connected to my body. I was carried into this place and I saw this portal. The best way to explain it would be like in the *Avengers* movie where something is shining down. That's what I see. I see this beam of light, this thick beam of light. And I knew I was being pulled toward it. I was being drawn toward it. It's not like I forced myself to be drawn. I was being led into it. My spirit was being drawn into it. And I got carried into this place, and I cannot say that I saw an angel, but I felt the presence of angels leading me on this journey. And I instantly knew that I was in Heaven.

Reflections on Alwyn Matthews's Experience

Like Fr. Cedric in our previous story, Alwyn had a spiritual transformative experience (STE). He was not sick or clinically dead, yet he had an encounter that featured many of the stages of a traditional near-death experience.

Take note that Alwyn had a strong sense as he went to bed that he had an appointment with God. His time on the other side of the veil would completely transform him, healing Alwyn of the depression and despair that had been weighing him down for many months.

9

MAN HEARS THE VOICE OF GOD TELLING HIM TO TURN HIS BIKE AROUND

Meet Ed Loughran

Ed Loughran is a lawyer. He was a good athlete, playing competitive sports into his early forties. Right before his 50th birthday, Ed got a new bike. He planned to take it out on a thirty-mile ride, and around ten and a half miles into the ride, he heard the voice of God say, "Turn your bike around now." Ed would make it all the way home but would soon drop dead of a heart attack.

was 49 years old in December of 2011 and I had a checkup that showed my blood pressure was normal. I had been a very good athlete in state championships and numerous things. I played ball competitively until I was 42 in an A-league in Chicagoland three times a week and stuff like that. I'm walking, I'm working out. So at 49 I got a new bike; I was going to turn 50 in a couple of weeks. My old bike was 15 years old and had the tar beaten out of it. I wanted to go on a 30-mile bike ride. When I went on my bike ride, it was probably 90 degrees out on the bike path. With about 10 and a half miles down, the Lord said, "Turn your bike around now." I had never heard a command from God. It sounded absolutely chill, patient, peaceful, and urgent. Just, "Turn your bike around now."

The key part of my story is the years I spent in prayer. I prayed in the spirit from 6:30 to 9:30 a.m. six days a week for 12 years—three hours a day of prayer. So I turned my bike around and started praying in the spirit, and I said, "Okay, God, what's up?" I started heading back. A cold front came through, and it dropped like 15 degrees. As I was coming back, there was a hill. As I came to this hill, He said, "Walk your bike up the hill." I walked up the hill and then I rode home.

I came back and I just sat down. I felt so tired. I didn't feel pain. After two minutes I kind of growled and got up and took a shower. When I got out of the shower I started feeling achy everywhere. I've been in worse pain, but in this case I was just kind of achy and sore. My wife came home and I said, "Molly, I need you now." She came upstairs and she said, "Well, if there's something wrong with you, I don't want anybody coming into our bedroom. We have six baskets of unfolded laundry in here. Walk downstairs."

I said, "Yes dear," and I walked downstairs. My wife was on the phone. I felt like I needed to sit down, and I just dropped dead in my living room. My wife, my oldest son, and one of my daughters were there. My wife stood over my body rebuking death. The paramedics said that they had never seen somebody with a massive heart attack wake up in the middle of the ambulance and look them in the eye. But my wife was following them, rebuking death and praying. The paramedics were there in six minutes. They told me I had been dead for approximately six and a half minutes.

Reflections on Ed Loughran's Experience

Just like Ian McCormack, whom you met in the first story of this book, Ed heard the voice of God directing him before he died and crossed over to the other side. As a man of deep faith and constant prayer, Ed knew to heed the voice of God, so he turned his bike around and headed back home. Ed would tell you his wife's violent prayer and intercession rebuking death played a huge role in his return to life.

10

SKATEBOARDING ACCIDENT PUTS YOUNG MAN IN A COMA AND LEADS TO A JOURNEY TO THE OTHER SIDE

Meet Gabe Poirot

Gabe Poirot is an evangelist with a passion for seeing young people enter into a life-changing relationship with Jesus. Back in 2021, he had a freak accident on his electric skateboard that would put him into a prolonged coma and a journey to the other side of the veil.

A little more than a year ago, I bought an electric skateboard that was capable of reaching speeds of 20 to 25 miles per hour. It really doesn't have a maximum speed limit, so I would kind of race cars sometimes on it. When I went downhill I felt like I was flying. I was like, *Wow, I'm a flyer now.* Some of my friends had this board as well, so we would all ride together. We had a fun time and it was a very high adrenaline push. There were multiple times when I knew I was going too fast. I wouldn't wear a helmet and the Holy Spirit would check me. I knew that what I was doing was wrong, but I just kept going. And it's funny too, in every other area of my life I was submitted to God, but this one area I was just going crazy on it. I really enjoyed riding on it. Fast-forward to October 25th, 2021. That's the day a lot changed.

My buddy and I were going around a curve and there were these markers on the road that made it a little bumpy. I hadn't actually ridden a skateboard before this one, so my balance wasn't very good. I wasn't good at falling either. I didn't know how to do any of those things. And when I hit the bump, I flipped off the board. We were actually chasing each other on the boards. And I flipped off the board and I landed directly on my head. The whole back of my skull instantly cracked and I was immediately unconscious. My lungs were only breathing at a rate of once every 60 seconds. Thank God my friend was there. He was able to hold me up and help me breathe. I'm not sharing any of these things from memory because I was out of consciousness. I don't have any memory of that whole riding trip. I'm actually very thankful that I don't remember, because it would not be a good memory.

My friend held me up, they called an ambulance, and I was rushed to the hospital. I was on a ventilator. They needed to drill a hole in my head to monitor the blood pressure. They called my parents because a lot of the doctors and nurses believed I was about to die. So my parents came from Virginia. They gave me 50/50 odds of living or dying as I hadn't woken up yet or regained consciousness. During all of this, as soon as the accident happened, I was with Jesus.

Reflections on Gabe Poirot's Experience

The conversation with Gabe was captured less than a year after his near-death experience. Dr. Jeffrey Long says it takes up to seven years for a near-death experiencer to fully process what they went through, so I suspect Gabe will have a fuller grasp of his encounter on the other side as time progresses.

While Gabe didn't hear the voice of God like Ian or Ed, he did experience a nudge from the Holy Spirit about not wearing a helmet when he rode his skateboard. Whether we hear the audible voice of God or receive a strong impression from the Holy Spirit, Ian, Ed, and Gabe's stories speak to the importance of responding when we sense God directing us.

CONCLUSION

As you've no doubt realized from reading these ten accounts, there are innumerable paths that could take you into the afterlife. While a couple of these NDEers were participating in activities that we could legitimately label as dangerous, most of them were just going about their normal day-to-day activities and had a medical crisis.

In three of these stories, the experiencers noted sensing guidance and direction from God relating to their own safety and preservation, which we've found to be a common experience in many of the afterlife stories we've encountered these past two years.

As noted in their respective accounts, two of the stories in this section of the book should be classified as STEs, where the experiencer walks through many if not all of the stages of a traditional NDE, but technically speaking was not ill or clinically dead. We plan to explore whether or not there is a measurable, qualitative difference between STEs and NDEs in a future book, but that is well beyond the scope of where we plan to go in this current volume.

Discussion Questions

1. In this section of the book, you've encountered both near-death experiences and spiritual transformative experiences. Do you feel those two different types of experiences are on par with each other? Would you put more weight on the experiences of somebody who clinically died? If so, why?

2. Have you ever been in a dangerous or difficult situation in which God attempted to give you a redirect? How did you respond? Did it make a significant difference in the outcome of your circumstances?

3. As many as 1 in 10 people have had a near-death experience. Have you or anybody in your circle of family and friends had this sort of experience? How does what initiated their/your experience compare to the ten accounts you read in this section of the book?

SECTION 2

OUT-OF-BODY
EXPERIENCE (OBE)

In some ways you could describe the entire NDE and STE journey as a sort of out-of-body experience, but what we want to get at in this particular section of the book is the point at which the experiencer departs from their physical body up until they cross some sort of border or threshold to the other side. Some of the frameworks we mentioned briefly in the opening part of the book differentiate the OBE from experiences of going through a tunnel and being drawn toward a bright light. For our purposes in this book, we're putting all of those sorts of experiences under this heading of out-of-body experience.

11

PILOT SHARES DETAILED TESTIMONY OF OUT-OF-BODY EXPERIENCE

Jim Woodford

When we last encountered Jim Woodford, he had just walked back to his truck and realized that the man slumped over the steering wheel was in fact Jim himself. This is when he began to comprehend that something had gone terribly wrong and he was dead.

My mind was trying to reconcile that I am here and yet I am there at the same time. How can this be? And of course, being a guy who could fix anything, in my arrogance I immediately concocted a scheme that if I could just get over there and get back in my body, everything would be okay. So I struggled to get over there. And I knew it was me because my head was turned this way on the steering wheel. There was blood gushing from my mouth and nose. I struggled to get closer to get back into my body, but suddenly I began to rise.

Now, as a pilot, I'm a good judge of altitude. And as I was rising, I was stunned because how could this be? I looked, and now I was drifting slowly backward, rising continuously. I could look down and see the bed of my truck, see my toolbox, and I was stunned.

I rose a little higher and then something made me look up instead of down, because I could see the surrounding area. I could look through the back window of the truck. I could see my body slumped over the wheel. And then I turned and I looked up, and there right in front of me was this golden circle. It was maybe 200 feet away. It was about 60 feet in diameter, and it was like the gold of a wedding ring. And then suddenly the center of it filled with a golden light. I had the impression that it swung inward and backward, like the door of an old-fashioned safe.

Immediately my body went into a reclining position of about 45 degrees. And I mean, unless you've lived under a rock in a cave, I think everyone has heard of the tunnel of light, but I never paid any attention to it. Suddenly I began to go forward toward this tunnel of light. As I went through the ring, I could see an immense distance. All of it was covered with a cloud that was golden, but there was a distinct path through the center. Once I realized what this was, it was as though I had pushed the throttles on an L-1011 forward to achieve V-1 on takeoff. I felt this tremendous force of speed. And I went at tremendous speed into this tunnel of light reclining backward about 45 degrees.

To give you an idea of the speed, I could feel and see the stars streaming by. I mentioned that in Baltimore one night, and there was a young guy in the front row and he said, "Sounds like the opening of *Star Trek* to me." That's a pretty good analogy. It was the stars streaming by. I was terrified because I'm a technical person, always understanding why things are happening, wanting to learn. But I was absolutely baffled. There was no rationale, no technical reason I could attach to this. The other thing that I remember vividly was that when you're going fast, whether you're in your convertible or in a speed boat or on your motorbike, you hear the rush of the wind. You hear the noise of the air. But right now? Nothing. Complete silence. And yet the sensation of tremendous speed.

Reflection on Jim Woodford's Experience

It's always fascinating to see how a person's expertise comes to light in the midst of their NDE. Jim Woodford is an accomplished pilot, which empowered him to give what I think is one of the most comprehensive descriptions of what it is like to float up into the air toward that tunnel or light. Take note of his comments on the altitude, angles, and speed, and you can realistically begin to imagine what it must have felt like.

Jim is the first NDEer we encountered who tried to solve the problem of being disconnected from his physical body by putting himself back in his body. Unfortunately, before Jim was able to fully execute that plan, he began to rise into the air. It would've been fascinating to hear what it felt like for his spirit body to come back into contact with his physical body.

12

DEMON YANKS MAN'S SPIRIT FROM HIS BODY AND HE KNOWS HE'S DESTINED FOR HELL

Meet Ivan Tuttle

In 1978, Ivan Tuttle was living a carefree life, going from one party to the next, from one high to another—when his fun, free life was interrupted by a pain in his leg. Doctors told him he had a dangerous blood clot—but Ivan didn't pay much attention to that. He was 26 and felt fine; blood clots were a problem for his grandfather, not him. Then the clock ran out.

Even to this day, I'm usually still up until 2, 3, 4 a.m., it just depends. It was nine o'clock and I'm like, "You know, something's wrong. I feel really tired. I feel really sleepy." And I told the girl I was with, I said, "Hey, you know, just sit out here and watch TV a little bit or do whatever. I've got to go lay down. Something's wrong." I went into my bedroom and I lay down on my free flotation water bed. I had one of those. I loved that thing. I wish they still made them.

I was sleeping on my left side; I always liked to sleep on my left side, because I had something called hypertrophic cardiomyopathy at the time. When you have hypertrophic cardiomyopathy, if you sleep on your left side, it helps the heart to be better. And so I lay down and I was sleeping on my left side and I fell asleep. I mean, I fell asleep fast. All of a sudden, something grabbed a hold of my left wrist and yanked me straight up out of the bed. And when I say yanked me, I mean, this thing grabbed a hold of me.

Now, as I told you, I was in good shape back then. I was one of these people that if I ever had to defend myself, it was usually one punch and it was over. I was very strong and I hit this thing as hard as I could. It had zero effect on it. And it just looked at me. It was the most demonic-looking thing. And I was like, "Wait a minute. What's going on?" And I turned around, you know, and looked at my bed like, "How did you get me out of the bed? I'm still in bed. Wait a minute. Oh." And then I'm thinking, "This is a bad dream, a bad nightmare." I went to turn on the light switch and my hand went right through the wall and the light switch didn't work. And then I knew I was dead.

It's kind of hard to explain, but it's like your spirit wakes up and your spirit goes, "Buddy, you're dead. I'm out of your body now. I can start doing the thinking instead of your brain doing it. Let me tell you what's going on." And I was looking at this thing and realizing this thing is taking me to hell. I knew it. I knew what was going to go on. I knew I was going to hell and next thing you know, we're going.

Reflections on Ivan Tuttle's Experience

When you consider that it was a demon yanking Ivan's spirit out of his physical body, his transition into his out-of-body experience is definitely part of one of the more traumatic stories we've shared on our podcast. Similar to Jim Woodford, Ivan had a limited amount of time to interact with his environment before crossing over to the other side. He quickly discovered his movements had little to no effect. His attempt at punching the demon made no impact, and when he attempted to flip on the light switch his hand went right through the wall.

A degree of confusion as you attempt to come to terms with your spirit having just left your physical body is common during the OBE stage of the NDE journey. Also, since it was a demon rather than an angel greeting Ivan when he was newly disconnected from his body, he put two and two together and realized he was destined for hell.

13

PLANE SLAMS INTO BUILDING AND PILOT FINDS HIMSELF FLOATING ABOVE THREE LIFELESS BODIES AT A CRASH SITE

Meet Captain Dale Black

At age 19, Dale Black was the only survivor of an airplane crash. In the aftermath of that fatal crash, Dale suffered extensive life-threatening injuries and was taken into Heaven where he received a deep revelation of God's love and God's ways.

Following the crash, it would take supernatural intervention from the Lord if he was ever going to walk again, use his left arm, or see out of his right eye. His dream of becoming an airline pilot now seemed impossible. As Dale's story unfolds, you'll see how God equipped Dale with the faith to overcome impossible obstacles again and again.

"Oh my gosh, we're going to be the headlines of tomorrow's newspaper."

Strange, but that was my last thought. I watched Chuck grab the flight controls with both hands and turn them all the way left, all the way back against his chest. And that was my last memory. And the rest of it took place. I found out later, we had slammed into a building—my book says it was 70 feet tall, but on the 50th anniversary we had a ceremony there and the curator and the people who designed the building indicated it was 120 feet tall. That's quite a difference.

But it doesn't matter how tall it was. It was a big building. And we impacted that at about the 75 foot mark at 135 miles an hour. And with that impact, the airplane just broke into a couple thousand pieces and there was no cockpit to be in anymore.

It's not like a big jet. This is a small airplane, maybe as big as your living room, but still that's not that big. And the three pilots, all three of us slammed into this immovable object, kind of like two cars going head on, on the freeway—that kind of impact. And it was lethal. It actually caused fatalities, of course, that impact, that blunt trauma. And then the three pilots fell, all three of us, just right next to each other on the ground. And the strangest part is right now. This is where I can tell you that I was looking down, confused, looking down at three pilots, not knowing that I was in that airplane—really not knowing anything was wrong. But in a sense I was scratching my head, looking down.

I looked at the first pilot in uniform and I went, "Man, he's dead, no doubt," but I didn't recognize right away who that was. And then I looked at the second pilot and, oh my gosh, that's Chuck Burns. He's my flight instructor. He's my good friend. And he looked dead. And then the third body was me. And I looked down—and I'm trying to say this quickly—but I had no pain, I had really no worry, but I was completely confused as to why I'm looking down at three pilots. One of those people was me, and it hit me all of a sudden, not about the cause of the crash, but what hit me was that I realized, "Oh my gosh, that's not me. I'm up here. That's not me. That's my body. I'm Dale Black. Not that my name means anything; it doesn't. That's just who I am. That's my name. And I'm Dale Black. And I'm up here. I am a spirit and I have a soul and I used to live in that body, but I'm not that body."

All of a sudden I realized in my youthful 19 years, I had always thought that I was my body. Maybe no one else has, but I sure have—I thought that was me and that maybe I have a spirit. I don't know what that means. And I have a soul. I don't know what that means. And I guess the soul lives forever, but at age 19 I had never understood this. And right then above my body, I realized I'm a spirit. I have a soul—my mind, my will, my emotions, my spirit, and my soul. They live forever. And that's who I am. And my body is nothing more than the tent. The thing that houses my spirit and my soul, but that's not really me. And I understood the eternal perspective. And I got that before anything else.

Reflections on Captain Dale Black's Experience

As Captain Dale Black describes above, immediately after their airplane slammed into a building, he found himself outside of his physical body confusedly looking down at three pilots strewn about the crash site on the ground. He soon realized that he was one the pilots and that his essence, his being, was so much more than his physical body.

Dale processed many profound theological and philosophical revelations in those moments following the crash as he attempted to come to terms with the implications of his spirit being separated from his physical body. As many of the people we've interviewed have indicated, those initial moments when the spirit is separated from the body are extremely confusing as you try to come to terms with the journey that is beginning to unfold before you.

14

MAN HAS OUT-OF-BODY EXPERIENCE CHASING HIS AMBULANCE FROM ACCIDENT SITE TO THE ER

When we last encountered **Captain Dale Black**, he was floating in the air above three lifeless bodies strewn about the ground at a crash site. Here's the next part of his out-of-body experience.

Anyway, the ambulance showed up. There was life left in me. Thank God for this third paramedic who resuscitated me on the scene. I was put into an ambulance with Chuck—back in those days, that was common. We were thrown in the same ambulance, two paramedics working on us, and strangely my body was in there. I was looking through the window the whole time. I called it an ambulance chase. It makes no sense. You know, I love things that make sense. I love logic. I like business. I like math to a point. I like things that are quantifiable and that you can prove. Anything that you can't prove, I don't like. I'm not really the kind of person who talks like this. And yet here I am. God gave me this experience.

All I know is that my entire life changed in that moment when I woke up in the hospital. But anyway, back to the hospital. I was put on a gurney. Chuck was put on a gurney. I watched this from about five feet above my body. We were raced into the emergency room. Chuck went into one room, I lost track of him, and I went into another. And I was hovering above my body, just below the acoustical ceiling, watching them cut off my gray slacks, my white shirt with the epaulettes, and my wingtip shoes. A gray-headed doctor came in and started giving me the paddles. I guess I had been in and out of consciousness—life. I don't know if I was clinically dead. I would say I was clinically not dead. It doesn't matter. The point is I was right on the verge of life and death. I remember none of this in my brain. I remember every second of it in my heart. That's my spirit. And you are a spirit. That's your heart, and that's what God gave you. Okay? So make sure you understand what I had to learn the hard way—that you are a spirit and you have a soul and you live in this body temporarily.

I was in the hospital. I watched all of this. While I was looking down at my body, and I was still a little confused, I was not hurting at all, but I was thinking thoughts: "It's too bad. It's too bad. I'm only 19. Wow. I wish I had done more. I wish I could have lived longer, but okay. All right. I sort of deserve this." And then all of a sudden, a movie started playing in my mind, like a rewind of a certain part of my life. And I was 12 years old at a church camp in southern California called Cedar Crest. I had come down to an altar at a cabin and there was this athletic minister who had invited the kids, me being one of them, that if they wanted to receive Jesus Christ and you were honest and sincere, come forward and he would pray for us.

Well, I did, and he was praying for me. And I watched this event in my mind while looking down at my body in the emergency room, still July 18, 1969. And I realized that I had given my heart to the Lord Jesus Christ. I invited Him in. I meant it. I was serious. I was genuine and I had a zeal for Him afterward. And then I realized, wow, I gave my heart to the Lord when I was 12, and look at me now—full of myself, self-centered, self-absorbed, selfish to the maximum. I was friendly, but inside I was about as self-absorbed and self-centered as anybody ever could be. And I was ashamed and embarrassed and realized that I didn't deserve to live. I was a humongous disappointment to God as a Christian. Yet, for some reason, that's the only event that played in my mind—that one little section of my life. Of course, I had time to think about it.

Interesting—the most important decision, the most important act I ever did was back when I was 12. When I honestly, sincerely invited Jesus to take over the controls of my life. I guess that's kind of important because I'm alive now and I've survived over 50 years since that crash. I was born again, and God in His mercy answered the prayers of my grandparents who prayed for me daily by name. I think God actually spared my life in answer to their prayers. Not that I deserved anything, because I didn't.

Anyway, I started moving out of the hospital room backward, looking at my body and moving back, and I couldn't control it and I couldn't steer it. I didn't know what was happening.

Reflections on Captain Dale Black's Experience

Captain Dale Black has one of the longer out-of-body experiences we've encountered that includes not only viewing his body from above the crash site, but also following his body in an ambulance and observing the medical care he was receiving in the emergency room. Throughout this time he is continuing to wrestle with his spiritual state and even has a flashback to a pivotal moment in his childhood when he had given his heart to the Lord.

Although Dale's flashback would not in my mind qualify as a full life review, which we'll get into in section 5, he does use the phrase "a movie started playing in my mind," which is what people generally describe during their life review.

15

MAN FLATLINES DURING ORGAN TRANSPLANT AND ENCOUNTERS ANGELS SINGING, "MIKE'S COMING HOME!"

Meet Mike Olsen

Louisville, Kentucky pastor Mike Olsen suffered for several years with idiopathic pulmonary fibrosis, a disease that kills almost as many patients as breast cancer. Mike was relieved when he received a call from the doctor letting him know that they had received a pair of lungs for him.

During his much-needed lung transplant surgery on January 7, 2019, tragedy struck when the last clamp was removed. Mike bled out, flat-lined, and was dead for a period of time.

Mike had many wonderful experiences on the other side of the veil, most notably meeting his organ donor!

The second lung went in, and as they were closing me up, the doctor took the clamp off too early. And I bled out. I died on the table. So in that situation, they were trying to get me back to life. They transfused me with a bunch of blood. But during that time, I saw myself rising off the operating table.

I'm a jokester. So I just said to myself, "Well, at least I'm going up." You know, because that's a good thing. So now, as a pastor, I had the assurance. I knew the Scriptures. I knew that I would be going to Heaven if I ever died, but I just found it kind of comforting to know

I was rising off the table. But as I got off the table, all of a sudden I heard all these negative voices, and they were saying, "You're not good enough. Who do you think you are?" And just taunting me. I thought, "Well, I know what that voice is." And I said, "In the name of Jesus, leave me alone and shut up because I'm a child of God and you can't say those things," and all those voices silenced and never spoke again.

This is where I get emotional. So as I was rising off the table, further toward the ceiling, I saw these rainbow lights swirling all around me. I was like, "Wow, what is this?" I was trying to discern— I still had my mental faculties, so I was trying to discern, "Is this the medicine? What is this?" And then these bright rainbow lights started singing. And then I knew it was angels. And I saw myriads of angels and they were singing, "Mike's coming home, Mike's coming home." They were so happy. And then I heard a voice saying, "No, he's just here for a visit." And as I rose into this bright light, I was just overwhelmed. I was like, "I'm standing in Heaven." As far as the eye can see, it's bright light.

It was just a feeling of total bliss, total. Like I can't explain. I just felt like I was engulfed in light. And then I started thinking about things in my life that I had done. And it was like, that realization came right there in Heaven, and it was like, "It's all taken care of, Mike." And then the thought came, "Jesus is all in all." Every molecule, I felt His presence throughout this expanse.

Reflections on Mike Olsen's Experience

Mike is the only person we've encountered who still had his faculties together at the start of an OBE to the extent that he could operate from a place of spiritual authority and command evil spirits to cease their harassment.

Mike encounters swirling rainbow lights that were singing, which he discerns to be angels. People's descriptions of angels vary greatly during these experiences, but what Mike shares still falls within the range of what would constitute normal angelic or spiritual activity during an NDE.

Although the angels were singing, "Mike's coming home," another voice called out making it crystal clear that Mike was only there for a visit. Unlike many of our NDEers, Mike knew from the very start that his time in Heaven would be limited.

16

MAN DIES FROM NEUROTOXIN IN HOSPITAL AND ENTERS A REALM OF COMPLETE DARKNESS

When we last encountered Ian McCormack he was on the beach wondering how he was going to make it to the hospital. Below we pick up his story where he has already made it to the emergency room and the medical staff has done all they can for him, but they're unable to reverse the effects of the neurotoxin injected by the five box jellyfish.

When I shut my eyes, it felt like the battle to stay alive had finished. As I was feeling this extraordinary release, I heard the flatline alarm go off on the heart monitor. My pulse was gone. Some people see a lot of stuff once they are dead, and of course this was not just heart dead because it was a neurotoxin. This was not a heart attack where you can be heart dead but not brain dead. I was killed by the poison. I was flatlined, everything, heart dead and brain dead. At the moment of death, I felt this extraordinary release and suddenly I was out of my body.

Many people talk about being able to look down and see people standing and talking during their out-of-body experience. Of course, what Jesus said is that when a man dies, his spirit leaves his body. You know, the physical body is just a clay vessel. It is ash to ash, dust to dust. Jesus said, "I am the resurrection and the life. Those who believe in me, even though they die, yet they will live." So the physical body dies but the spirit of the man created in the image of God leaves. So, in a second, I was out of the hospital, in a completely different realm. But now I was awake, standing upright, and everything was pitch black.

I thought, *Did I just die? Have I just died and left my body or have I just woken up in the dark?* I was not sure how long I had been asleep. Well, I had to be alive, not dead. It was dark. Obviously my pupils were dilated and I had been asleep longer than I thought. Sometimes you can go to sleep for what feels like a few seconds and it ends up that a few hours have passed. I thought, *Well, do not panic. Your pupils are dilated. Let them adjust to the dark. You will see some light.* So I then turned 360 degrees around looking for light. I began looking for a light switch, reaching out to my right, trying to not trip over anything. Of course, to my amazement, there was no wall. I went back to where my hospital bed should have been, looking for a lamp or a table.

Nothing. It was so dark I could not see my hand in front of my face, so I brought my hand toward where my face should have been and my hand passed straight through my head. That was impossible. I tried two hands. They both went straight through my face. Yet I could feel that I was there and my hands were there. When I tried to touch my body, I discovered there was no physical form. I was now in a realm where I was dead and out of my body. The only thing I could relate this to was Grandfather telling stories of people who had lost limbs in the war but who continued to experience what they call phantom pain. In my mind I was going, *Well, forget just losing an arm or a leg. You have potentially lost your entire human form that is back in that hospital, and you are potentially dead but also alive in a realm of complete darkness.*

Reflections on Ian McCormack's Experience

While many people describe being able to see their body and its surroundings when they enter into their OBE, that was not Ian's experience. He transitioned into a different realm that was pitch black. He does describe an extraordinary feeling of release as he left his body, which we've found to be especially typical of people who experienced great trauma and pain before they crossed over into the afterlife. He also wrestled with the typical level of confusion reported by most NDEers as they try to reconcile what has just happened.

17

MAN TAKES HIS LAST BREATH AND FLOATS THROUGH THE CEILING AND PAST A SWAMP COOLER TOWARD A BRIGHT LIGHT

When we last encountered **Bryan Melvin**, he was lying on his bed and had just taken his last breath. What follows is what happened when he transitioned into his out-of-body experience.

was not wearing my glasses, but as soon as that happened, I noticed I could see clearly across the room. That was odd because I am very nearsighted.

My clock was in front of me and showed that it was ten minutes before noon. I tried to pet my dog, but my hand went through him. I saw a hand come out of my own hand and go through my dog's chin. My dog started whimpering and crying. And then I began to float above my body. Let's just say I lost my atheism as soon as I started floating above my body, because I realized that I was still alive. In fact, I was more alive after I had left my body than I am right now. It's hard to explain, but that is how it felt.

There was no more pain. I felt good and totally at peace, the most peace I had ever felt. I did not want to go back into that old body and go through all of this stuff. The next thing I knew, I went through the ceiling and passed the swamp cooler on the roof, and on up into what I would call a black void heading toward a light.

Within that black void, I was drifting toward this light. I felt peaceful. It was the most joyous experience I had ever had. I felt **love** and compassion and heard this beautiful music. This music **was in** another language, but I could understand what was being sung. **It** was praising God. They were praising Him for the mysteries of **the** universe. And I was floating there, getting a life review. I did **not** realize that I was headed toward a reckoning. If my neighbor **would** have found me at that moment and gotten me to the hospital **and** resuscitated me, I would have a vastly different testimony, because **I** would tell everybody to go to the light. I was up for a rude awakening and a reckoning just around the corner.

Reflections on Bryan Melvin's Experience

As Bryan recounts this part of his story, he notes that he felt more alive after he left his body than he does today, a sentiment that we've heard many times from other NDEers. Although he is very nearsighted in his physical body, in his spiritual body he was able to see clearly across the room without glasses. He also reports feeling no more pain.

Bryan had an experience similar to many others when he tried to interact with his physical environment. As he attempted to pet his dog, his hand went right through the dog's chin.

Although he doesn't give much detail, Bryan does describe floating through the ceiling and past the swamp cooler on the roof into a black void toward a light, which are all hallmarks of the traditional out-of-body experience.

18

JEWISH TEEN SURPRISED TO ENCOUNTER JESUS AS SHE LEFT HER BODY AND FLOATED TOWARD A BRIGHT LIGHT

When we last encountered **Heidi Barr,** her horse had crushed her as it rolled across her body. Heidi was immediately ushered into an out-of-body experience.

I instantly left my body and was 30 to 40 feet up in the air. I saw my horse roll over my body and my body being tossed like a rag doll. I did not care. My body meant nothing to me. I knew it was me immediately, but I did not care.

I saw my horse slide down the slope, right herself, and head to the barn. My middle sister put her hands against the car window with a look of horror on her face. My little sister screamed and covered her face with her hands. I saw the man on the Arabian run. The Arabian turned and ran down the other trail toward the barn. I saw a lot of commotion in the barn, which was odd because the barn faced away from me, but I could see into the barn. The one thought in my head at that moment was that I wished my sisters did not have to see me die. I did not care that I was dead.

At that moment I noticed there was a light over my shoulder. As I had that thought, I saw that the light was illuminating everything before me, and suddenly I realized it wasn't a light but a man.

The light was emanating from this man. He moved forward until He was beside me. I looked at Him and recognized Him immediately. It was as if I said, "Hi, how are You?" I knew Him. I had always known Him. I had known Him since I was a small child. It was Jesus, which did not strike me as being odd at all. At that moment, it should have been odd because my father was an atheist and my mother was an agnostic. Even though we were part of an Orthodox community, my father told us on an almost daily basis that Jesus Christ is the biggest hoax ever perpetrated on humanity, Christianity is a hoax, and Christians are stupid for having hope—all this because my father believed there was no Heaven, hell, or God. When you die, you are buried and forgotten. You are no more significant than the tiniest speck of dust in this infinite universe. So Jesus was the last person I should have encountered, yet He was the first person I encountered.

Reflections on Heidi Barr's Experience

As Heidi's horse rolled across her body, she immediately entered into an out-of-body experience in which she could see the end of her accident unfolding from a vantage point of 30 to 40 feet up in the air. This quickly transitioned into an encounter with a person whom she understood to be Jesus. Even though she was religiously raised in a Jewish Orthodox community, her father was an atheist and her mother was an agnostic. Yet Heidi still knew this person she encountered to be Jesus; in fact, she realized she'd known Him since she was a small child.

19

MAN LEAVES HIS BODY AND SEES ANGELS AND DEMONS WARRING OVER HIS SOUL

When we last encountered **Randy Kay**, he had just died in the hospital due to an MRSA bacterial infection, which caused a state of hypercoagulability throughout his body.

could feel a tugging at my shirt. It literally felt like something was tugging at my shirt, and then everything went dark. Then I was in a space of almost nothingness, being pulled toward a light. I could see my body as a third party now because I was still on the bed and I could see these warring figures in the distance that I couldn't figure out. I had traveled through what was like a spiral galaxy, a galactic space, and I didn't have a sense of anxiety at this point. It was peace, but I was just soaking it in because everything was ethereal and unlike anything I'd ever seen.

These spiritual beings were in the background. On the right side were these tall figures with glistening armor, and light was shining against them. They were wielding what looked like swords, and they were brilliant. And on the other side were these decrepit-looking figures equally as towering, but they looked like they were morbid creatures also fighting with swords. It was the most bizarre thing. And I just couldn't assess what was going on because everything at that point was somewhat ethereal. I figured out later that they were warring over my soul because I'd been in this state of questioning

God. *Why, God, did You abandon me? I served You all of these years and now You're not answering my prayer.* So that was the state of mind I was in at the time. But I knew enough as a believer in Jesus Christ to cry out His name, and I knew He was the only one who could really save me from whatever was going on.

Reflections on Randy Kay's Experience

Earlier when we heard from Ivan Tuttle, he described a demon grabbing his left wrist and yanking his spirit out of his body. Now, Randy talks about experiencing what felt like a tugging at his shirt as his spirit departed from his physical body. Randy immediately began to rise up, and he soon encountered what he would eventually come to understand were angels and demons warring over his soul. It is not uncommon for NDEers to describe some sort of an encounter in the midst of their OBE with angels and demons or coming to some sort of crossroads between Heaven and hell.

Randy was in a dark place spiritually in the days and weeks leading up to his NDE, and this continued after he crossed over to the other side. Randy knew that Jesus was the only One who could rescue him in that moment of despair, and that's precisely who he cried out to.

20

TEEN RECEIVES BURNS OVER 65 PERCENT OF HIS BODY AND HAS AN NDE WHEN HE BLEEDS OUT DURING SURGERY

Meet Mark McDonough

When Mark McDonough was a teenager, a catastrophic house fire claimed the lives of his mother and younger brother. Mark had burns on over 65 percent of his body. Ten days after the fire Mark experienced a life-altering NDE during surgery.

It was exactly ten days later, because August 3rd was the fire. It felt like a million days, but really wasn't that long. During that whole ten days, all I can remember thinking is *How could God let this happen?* When they finally said that Toby didn't survive, I couldn't believe it. He was a six-year-old boy. Six is innocent. And then Mom was taken off the ventilator on August 5, when her official death occurred. August 5 is significant to me because I suffered a stroke 30 years later on the anniversary of her death.

When my dad saw me for the first time, I was so swollen like the Pillsbury dough boy. I was wrapped in gauze and twice my size because my body was ballooning and bloated from fluid. My face was swollen from the burns. I remember during those ten days thinking, *How could God let this happen?* It was almost like it took ten days for that question to be answered. And the answer was, *I know you're confused. I know you're hurting, and I'm with you. I got you.*

I know God can handle the anger, but today I sometimes break a shoelace and feel like I'm just as mad. So I say, can You give me some credit for back in 1976? But yeah, up until that moment, ten days felt like forever. I was trying to negotiate or to say, *Come on, I'm willing to listen. Just tell me why and I'll do what You want me to do, but just give me some insight.* I'm not sure He gave me a whole lot of insight. But the double-edged sword is He gave me enough certainty to know, okay, I can trust. Just like when my dad said, "Jump off the sideboard counter, I'll catch you. You can trust me. I'm your dad."

That was the feeling I had in that near-death experience. The doctors kept saying it was interesting. The director of the burn unit is a Christian. He's still alive, and I just celebrated his 91st birthday with him last fall. He would say, "We don't know why God does some of the things He does or whether He allows them or whether we cause them, but we do know He is there when we need Him, and He is the strength that we need to get through the tough times."

What a blessing that the surgeon running the burn unit had that faith. But in the NDE it felt like I had been screaming for ten days, right up until that second. I felt like, "God, You must take me. I cannot survive this feeling." The resident would lift my arm off the table, "Excuse me," and blood was dripping to the floor and the skin was being peeled from my abdomen and the pain was just unbearable. I'd be saying, "I can't stand one more second," and one more second would carry on. But then all of a sudden there was this sense that I was in a recliner and just floating up toward this nice, soft, warm light. It was as though I were lying on a beach and my eyes were closed and I could see that light on the other side of my lids and feel this comfort and warmth and safety. I had the feeling that I'm forgiven and I'm loved and it's okay, and we're going to get through this. And it was.

Reflections on Mark McDonough's Experience

This does not come across well in the words Mark used for his experience in our interview, but he was able to feel the excruciating pain of what was happening during surgery even though he was anesthetized. While many NDEers describe a sense of floating, I particularly like Mark's description of feeling like he was in a recliner as he floated toward the light. Having just come through a very traumatic ten days leading up to the surgery, let alone the pain experienced during the procedure, the sense of comfort, warmth, safety, forgiveness, and love he was experiencing was exactly what he needed in that moment.

21

MENNONITE TEEN SNAPS NECK AND AN ANGEL TELLS HIM, "IT'S TIME FOR JUDGMENT"

Meet Joe Joe Morris

Joe Joe Morris grew up in a family that bounced around between multiple Mennonite communities. His life was plagued by depression, anger, sleep paralysis, bedwetting, and other challenges. After hearing his neck snap, Joe Joe discovered that he was out of his body and found himself in Heaven's throne room.

I went into my room, I slammed the door, I grabbed the pillow, and I said, "God, why did You make me? I don't want to live." And I cussed God out. I was so upset. I was so upset at the Creator for placing me on this earth because I felt like everything I did was worth nothing. I was wasting space, and it's a very desperate place to be. And I said, "God, if You don't show me what I'm here for, I don't want to be here anymore." I gave Him an ultimatum.

A week later, I was just going through my everyday schedule. We had a very rigid schedule, because in a community without a schedule, you fail. So we went through the motions in 30-minute to hour-long segments. We were very, very, very structured. I went to take a three o'clock break, I set my timer for 29 minutes, and I lay on my bed for my three o'clock nap.

In the moment I lay on my bed, I felt my neck snap. A paralyzing feeling swept over my body. I could not move. Moments later, I saw the back of my head. I started hyperventilating because I was now in spirit form, yet I could see everything crystal clear. I realized that I could go through things, my hand would phase through my desk, and I tried to get back into my body, but it didn't work.

In a panic, I just ran out my door, but not my door. I ran out my wall and treated it as a door. I sort of felt this light wind as the sheet rock passed through me. Then I was outside and I started yelling at this lady who was going to the washhouse in the center of the colony, "Help, my body's in the room. It's not breathing." She couldn't hear me. Her eyes were glazed over. She had a baby on her hip and she was pulling a cart of laundry.

I remember thinking to myself, *She can't hear me.* Then someone walked through me and I thought, *I am a spirit.* At that time, it felt like a cheese grater on my mind because my senses became so sharp. I could hear miles away. I could hear a car starting miles away. I could hear children laughing at a great distance off. I started thinking to myself, *Oh God, this is too much for me to bear.* At that moment of desperation, angels showed up and said this one line: "It is time for judgment."

I remember thinking to myself, *Okay, I'm trapped out of my body. I know I'm dead.* I looked at my body and it was not breathing. And I remember thinking to myself, *Okay, it's time for judgment. I am definitely not doing anything here on earth.* So I agreed to leave with them.

Reflections on Joe Joe Morris's Experience

Similar to Jim Woodford and Captain Dale Black, Joe Joe had a significant amount of time to interact with his environment. Initially, he tried to reenter his body, but that didn't work.

Eventually, he panicked and ran through the wall and attempted to communicate with a lady outside, but she couldn't see or hear him. In addition to, as Joe Joe described it, being able to phase through things, he also had extremely sharp senses to the point where he could hear sounds that seemed to be coming from miles away. His OBE comes to a close with an angel coming on the scene to tell him it's time for judgment.

While this experience isn't as terrifying as a demon yanking your spirit out of your body as in Ivan Tuttle's case, an angel telling you, "It's time for judgment" has to be a close second.

22

WOMAN DROPS DEAD IN BACKYARD AND IS PULLED INTO A DEEP, DARK, COLD PLACE

Meet Karina Ferrigno Martinez

Karina Ferrigno Martinez left the hospital to be with her kids on Mother's Day and died in her backyard.

I fell down and I started breathing so fast, and I'm sure many of the viewers would understand this, but when someone is passing away, you will see this breathing pattern and all of a sudden it just stops. And that's what happened to me. I was breathing so fast and it stopped. My husband was sitting next to me, by the way. He put on my Apple watch to check my heart rate and he was so concerned. He was unable to call 911 because we had called 911 on Monday, Tuesday, Wednesday, and Thursday. Finally, he was like, "I'm not calling 911; I'll call your sister." So he kept checking my heart rate and my heart rate was dipping; it just never wanted to go back up. It was always going to 60 on the pacemaker.

Then my breathing stopped, and I just heard this beautiful, peaceful voice that I recognized. I had always heard it, but I never heard it. All of a sudden it asked me, "Are you ready to come home?"

It was just so beautiful, gentle, and peaceful. It was just like everything at once. And I said, "Yes" in my heart, not my mind. I was with my kids and I didn't feel like I had to stay. From that moment, what I felt was my spirit. It started coming out at an angle. I was lying down and I just went through my husband. I went up and I stopped and I said, "Wow, I'm dead. I died." But I was at peace, and I still felt that beautiful presence.

I looked down and I looked through my house and my twins were fighting because my daughter always knew something was wrong with me. Now I understand why—she was the only one who knew that I was gone. She was arguing with her brother because he's a boy. He was like, whatever. She was telling him to stop being the way he was, and I could hear their conversation.

My 14-year-old daughter used to have so many health issues too and a lot of medication. She would be on the floor with a lot of anxiety and panic attacks because she knew how sick I was. And I just said—I didn't even speak anymore at this time, it was just my mind—"Who's going to take care of my kids?" And this beautiful voice just said, "It'll be okay." And I trusted Him for the first time. And in the blink of an eye, I just poof went into this darkness—this really dark, dark place. I tell people it's like if you ever build something underground and you seal it; there's no windows. You go in there, and there's darker than that. And then I hit cold. How cold it was in there has never left me.

I heard the voice again. It was beautiful. He said, "Close your eyes and don't turn around." So I closed my eyes and I didn't turn around and I had that fear in me. I started praying and praying and I prayed even in languages I've never spoken. I'm Colombian, so I speak Spanish. So I started praying the Our Father. I was raised Catholic, so I began repeating that, saying, "I'm sorry. I'm repenting." I didn't even know what the word *repent* was in English; it's not in my vocabulary, but I said it that day.

I saw satan's face, and then this blue light, this spirit passed through my entire being. All of a sudden, this white light passed and these gray clouds started opening up. I was head first down in that tunnel and my feet were up. I could not see my feet, but I felt those were my feet. My eyes were still closed, but I could see the light. This golden light just kind of started opening. Then all of a sudden, my head went up into a golden light and I immediately experienced a shower of intense love like I had never felt. And not only just love, but everything that came with it is literally everything.

The peace, no pain, no anger, nothing that I'm feeling at the moment. Right now I feel mad because I want to go back. But it's not the anger you normally have; it's just all these feelings. And I also feel the peace and the love, but it's just this warmth. Then I could see all these other beings and the people calling my name, and they were celebrating me saying, "Come, come." I still had my eyes closed. And He said, "You're home." And I knew that I was in Heaven.

Reflections on Karina Ferrigno Martinez's Experience

When Randy and I interviewed Karina, she was less than two years removed from her near-death experience. As Dr. Jeffrey Long's research shows, it takes an average of seven years for somebody to fully process their afterlife encounter, so it'll be interesting to speak with Karina in the future when she is further removed from her NDE to see how her perspective on her experience has shifted and expanded.

Throughout her OBE Karina encounters a beautiful voice that is guiding and comforting her along her journey. As we've already seen earlier in the book with Ian McCormack and Ed Loughran, it's not uncommon to hear a voice of divine guidance as you're transitioning to the other side of the veil.

Although we didn't ask her to explain further, Karina mentions that her spirit passed through her husband's body. In all of the people we've interviewed to date, we've never had anybody mention anything similar.

Karina has a brief DNDE encounter before she's drawn up into a tunnel of light and is covered by an intense shower of love. Her OBE wraps up with what is commonly referred to as a welcoming committee as she's arriving in Heaven.

CONCLUSION

After making your way through these twelve out-of-body experience accounts, you no doubt have realized that there is great variety in what people experience as their spirit leaves their physical body. While some NDEers like Captain Dale Black and Joe Joe Morris were allowed a significant amount of time to interact with their environment before they crossed the threshold to the other side, others like Randy Kay experienced a rapid and seemingly instantaneous transition to the other side.

These OBE stories strongly reinforce the traditional elements reported by experiencers in this stage of the near-death experience journey, which generally includes a level of confusion as they try to come to terms with what has just happened, a feeling of rising or floating in the air, and being drawn toward a tunnel and/or bright light that seems to indicate the threshold you must traverse to get to the other side.

Several of these OBEs featured angels and demons. By and large, in this stage of the NDE journey angels come on the scene to either announce something or offer help and comfort. Demons may be indicative of an experiencer's upcoming journey to hell, or they may be there to inflict pain and fear in the NDEer.

Discussion Questions

1. You just finished reading twelve different out-of-body experiences. Is there one in particular that

you connected with? What about that story made it stand out to you?

2. The NDEers you met in this section of the book shared both comforting and distressing elements from their OBEs. Did you notice anything in these stories that illustrated either a characteristic of the Kingdom of Heaven or a characteristic of the kingdom of darkness?

3. During some of the OBEs, experiencers were allowed a significant amount of time to interact with their environment while they were in spirit form. Do you see something purposeful in that?

4. As you read these OBEs, how did they make you feel? Were you strengthened and encouraged about your future appointment in the afterlife or were you filled with fear? Why were your emotions kindled to move in that direction?

SECTION 3

HEIGHTENED SENSES

Most near-death experiencers report having a heightened sensory experience when they are no longer tethered to their physical body. The typical senses we associate with our physical body such as taste, touch, smell, hearing, and sight are cranked up to a superhuman level. Experiencers report not needing to talk when they are in their spirit body. Communication is a sort of instantaneous thought-to-thought or perhaps better stated spirit-to-spirit exchange. Many also report receiving or having access to knowledge that gives them a deep understanding of the things they're encountering on the other side. Sometimes that might look like receiving a massive knowledge download in Heaven and at other times that looks like fully understanding why the people you see tormented in hell are there.

23

THE HEAT, THE DEMONIC TORMENT, MAN RECOUNTS THE HORRORS OF HIS TIME IN HELL

When we last encountered Ivan Tuttle he was nearing the end of his out-of-body experience. What follows below is some of his sensory experiences in hell.

As I looked at these people, so many were wondering, "Why am I in hell? What am I doing here? What did I do wrong? Get me outta here. I need to get out of here somehow." But they all knew, even those who were Christians at one time in their life, they knew that they were in hell. All their prayers, when they try to pray from hell, it's like an iron dome is over it. They're not going anywhere. It's like it just hits something and it stops. And these people were screaming. The smell, the stench was horrible.

Now I never saw flames, but I felt this intense heat all the time. It was an intense heat. These demons would sit there and I'd watch them with other people. They did the same thing to me. They stab you with things. They pull on you. They jerk on you. They stick you with great big, long thorns or something. They stick them into you. It's the most horrible feeling. On earth, when you get a splinter, you know that that little dinky splinter hurts so bad in that finger. Can you imagine that same pain from a little splinter through your whole body? That's what it's like—your whole being, your whole spirit being, it feels every ounce of the pain. So intense. But the difference is when you're in the flesh, you can pass out. In the spirit, you live with that pain. And here's the thing to remember—that pain lasts forever. It never stops. It keeps going and going. Listen, a hundred million years, we can think, "Okay, a hundred million years," our mind can kind of grasp that. But a hundred million years isn't even a tenth of a second in eternity. It's like nothing.

I think the thing that was the worst of all was knowing there's no hope. When you are in hell, all those people in there, they know there's no hope. I mean, they want to get out, but they know it's over. It's over, man. Once that happens, there's no getting out of it. You know, I'm one in like 500 billion. I don't know if there's anybody else that's ever gone through what I went through. I just know that when I was in hell, I knew this was it. It was final. And I didn't think I was ever going to get out of this. It was the most horrible, horrible feeling. Even when I talk about it today, my eyes are tearing up. I'm trying not to, here, but my eyes tear up because of the hopelessness that you feel, the horrible feeling that you have because the pain is so intense, the smell is so gross, and it never stops.

Reflections on Ivan Tuttle's Experience

When you take into account that your spirit body's senses are unhindered, that makes what Ivan shares about hell that much worse. Note his descriptions of intense heat and intense pain from how the demons were tormenting and assaulting him. Even if we think of our worst day, it's hard to fathom the depths of despair one must feel in hell when you know you belong there, there's no hope for your prayers for help to reach Heaven, and that it's final.

24

WHEN IT COMES TO EXPERIENCING COLORS, EARTH IS LIKE THE WALMART VERSION OF HEAVEN

When we last encountered **Gabe Poirot**, he had just had his skateboard accident and as soon as he hit his head he was with Jesus in Heaven. What follows below is Gabe attempting to quantify some of his sensory experiences in Heaven.

My visual memory is mainly Jesus. The best way I could describe this to you is when someone is looking at you and it's a very real moment—their eyes are the only thing that you're processing. When I looked into His eyes, they were the only things. I was captivated.

The colors were amazing around Him, the floor, everything was amazing. The best way I can describe the colors is earth is the Walmart version of Heaven color-wise and everything-wise. It's like the TV my grandparents had and all the pixels and their correlation to how you would see things. It was just barely fuzzy. You couldn't really make things out clearly. Well, when it comes to the colors, we're living on an earth that's just fuzzy and we think things are clear, but they're not that clear compared to Heaven. And in Heaven the colors are so much clearer. The green on earth is just like one thousandth of the green in Heaven, if that. One thousandth to a thousand. It's just a taste. When the Bible says in James 1 that the good things down here on earth reflect the Father of lights, with whom is no variableness, neither shadow of turning. That Scripture is very accurate.

Reflections on Gabe Poirot's Experiences

Throughout our many interviews, we've had people describe how the colors here on earth pale in comparison to the colors in Heaven. Some people have even told us that the colors they've seen in Heaven don't exist on earth. It was helpful that Gabe attempted to quantify the difference between the colors he encountered in Heaven and those here on earth. If the colors we see on earth only display one thousandth of their brilliance, then it must be quite an amazing display when you encounter them in their fullness on the other side.

Gabe's description of being wholly captivated by Jesus fits well with so many of the Jesus encounters that have been shared with us. When you're with Jesus, everything else fades to black and He is the only thing that matters.

25

MAN DESCRIBES THE LANDSCAPE OF HEAVEN AS BREATHTAKING TO THE EXTREME

When we last encountered **Randy Kay,** he saw angels and demons warring over his soul and he had just cried out to Jesus to rescue him. Below Randy describes the landscape he encountered during his time with Jesus.

I was so immersed in His presence, and He carried me through that as His arm was around me. He'd never let go. I didn't really look at my surroundings until after some time. When I did, the brilliance of what I was seeing was just breathtaking to the extreme. It was as though in this world, shades of colors and fragrances and other things we see as though a film was covering them. And in Heaven, that film was pulled off. I saw shades of colors and greens and yellows I had never seen before, the fragrances of flowers that I had never experienced in my lifetime. In my physical body, I have nasal blockage, so I'd never really smelled fully until then. All of my senses and my physical abilities were peaked. This was the best I'd ever felt in my life.

There was a landscape, as I mentioned before, the hills and everything was alive. Everything speaks life. Life was coming forth before my eyes. The flowers were growing and there was a river pouring forth. And from my perspective, it seemed like it was coming from Jesus. Everything came alive through the waters and the streams.

And I looked to the right, and I could see these figures and they were joyful. And it was a cascading, kind of linen-like columns and flowing linens amidst the grass and the beautiful colors of the hills and the landscape and the trees and the flowers and so forth. And my sense at that time was that the joy of the Lord was somehow reflective of the life that they lived. That was a reward that they had. And the children that I saw were extraordinarily joyful. And there were angelic voices just echoing throughout, again, more brilliant, more harmonious than I'd ever experienced in the most beautiful symphonies I had attended times infinity, and I was in a place that I never wanted to leave.

Reflections on Randy Kay's Experiences

Similar to what Gabe described in our last story, Randy also recounts being fully immersed in Jesus's presence. Randy not only comments on colors, but he also talks about the fragrances he smelled in Heaven, both of which he said are beyond their counterparts on the earth. In fact, he says it's as if the colors and fragrances on earth are covered by a film, so think of either looking through or trying to smell through a piece of plastic wrap and how that would obscure what you're able to take in. That's an intriguing way to grasp the difference between what Randy encountered on earth versus Heaven.

It's also worth noting that Randy recounts how his physical body has nasal blockage back on earth, but he is not hindered by that in Heaven. He says not only were his senses and abilities peaked, but this was also the best he'd ever felt in his life. This is such a great illustration of the relief and euphoria NDEers experience when they are no longer held back by the limitations of their physical body.

26

MAN VISITED 52 COUNTRIES, THE MOST BEAUTIFUL PLACES, BUT IT ALL PALED IN COMPARISON TO THE LANDSCAPE OF HEAVEN

When we last encountered **Jim Woodford,** he was rising into the air during the latter part of his out-of-body experience. Below we jump into the middle of Jim's Heaven experience in which he describes some of the things he saw in Heaven.

The mist cleared in front of me. I looked up and to my right, where this beautiful mist was lifting off this field. The field was covered in flowers of so many colors—colors that I have no name for. I've traveled to 52 countries in the world. I've been to the most beautiful places, but nothing compared to this. I was stunned by the beauty of it and the rolling fields that seemed to go on forever and this beautiful vault of a darker blue sky than we're used to here on earth—but no sun. As a pilot, I was trying to orient myself and I thought, "If I could find the sun, I'd know my southeast, southwest." No sun. Everything seemed to generate a light that created this fusion of color.

I'll skip forward—they showed me many things, told me many things. I'd developed 360-degree omnivision, I call it. I heard everything. I understood everything. The beautiful flowers spoke to me, sang to me.

Reflections on Jim Woodford's Experiences

As a pilot Jim Woodford was an accomplished traveler who had been to 52 different countries, yet even the most beautiful places he'd seen on earth did not compare to what he saw in Heaven. As Jim and others have described, the colors in Heaven are so far beyond what we have on earth.

Jim also noted that everything he encountered radiated a light that created this fusion of color. He even said the flowers seemed to speak and sing. Several of the NDEers we've encountered have shared similar experiences of everything in Heaven reflecting the light of Jesus as well as others who have said even the plants sing.

Last, it's worth noting that Jim's senses were heightened. Not only did he have 360-degree omnivision, he could also hear and understand everything. This is in line with what other NDEers have described when they are no longer hindered by the limitations of their physical body.

27

NEAR-DEATH EXPERIENCERS SMELL GRANDMA'S COOKIES AND TAPIOCA PUDDING IN HEAVEN

There is something special that happens when you bring two near-death experiencers together for a conversation. It's happened many times when Randy and I are interviewing somebody about their experience—the guest will share something with us and then Randy will go, "Wow, me too." **Jim Woodford** and **Randy** share about a similar experience they both had in Heaven.

Jim: So there I was cuddled up to something that I thought was just a myth, a legend, and I felt so safe and warm. And I know we're running late, but I have to tell you this. As I was being hugged, I suddenly became aware of the incredible smell of warm tapioca. And I'm not here to start the church of the holy tapioca. I'm not, but here's something you should know, because you will all experience this. God knows what a huge difference this makes for us when we encounter Him and His beings. He gives us something that we loved as a child to make us feel we have come home. And when I was a young boy walking home through a snowstorm in Northern Canada in the middle of June, I'd get to my grandmother's house and I'd go in and on her woodstove she would have made warm tapioca for me. Isn't that wonderful? And for some of you, it may be the smell of your mom's perfume. It might be any of those things that brought you joy as a child. For me, it was the smell of tapioca. So I don't mean to digress.

Randy: I'll help you digress a little bit again, because for me when I met my grandmother in Heaven, it was chocolate chip cookies.

Jim: Really?

Randy: Yes, when I visited her home that's what I smelled, those chocolate chip cookies. That was the fragrance in Heaven. Jim, our audience has sometimes noted the variance in the stories—that is, each of us recounts things a little bit differently, or sometimes significantly differently than what others have mentioned. I know it doesn't bother you or me to hear these different accounts, because we each reach a destination. Along the way, our travels to that destination and even our expression of how that destination looks and appears to us is relevant to our own experiences or personality and all of those things. I just think it reflects the glory of God to know us and what we need.

Reflection on Jim Woodford's and Randy Kay's Experiences

I believe Jim hits the nail on the head when he says that God gives us something that we loved as a child to make us feel we have come home. For Jim, that was the smell of his grandmother's warm tapioca, and for Randy that was the smell of his grandmother's chocolate chip cookies. Randy rightly says that this "reflects the glory of God to know us and what we need."

28

MAN GOES FROM FIVE SENSES TO 3,000 SENSES IN HEAVEN

When we last encountered **Alwyn Matthews**, angels were lead-ing him into Heaven. Below, he shares some thoughts about our untapped spiritual potential when he considers what he encoun-tered in Heaven along with a conclusion he draws from the Gospel account of the exorcism of the Gerasene demoniac.

Our spirit is so incredible. There's a story in the Bible where Jesus is casting out demons from a guy in the region of the Gerasenes, and the demon says he identifies himself as legion. And theologians say that literally what he was telling Jesus was that he had 4,000 to 5,000 demons. Now, what that tells me is it's possible for 4,000 demons to occupy a single person's spirit. That's a lot of demons. That tells me there's a lot of bandwidth in our spirit. And so, what we must under-stand is that as spiritual beings, we have incredible bandwidth and incredible capacity.

That's what happened when I went to Heaven—I went from sensing things around with my five senses to my 3,000 senses. I'm just using a number to get my point across, that when people come in contact with Heaven, they will feel alive for the very first time.

Reflections on Alwyn Matthews Experience

Many NDEers reference the Bible when they're trying to make sense of what they encountered in Heaven. Alwyn surprisingly draws a unique conclusion from the story of the Gerasene demoniac to illustrate that we have much more spiritual bandwidth than we usually realize. To illustrate the wide chasm between our earthly senses in our physical body and our spiritual senses, Alwyn says it's like we have five senses on earth and 3,000 senses in Heaven. That's a 600-time increase!

29

WOMAN RECOUNTS HOW EVERY BLADE OF GRASS IN HEAVEN SINGS PRAISES TO GOD

When we last encountered **Heidi Barr**, she had just come to the end of her out-of-body experience and had a surprising encounter with Jesus. We're going to jump a bit further into her Heaven journey after she had just spent time with God the Father. She describes the wonderful things she saw in Heaven.

I could see what I can only describe as Heaven. And the first thing I saw was grass. It was this amazing green grass. This was infinitely far away, but I could see every single individual blade of grass and it was a brilliant green. The colors were beyond what we have here on earth. The most beautiful colors here are merely a shadow by comparison. They are only a reflection of the colors in Heaven. I could also see flowers. I could see every petal of every flower and every vein in every petal of every flower and every pistil and stamen of every flower and every grain of pollen. I could see trees. I could see every leaf on every tree, every individual leaf, every vein on every leaf.

They were all moving, but there was no wind; they were moving with the light and they were singing the praises of God. The grass was singing. That was the thing that just awed me—the grass. Every blade of grass was singing the praises of God.

I could not look away. And then I saw, as I looked farther, that there was a meadow and I could see a misty pathway that was shrouded in clouds. It was as if there was a veil between what was coming down the pathway and myself. I could see people were coming. I could hear singing, but I could not make anything out clearly. I just saw people were coming toward me on that pathway.

This was all far away, but I could see every detail. And it was at that moment, as I was staring at this, that Jesus came and stood right next to me.

Reflections on Heidi Barr's Experience

Like the other NDEers whose stories you've encountered in this section, Heidi also describes the colors in Heaven as beyond what we have here on earth. What is very unique about Heidi's experience is she recounts how she was able to see everything in extreme detail down to every blade of grass, flower petal, and even every single grain of pollen.

Similar to what Jim Woodford shared about the flowers singing during his time in Heaven, Heidi recounts how she encountered every blade of grass singing the praises of God. As we consider so many of these stories, it appears that everything in the environment of Heaven sings praises to and reflects the glory of God.

30

IN HEAVEN YOUR MIND CAN OUTPERFORM GOOGLE

When we last encountered **Ivan Tuttle**, he was in utter despair and torment in hell. We're going to go a bit further down the road in his near-death experience where he recounts what he experienced and felt in Heaven.

One word describes it. Euphoric. You go from total desolation, no hope, no anything. You're so burdened and heavy that all of a sudden now you're, "Oh yes, oh man." You know, you feel everything. You feel the glory of God going through you. It tingles everything that you have, all your senses are tingling. And it's like, oh, you can taste it. You can feel it. And all that smell that was on you is gone and it smells beautiful there. You smell good up there. Your senses are so heightened, even more so than ever.

Even the spiritual senses that you have become so great because now you can look at something and instantly know everything. You can look at Google and you can outperform Google. If somebody was typing something in, you could answer it before they even finished asking the question. That's where you get to when you're in the spirit, especially when the glory of God is all over you, because that's what happens when you go into Heaven—His glory is over you. There's nothing like it.

Reflections on Ivan Tuttle's Experience

Since Ivan Tuttle's experience began in hell, I believe the depths of his heightened senses in Heaven felt that much more extreme. Note how he described the tangible experience of God's glory in Heaven. You feel it going through you. It tingles. You taste it, you feel it, you smell it. Whether talking about God's glory or the love of God, many of the NDEers we've encountered say one or both of them absolutely permeates every part of your being while you're in Heaven.

While other NDEers you've encountered in this section of the book have mentioned having a heightened cognitive ability—just knowing things—Ivan's description of your mind in Heaven being able to outperform Google search was a tangible way any of us can understand to illustrate the instantaneous nature of it.

CONCLUSION

Regardless of whether an experiencer ends up in Heaven or hell, the stories in this section of the book clearly illustrated the heightened sensory experience that is possible when a person's spirit is no longer tethered to and, maybe better said, hindered by the physical body.

We don't pretend to understand how it works for somebody to experience the five senses of sight, hearing, taste, touch, and smell in a spirit body, but outside of the typical travel narrative used to recount a journey on the other side, most of what people share relates to experiencing something in either a hellish or heavenly environment through their core five senses. All of those senses are dialed up to eleven.

Beyond the five senses, many experiencers also report an enhanced cognitive ability where they just know and understand things. In fact, communication with other beings on the other side of the veil is instantaneous, in a sort of spirit-to-spirit communication.

The consistent thread throughout many of the stories you just finished reading in this section of the book is that everything on the other side is brighter, more colorful, more beautiful, and more intense than anything we experience on earth. I appreciated Randy's description of the difference between Heaven and earth—that it's as if the things on earth are covered by a film that mutes what we experience. That is one of the best tangible and understandable analogies we've encountered that clearly illustrates the experience.

Discussion Questions

1. Have you ever had a feeling of your senses somehow being limited or muted here on earth in your physical body? Have you ever felt that limitation temporarily lifted during a time of prayer or a season of particular closeness to the Lord?

2. Throughout the stories in this section of the book, people have shared many beautiful things they encountered in Heaven. What aspects of the environment and landscape of Heaven most excited you?

3. As you consider the heightened five core senses and enhanced cognitive ability available when you leave your physical body, which one do you look forward to most?

4. When you realize that you can experience heightened senses in both Heaven and hell, does that give you pause when you think about your current spiritual state and your final eternal destination?

SECTION 4

ENCOUNTERING OTHER BEINGS

Near-death experiencers often share about beings they encounter on the other side during their afterlife journey. These beings can include:

- Angels, demons, and even satan
- Divine beings: Jesus, God the Father, and the Holy Spirit
- Deceased people: family, friends, strangers

The above beings are the less controversial of the bunch. Some experiencers also report encountering animals in Heaven. We've heard stories including:

- Lions
- Horses
- Deceased pets

Given the scope of who or what we're putting under the heading of beings, this is the longest section in the book.

31

MAN ENCOUNTERS THREE ANGELS RANGING FROM 10 TO 15 FEET TALL

When we last encountered **Jim Woodford**, he was being comforted by the smell of his grandmother's warm tapioca in Heaven. Below we get into his encounter with three magnificent angels.

I turned back to look. I might not have gone to church, but I knew what an angel was. And suddenly I was looking at three magnificent beings coming toward me—very tall, very elegant, silver long hair, beautiful golden light, which was, as I learned later, a refraction of their golden wings that creates what we call a halo. It's the light of their silver hair from their wings when their wings are extended. I remember being astonished because of the feeling of love and peace and safety that flooded over me was truly overwhelming, and just mere seconds before I felt all this hatred and evil toward me.

They came right up to me, and the first one approached me. And of all the things that I will always remember about this incredible encounter were their eyes. Now imagine these beautiful creatures—ten feet tall. Another one about 12 feet tall. And then the one coming behind dressed in warrior gear, truly a guardian angel, about 15 feet tall. These were wonderful creatures. The first one walked up to me and looked down at me. And the thing that I'll always remember is their violet eyes. Then he spoke to me and his lips didn't move. It was more than telepathy. He was in my mind and I was in his. And I say "he"—I don't want to use the word *androgynous*, but they looked like the best of all of us. They had the gentleness of a female and the strength of a warrior—just this incredible combination of everything that's good.

All of a sudden, I felt this wonderful arm come up and around my shoulder. And then this magnificent, huge, feathered wing came out around his arm and he pressed me into his chest. And I looked up into those violet eyes and heard this beautiful voice in my mind that said to me, "Fear not, James, for we are your constant friends." And now as you gentlemen probably know, whenever you get an email or a text or a letter from me, I always sign it, "Your constant friend."

So there I was cuddled up to something that I thought was just a myth, a legend, and I felt so safe and warm.

Reflections on Jim Woodford's Experience

These three angels came on the scene shortly after Jim had encountered a demonic creature who was trying to pull him into hell. He was in a state in which he needed a lot of comfort, and that's precisely what these angels provided.

Of all the interviews we've conducted in the past few years, Jim provides one of the most detailed descriptions we've received of the features of angels. The features that really stood out as unique in comparison to other descriptions we've heard were their violet eyes and that, while they were neither male nor female, they were an incredible combination of the best of us with the gentleness of a female and the strength of a warrior.

There is a divide among scholars about whether or not angels have wings. In Jim's experience the angels had wings, so we'll just have to take his word for it.

32

MAN WITNESSES AN ANGEL SHOWING JESUS THE BOOK OF HIS LIFE ACCOMPLISHMENTS

When we last encountered **Jim Woodford,** he was with three angels. Now we're going to jump further ahead in his Heaven journey to where an angel has just finished showing a figure the book of Jim's accomplishments during this life. That figure was none other than Jesus.

I was watching and this figure was leaning forward, clearly intent on the little bit that was written in there. Suddenly the figure straightened up and the angel folded up the book, put it in his sleeve, and disappeared. And then this magnificent figure turned toward me. As He turned from profile to direct-on, suddenly the shimmer that had covered His features vanished. And I found myself face to face with none other than Jesus Christ, the Son of God—someone I thought was just some old Jewish legend that people had made up. I was looking at this figure and the magnificence of this figure. Not just the look of intense love and concern for me, but this golden light flowed out of Him. It seemed to start at His head and flow down His body. It was light that behaved like slow-moving water. It flowed off Him and it flowed down that slope. I fell to my knees and tried to crawl toward Him. I had to get closer. It was as though I had finally come home; I had found what I had searched for all my life. And I started to crawl toward Him to get closer. And then His eyes looked into mine. When I looked into those eyes of gray and green blue, I was lost in the love of eternity.

This magnificent creature knew me, too, but this was a creature of love and forgiveness and He desired to know me better. For a split second, although my intellect knew better, when my eyes met His it was as though I was the only one in creation, the only one He had ever created. He knew me that intimately and loved me that deeply. In that moment I knew from then on, whatever happened to me, I was His forever, but I just wanted to be around Him.

I tried to crawl closer to Him and two guardians appeared beside me and held me back. I struggled free and continued to climb toward Him. Suddenly He raised His right hand and there was no mistaking what the gesture meant. He was still smiling in a gentle way, but this was a definite command to stop. I remember the feeling inside of me of not being allowed to come closer. I waited with bated breath, I guess—if I was breathing. But I was just completely enveloped in the love of His eyes. And then I guess I must've taken another step or two or crawled on my knees. All of a sudden, He raised his hand even higher. When He raised His hand, His cloak fell back and I saw the remains of the crucifixion. And then He looked intently at me and He began to speak to me.

People say to me, "What did He sound like?" How can I possibly be accurate? But suddenly I heard His voice. And with Him, unlike the angels, which was more of telepathy or a mental thing, Jesus's face moved just as you or I would when speaking to each other. And then I heard the voice of the Son of God, and it stunned me that He knew my name. He knew me.

He looked at me with the gentlest of smiles—hands still raised, meaning to not come forward. And He said to me, "James, My son, this is not yet your time. Go back and tell your brothers and sisters of the wonders we have shown you." And His hand slowly came down and crossed over His left.

I was overwhelmed with the fact that He knew my name, but more than that I was now coming to the realization that I wasn't being allowed to stay. And I began to plead. I began to beg, "Please let me stay. This is what I've yearned for all my existence. I just want to be wherever You are. Please don't send me away. Please let me stay." I remember saying this: "Please let me stay. I won't be any trouble." Can you imagine saying that to the Son of God? "I won't be any trouble!" But I was desperate.

Reflections on Jim Woodford's Experience

There are so many things to unpack from Jim's encounter with Jesus.

Although it's a small part of the overall encounter you just read, don't miss the little book that the angel shows Jesus and then puts back in his sleeve. Do each of us have a guardian angel that follows us around and records our life? That's what this part of Jim's encounter seems to imply.

When Jim looked into Jesus's eyes, he said he was lost in the love of eternity. This is a typical response from NDEers who report spending time with Jesus. They all say that they were lost in or overwhelmed by His love.

Like many NDEers who experience Heaven, Jim did not want to return to earth, but Jesus told Jim it was not his time. In fact, he was given the assignment of telling his brothers and sisters about all the wonders he had seen in Heaven. Not everybody who goes to Heaven is given a specific assignment before they are sent back, but for those who do, that divine assignment seems to profoundly mark the course of the rest of their life.

33

MAN WITH LIFELONG LOVE OF HORSES ELATED TO DISCOVER THEM IN HEAVEN

When we last encountered **Jim Woodford**, he was with Jesus and had just been informed he could not stay in Heaven. He must return to earth to complete his assignment. Below we jump into another part of his heavenly experience in which he encountered one of his loves on earth, horses.

They wanted to show me something that would really make me happy. The second guardian raised his hand, and suddenly horses came from around the grove of trees toward me, and as they trotted across the grass, the grass lit up with the light from their hooves. Three of the most magnificent horses came toward me.

Now, I had never studied the Bible. I had no idea at that time that when Jesus comes back, He'll be riding a white horse. It's in the Bible. I was stunned, because as I stood there they came right up to the fence. I had loved their kind all my life, and they seemed to know that. They looked at me with such love in their eyes. And I reached forward to stroke the neck of the lead horse, and my hand sank right into the body of this being of light. And when I pulled it back, the light of the horse's body stuck to my hand until I got 10 to 12 inches away and then it went back into the horse's body. It was just phenomenal to watch and to experience. I've come to call it the sticky love of God, not something you hear every day. So those were the horses.

Reflections on Jim Woodford's Experience

The angels who were leading Jim around Heaven wanted to show him something that would make him exceedingly happy. He has been a lover of horses his entire life, so imagine his delight when three magnificent horses approached him in Heaven.

As you've seen in many of the other stories you've already encountered in this book, God has a tendency to bring people things that will bring them joy and comfort when they're in Heaven. On the one hand, this illustrates just how much He loves us, but on the other it also shows just how deeply He knows us.

Note Jim's experience of stroking the neck of the lead horse; his hand sank right into the horse's body. The light from the horse's body stuck to Jim's hand until he moved about a foot away. Even the animals in Heaven reflect the light of God or, as Jim says it, that sticky love of God.

34

MAN RECEIVING DOUBLE LUNG TRANSPLANT MEETS HIS ORGAN DONOR IN HEAVEN

When we last encountered **Mike Olsen,** he had died on the operating table and was transitioning from his out-of-body experience
into Heaven. Below we get into the next part of his heavenly journey in which God allows him to meet his organ donor in Heaven.

thought, "Oh my goodness. I worried about way too much stuff on
the earth." I was worried about my finances. I was worried about my
health. Even as a Christian, I was worried about my spiritual condition—did I do enough? You know, was I good enough? I knew Jesus
took care of it. But when I got there, He did take care of it. It was like
the slate was washed clean. The realization was, "Mike, it's not you
anyway. Why, why were you even thinking that? It's all Jesus." I mean,
the whole place was filled with His presence. The glory of the Lord fills
the temple—that was the Lord.

As I stood there, all of a sudden I got emotional. I started thinking about the donor. I thought, "Oh my God, this guy died so that I
could live. This guy died so I could have his lungs." I thought I'd said
it out loud, but I think it was in my spirit man, because in Heaven
when I was talking back and forth, it wasn't like speaking. It was
like, my spirit was speaking, I guess.

So anyway, I cried out through my spirit and I said, "I want to thank
my donor." All of a sudden, I looked behind. I don't know why. I just

felt a presence behind me. I looked over my left shoulder and there was Jesus, and there was the donor. How did I know it was the donor? I just knew. It was as if Jesus said, "Here he or she is." I don't remember. The figures were like, I couldn't see them fully, even Jesus. I don't know why that was. Anyway, the Lord came up to me and He put His hand on my left shoulder and He said, "Mike, these are your new lungs because you just received them."

I said, "Yes, Lord." And at that moment, when I said, "yes, Lord," I started floating back down to the OR table. I just had the feeling that I had to agree with Him. I had to agree that I would take this person's organ into my life, into my body. As a transplant patient it's so strange to even think about having somebody else's organ in your body. So God gave me the comfort to know that He knows about it. He knew about it before I'd even got the transplant done. He knew all things.

Reflection on Mike Olsen's Experience

The majority of the NDEers who share about meeting Jesus in Heaven describe being completely overwhelmed in His presence. Everything else simply fades into the background. It's very intriguing that Mike had the wherewithal to make a request of Jesus—a request that Jesus immediately granted.

Mike was able to briefly meet and thank the donor who had given up their life and specifically their lungs so Mike could keep on living. Note that Jesus told Mike that those were his new lungs because he had just received them. When Mike said, "Yes, Lord," he began floating back down to the OR.

In our multi-year journey of collecting and telling stories of the afterlife, Mike's continues to stand out because he's the only NDEer we've encountered to date who has met their organ donor in Heaven.

35

MAN LEARNS ALL ABOUT DIFFERENT TYPES OF ANGELS IN HEAVEN

When we last encountered Ivan Tuttle, he was sharing about things he was experiencing and feeling in Heaven. Below we jump to a part in our conversation where we asked Ivan how he knew so much about the angels he encountered in Heaven.

Well, I was told what they were. I cheated. I paid attention for once. You know there's a power that angels carry, and the most powerful angels are archangels. When you're in their presence, it's almost like being in the presence of God—it's that strong. It's that powerful. When an archangel appears, do not mess with it because they're going to appear for something that's really special.

There are angels that have wings; there are angels that don't have wings. There are angels that look like you and me, and to prove a point, I don't have the passage in front of me right now but it's in Acts. If you remember, when Peter got out of prison, he went up and he knocked on the outer door and the girl ran and said, "Oh, I forgot to unlock the door." She said, "Oh, it's Peter," and ran back in to everybody, and they said, "No, it must be his angel." Well, why did they say that? Because there are angels that can look just like you and appear someplace where you might not be.

Sometimes you hear people say, "Oh, somebody was in someplace." I've had people tell me before, like I'm up in the state of

Washington and somebody in Florida says, "Hey, I saw you today. You talked to me."

And I'm like, "Really?"

"Yeah, I was talking to you about your book."

And I'm like, "Okay, where?"

"Down here in Florida."

And I'm going, no, I wasn't there. So as far as I know, that's one of my angels. That's all I know. And so those things happen. There are messenger angels, there are angels that are dispatched to bring you a message that is coming. You'll have angels that can appear in the middle of the night or just be standing next to you and constantly talking to you in your ear. Hopefully you can hear them. Your spirit hears them, but you have to get your mind in tune to it by allowing the spirit.

Here's the key to listening to God and listening to things that God wants you to hear—you have to allow your spirit to rule your brain, not your brain rule your spirit. We've been taught through religion that our brain must control our spirit. The reality is our spirit must control the brain because that's the way it was designed. We were designed so that when God breathed into the nostrils of Adam, it was to activate his spirit so that he can keep his mind going. We need to learn to do that.

You have a guardian angel. You really do have one. There's one there. Some people can see angels and some people can't. I can't tell you why, but these angels have different assignments. Angels are coming to bring you things. You've heard of people getting in a wreck, about ready to hit a cement truck, and all of a sudden their car veers off to the right and they never turned the steering wheel. Well, that's your guardian angel that did that. People can say what they want, but they're real.

Reflections on Ivan Tuttle's Experience

We're fortunate Ivan Tuttle cheated and asked questions about the angels he encountered in Heaven. He offers us a good overview of some of the different types of angels people sometimes encounter.

If you ever encounter an archangel, know that something special is about to happen.

36

MAN ENCOUNTERS JESUS ON THE OUTSKIRTS OF A GRAND CITY

When we last encountered **Bryan Melvin** he had come to the end of his out-of-body experience and entered a life review (which we will read about in more detail in Section 5). Below we step into his encounter with Jesus.

What happened next was, I was going through this void and I was having this sense of love and compassion. When I got to where the light was getting bigger, I could see that it was coming from a person who was standing on a rock, and behind Him it opened and I could see a grand city, but then it got dark and I could see something else, but I could not make it out. I floated toward the rock. I landed feet first on the rock and the person who was on the rock was wearing a robe and light was coming from Him.

It was a brilliant light of many colors and shades. I cannot even explain this brilliant white light; it was phenomenal. It was coming from the person and He had His hands in His robe. When He took His hands out, it really got bright. Like I said earlier, I landed feet first before Him and then I fell down face first. Then somebody or something picked me up, even though I did not want to get up. I was right in front of Him. He had a hood on and I recognized who it was. It was Jesus!

Reflections on Bryan Melvin's Experience

Many of our NDEers have described coming to some sort of gate or boundary that they are not allowed to go beyond. In Bryan's case he meets Jesus on the edge of a grand city. Like others have described, there is a brilliant light emanating from Him.

Although Bryan describes landing feet first in front of Jesus, he says he immediately fell down face first. Many have told us about being unable to stand in the presence of Jesus. The glory in His presence is so weighty, you can't help but kneel or lay face down before Him.

37

MAN ENCOUNTERS ADOLPH HITLER IN HELL

When we last encountered **Bryan Melvin** he had had been before Jesus on the outskirts of a grand city. Below we move on to part of his time in hell in which he encountered two very prominent and recognizable people.

To make a long story short, we came to a row of cells and I saw some Nazis, people who had committed horrible atrocities, and they were experiencing being shot and killed. I saw the man who was known as the blond butcher. He orchestrated and laid the foundation for the final solution. He was killed in Czechoslovakia in 1942.

I walked to another place and there were all these entities around and I stopped and looked inside this one cell that looked like the inside of a furnace. Inside I saw Adolph Hitler. You could not mistake him. People do not realize the depth of the vile hatred that he had and how much he was involved in the occult. His powers of deception were acquired through luciferianism, a religion practiced by the ancient Nordic pagans.

He was being gassed and cremated repeatedly. His flesh would be consumed, burned off by the flames, and then come back. I cannot explain it. He was feeling the pain, yet he was also getting violently angry.

The part I saw was him experiencing the flames of the furnace, but I knew intuitively that he also experienced the gas chambers. He experienced being stripped. He experienced being raped. He experienced being buried alive. He endured all the atrocities that he put the Jewish people through.

It was unmistakably him. He had his little mustache and everything. He looked like a picture I had seen of him from about 1945, where he was pinching some German kid soldier on the cheek. That guy survived the war and talked about that. He looked like that, but he was bent over. Some people say that he might have had Parkinson's, or Parkinson's that was induced by the drugs that he was being given. He was a drug addict. People do not know it, but it has come out that Dr. Morell gave him shots and some synthetic form of methamphetamine.

Reflections on Bryan Melvin's Experience

Bryan's story is one of many near-death experience accounts we've read or shared about time in hell in which the experiencer describes seeing people being imprisoned in cells experiencing repeated torture.

While many often describe seeing less prominent, everyday people in hell, Bryan saw two men who are of historic significance. First was Reinhard Heydrich, and second was none other than Adolph Hitler. Both of these men were repeatedly experiencing the atrocities they had committed on earth.

38

MAN DEAD FOR 30 MINUTES IS USHERED INTO THE PRESENCE OF JESUS

When we last encountered **Randy Kay,** he and **Jim Woodford** were discussing the comfort Randy felt when the wonderful smell of his grandmother's chocolate chip cookies hit his senses in Heaven. Below, Randy shares details of his time with Jesus.

Everything went dark and I died, my heart stopped. And this was for, we think, a period of about 30 minutes. And that's when I met Jesus. And this is the part where, thinking about it, I start to become emotional.

It's a very ethereal experience, and putting much of it in words is extraordinarily challenging. From my perspective, I was looking at a beautiful landscape and then all of a sudden I was in the landscape and what I observed as beauty from a distance, now I'm immersed in it. John Burke's analogy is going from 2D or 3D to 4D. So there was a darkness, but there was a light that was shining from above. And that almost sounds cliché, but it was so bright, so brilliant that I felt as though I couldn't look at it because I would be blinded. The light was infusing through the dark space from above to the point where it was turning as I was rising. I could faintly see my body at the inception as I was rising above. It was turning from pitch black to lighter colors. And then I looked out in the distance and saw strange figures, and they seemed to be battling each other, kind of warrior figures on one side or the other. I didn't know what that was about, but I did know that I needed to call out Jesus—the name of Jesus Christ. And I did.

In the next moment, I was there with Him. This figure put His cheek against my cheek, and He was holding me, I mean tightly. I didn't turn to Him, but I knew that it was Jesus. And for a while we didn't have to talk because there was a communion. He knew my thoughts, I knew His, and He whispered to me, "Trust Me."

He didn't have to say "I love you" because Jesus is love. For the first time in my life, I felt the presence of love in a complete way. The Bible talks about now we see dimly. I knew love in the person of Jesus Christ in a way that was apart from an action or an emotion or anything of that sort. It was an immersion in the presence of the Lord Jesus Christ. He was my friend. He was my companion. I felt like I was an audience of one, that there was no one else in the world, even though I knew the cares of the world were on His shoulders. I felt like there was no one else but Him and me. And when I looked into His eyes, they tumbled through me, and everything that was dark was exposed by His light—everything that I had worried about, every fear. I was a fearful person and I didn't even believe in NDEs until I had my own. I was a skeptic of that. I even ridiculed some of those stories, and now I knew that He was going to take care of my children. I knew that He was going to do that. I just had perfect peace and comfort. Comfort is something that, again, almost sounds cliché, but I have never to this day felt absolute comfort and peace as I did in those moments.

Reflections on Randy Kay's Experience

When Randy comes into Jesus's presence, He is cheek to cheek with Him and Jesus is holding Randy in a tight embrace. Time and time again, when NDEers share their stories of encountering members of the Trinity, be it God the Father, Jesus, or the Holy

133

Spirit, it's always in a way that they can receive and meets a need that they have.

As Randy described earlier in the book, he was in a place of extreme turmoil and distress and was wrestling with his faith before he had his near-death experience. What he truly needed when he got to Heaven was a hug from Jesus.

Randy goes to great lengths to express his feeling of complete immersion in the love of Jesus and how that gave him an absolute sense of comfort and peace. Based on the many afterlife stories we've shared, that immersion in the love of Jesus that permeates all of your being seems to be a critical transformational moment in many Heaven experiences. When these men and women come back to earth, their personalities are profoundly shifted. Many of them have a love and empathy for the hurting and the lost that they'd never had before. It's almost as if they now see people through the eyes of Jesus.

39

MAN MEETS BELOVED CHILDHOOD PET IN HEAVEN

When we last encountered **Randy Kay,** he was in the presence of Jesus. Below we move to a part of his Heaven story in which he encountered his beloved childhood pet. We've heard a number of these pet stories through the years, and this seems to be another way God brings comfort to the experiencer during their time in Heaven.

I was seeing these animals throughout Heaven, even the ones like lions who prey upon other animals, but they were of a softer, gentler nature. But there was one instance that Jesus had picked out just for me because when I was growing up, I was bullied a lot. I was an overweight kid, and I was taunted. I suffered from asthma, so I was a sickly kid. I was in the hospital consistently with a collapsed lung and all kinds of things. So I wasn't in the least bit a popular kid. I was tormented by bullies most of my childhood, but my parents brought home this dog, Casey, a little rat terrier. I was more or less an only child who had an older brother and sister, but they were out of the house by this time.

So Casey became my only friend. Casey was the only one. I came home from school, running from school wanting to get away. And he was there all the time. He would hop on my lap when I was feeling down; he sensed that. He would crawl up and lick my face. He was my best friend and I miss him. Of course, by this time he had died when I was young.

When I was in Heaven with Jesus, He was showing me all of these wonders and then He turned to me, He motioned over to look at this little dog, Casey. Casey was just jumping up and down on me and He said, "See, I give you the desires of your heart." I realized He had given me Casey, and He said, "You'll see him again when you return." Then Casey went away.

Reflections on Randy Kay's Experience

Of all the things we could talk about related to near-death experiences, pets in Heaven is one of the more controversial ones. Many say animals do not have souls, therefore they can't or won't go to Heaven. Yet as Randy and others have shared, they encountered a beloved pet during their time in Heaven.

Based on the stories we've heard, God allows experiencers to encounter their pets in Heaven to bring them joy and comfort. He does it simply because He loves us.

40

WOMAN MEETS HER DECEASED PUPPIES MAX AND TASHA IN HEAVEN

When we last encountered **Karina Ferrigno Martinez**, she was being welcomed into Heaven. Below she recounts her experience of meeting her beloved puppies in Heaven.

I could barely go in because I felt so worthless. I said, "This is not good for me. Just send me back because I'm such a bad person. I did so many bad things." The voice said, "Just come, you're home."

I thought I wasn't worth anything at all. I didn't feel like I was worthy to be there. The voice kept saying, "Open your eyes." Earlier I had seen something evil in that darkness, so I didn't want to open my eyes. And the voice said, "Look to your right and open your eyes." So I just barely opened my eyes and I could see the shape of this beautiful dog that I lost the day before I went in to get my pacemaker. His name was Max. And then I saw the shape of my other dog, Tasha. Then I fully opened my eyes and I was full of joy. I was so happy.

Reflections on Karina Ferrigno Martinez's Experience

When Karina arrived in Heaven, she was struggling with feelings of unworthiness because of the life she had lived. She was also traumatized by the evil she had encountered in the darkness in the early stages of her near-death experience. God had to reassure her several times that she was home, that she belonged.

When she was finally brave enough to open her eyes just a bit, she saw her beloved puppies Max and Tasha. At that moment, she opened her eyes wide and was filled with joy and happiness.

Similar to Randy's story, God brought Karina her puppies Max and Tasha to give her joy and comfort as she was struggling to come to terms with whether she belonged in Heaven.

41

12-YEAR-OLD BOY MEETS ANOTHER BOY IN HEAVEN WHO SENDS HIM BACK WITH A MESSAGE FOR HIS PARENTS

Meet Retah McPherson and Her Son Aldo

Retah McPherson's son, Aldo, suffered a severe brain injury due to a car accident when he was 12 years old. During his coma, he had a supernatural experience in which he went to Heaven, saw God, angels, Moses, and Abraham. Aldo came back with one message: Jesus is alive!

While we were in the hospital and Aldo was in a coma, I had a message that somebody had phoned me. It was the day before they were going to turn off the machines. And this guy says to me, "Retah, I just want to encourage you. Our son had the same experience. He drowned in the sand and was also in a coma." I asked him this question. I said, "How is he today?" And then he said, "He died." I was in so much shock, I put the phone down. Well those people went and found our address, went to search for us, and they left a card.

So in the time that my son had this heavenly experience, he met this child. So then after three months we went back home. He had come out of the coma but was still lying flat, couldn't speak, couldn't talk, nothing, but he could write. One morning he was showing me that he wanted to write, and I gave him his pen and everything and he said, "I met this boy in Heaven and his name was Dwano. You need to find his parents and tell them he's so happy in Heaven. He doesn't want to come back. Tell his father and his mother that they need to give their lives to the Lord. That's what he requested." And then he went on and he said, "They need to sell their airplane."

Now, I thought, okay, now we lose it. Now we lose it. How many people do you know who have an airplane? And he said, "You must tell them today that he's very happy and he doesn't want to come back." And he said, "You have the details." He explained about that card, and I put one and one together. In those years, it was still fax machines. I thought to myself, *Lord God, You need to have grace on me. What if I send this letter to people whose son died and this is not right?* And Aldo wrote, "Mom, trust God. God wants to use his parents for His Kingdom." I was like, *God, this is a step of faith.* Sure enough, these people phoned and the mother said, "I couldn't wait any longer to hear from my son and I was ready to do anything and here I received this letter out of Heaven."

By the way, the guy had an airplane. He was a businessman.

About 15 years later, I don't know if you ever heard about Angus Buchan here in South Africa. He had a campaign and everybody came together on the field and this guy stood there and gave his testimony with this letter 15 years later. He was on his way to a mission trip. They sold everything and there they were ministering around the world. So for me, God was teaching me steps of faith. When God prompts you to do something for Him, write the letter. This is who I saw in Heaven. Tell his parents he's so happy. And this is something that we need to know. Heaven is a place where we are in God's presence all the time. Who would want to come back? But that place is also there for you and me right now as we can bring the Kingdom down to earth.

We know those people till this day, and we actually became friends.

Reflections on Retah and Aldo McPherson's Experience

This part of Aldo and Retah's story is an absolute favorite of ours. Of all the people we've talked to over the past few years, this is the only story we've come across in which an experiencer came back from Heaven with a very specific message from somebody who had already gone on to Heaven. What's even crazier is that Dwano's parents had connected with Retah while Aldo was still in a coma in the hospital.

Retah's heart must have been beating so fast when she faxed the letter to Dwano's parents. And then to hear the response that Dwano's mom had been praying for confirmation of what had happened to her son. And then fast-forward 15 years, they sold everything including the airplane and became missionaries. This is such an amazing story of a visit to Heaven making a dramatic ministry impact here on earth.

42

ANGELS TAKE WOMAN ON A TOUR OF HEAVEN AND SHE SEES GOLDEN STREETS AND THE TREE OF LIFE

When we last saw **Karina Ferrigno Martinez**, she had just encountered her dogs Tasha and Max in Heaven.

I saw this beautiful angel and this angel had wings. It was flying and there was a beautiful white light radiating behind this angel. And I heard a voice coming from the angel and he was holding this brownish, what I thought at first was a box. It was the book of life, my book of life. And I ran past my dogs and I started flying.

The streets there are gold, so the golden light was coming out of the city. I didn't see much of the structures because I was so focused on all the beautiful things that were happening on the ground. There was my dog and the beautiful golden streets.

When I was flying, I got to see the tree, the river, everything. I could see everything. I had these two massive angels next to me, just guiding me. I wasn't talking to them, but they knew what I was asking them, and they were giving me the responses to my questions. Finally we got to the ground that I know I wasn't touching and we were close to the tree of life.

Reflections on Karina Ferrigno Martinez's Experience

Following the time with her dogs, Karina encounters two massive angels. One is carrying the book of her life, which is similar to what Jim Woodford described earlier when he talked about an angel sharing the book of his life with Jesus.

Karina is unable to give us much detail of the city because she was so focused on only a few of the things she was seeing on the ground. This is very common in so many of these NDE accounts in which the experiencer is so overwhelmed by one or two aspects of the experience, they're unable to give much detail about the things that were in the periphery of their vision and their experience.

Karina also notes that she was able to ask the angels questions that they answered through what we like to refer to as spirit-to-spirit communication, something that we've heard from many of our NDEers throughout the book.

43

MAN ENCOUNTERS ALL THREE PARTS OF THE TRINITY IN HEAVEN

When we last encountered **Ed Loughran,** he had died of a massive heart attack following a ride he had taken on his brand-new bike. Below, he takes us into his Heaven experience in which he meets all three parts of the Trinity.

felt like I had 12 to 18 hours in Heaven, and I didn't see anything except the screen going black and there's just a purple line and then white in the far-off distance. And then I'm immediately standing next to Jesus. I'm standing right next to Him, and I looked and the first thing He said was, "Well done, good and faithful servant."

And I said, "How can that be, Lord? I don't get it. I've only accomplished this much of what You've called me to do with my life."

He said to me, "Have you connected well with Me?"

I said, "God, I don't know anybody personally who has spent more time in prayer connected to You. I've heard of people. I just haven't met them."

He said, "What you've done has flowed from that."

I said, "Yeah, I've connected well."

He responded, "What you've done is connected from that place of presence of spending time with Me. Well done, good and faithful servant." And then we talked a little bit more, and I still don't get it. He spent 45 minutes talking about courageous choices I've made.

The first thing I felt was the affection of God. Also, I knew He was a little taller than me. And I say He felt more like a Latino because He was close to me. I've been all over, everywhere but Antarctica. I've done ministry teams and trips and all that stuff. And so, the Latins, you know, you're not there unless you can smell each other's breath. "Hey, how are you doing?" Oh yeah, I smell your breath. And Jesus was like that. Not like, "Hi, I'm a German white guy from the United States." He just felt more Latino culturally, but I knew not to look at His face.

One of the things I share is that I've probably met 16 people with similar stories. And three out of four of them who saw His face, He had to command them to come back. If they saw His face, He had to command them to come back. "No, your mom needs you. No, this isn't your time. No, you have to go back." So I just knew not to look at His face. I don't know why. I don't remember hearing that. I just knew not to. It was just me.

It was a light place. I felt the affection of God. If I could bring one magic wand from there, if I could just say, "Here's what I have from Heaven," it's that everybody could feel this infinite affection of God. When I was dead, whatever sinful nature was no longer there. I didn't fight. I didn't resist. Whatever need for control I had was gone. I just received, I didn't fight it. It was just me and God. There were people way, way in the distance like a sliver. There's just a river of things way in the distance. But I didn't recognize or see anybody. It was mostly me and Jesus. It was infinite affection. I couldn't quantify it. I don't know, other than I encountered the Holy Spirit and the Father as well.

So anyway, there's the affection of God from Jesus, and it was just extraordinary. So then suddenly say 20 or 30 feet away, there was Holy Spirit. I didn't see Holy Spirit. And I'm like, "Hey, Holy Spirit, we've been buddies. We were friends for a long time." And I'm like, "Oh, Holy Spirit." But it felt like a distance and the thought came,

Holy Spirit's like a woman. And I'm like, "What?" And the thought was "easily grievable." And I'm like, "Oh, okay. Oh, Holy Spirit, I love You. I need You. What would life be without You? I love You, Holy Spirit." And immediately I was there and enveloped in the presence of the Holy Spirit. And I felt again, the first thing was affection, an infinite level of affection.

Then suddenly it turned into the jealousy of God. And this is where I say 12 to 18 hours, because this is where I had an ecstatic experience in the classic early church sense, where it was timeless. And the jealousy of God for me—God doesn't want me to settle for 99.99999999 percent of what God has called me to. God through Holy Spirit has the provision to accomplish everything Holy Spirit wants to do. And then the jealousy turned into this ferociousness against evil. I heard no profanity in Heaven, but there are no Christian terms to describe the intensity. When that evil comes at you, I want to rip its heart out. I never heard profanity, but I'm thinking of the most ferocious words for it.

So Holy Spirit was this easily grievable woman I had to woo. At the same time, once I was surrounded, Holy Spirit was so mama-bear-on-steroids for me and ferocious. The Holy Spirit is ferocious for the things of God and the Kingdom, does not want us to settle for anything less, wants us to continue to invite Holy Spirit in everything we do. So there's that timelessness there. If I just got one attribute of God, it was the jealousy of God. And I think the never-ending unfolding of God pouring forth the excellencies will make Heaven in and of itself an extraordinary joy, just in seeing who God is.

Then the Father was there. I found myself off to the side. So in a triangle—Jesus, Holy Spirit over here, and then I kind of met the Father over here. I didn't see Father, I didn't see Holy Spirit, but I encountered their presence. And the only way to describe the Father was a partier. I don't know how else to describe it. He came down and He sang a song over me, "My Eddie." My Eddie. And I felt Him dance around me. I was free to receive it without hindrance. And just the affection of God over me partying, celebrating me. He delighted in me. One of my taglines is "one of God's imperfect trophies looking to make Jesus famous." That's my tagline. But He rejoiced over me. It's as if it doesn't matter if you're a dented trophy that's been banged around and through the wars; it's on His mantle. It's like He celebrated me as His creation; and the affection is the thing.

Reflections on Ed Loughran's Experiences

In terms of encountering God, Ed has one of the more expansive testimonies. Although Ed was clinically dead for about six and a half minutes, he felt like he had between twelve to eighteen hours in Heaven. That he encountered all three members of the Trinity is quite fascinating. His time with Jesus is on par with what others have shared, so we're going to focus more on his time with the Father and the Holy Spirit.

He describes the Holy Spirit as a grievable woman whom he had to woo and a mama bear on steroids who was ferocious for the things of God and the Kingdom. Somehow those words feel so right and paint an interesting word picture of our relationship with the Holy Spirit.

He describes God the Father as a partier who sang over him, danced over him, and simply celebrated him. Doesn't that just sound like a dad who is totally for his kid?

Don't forget early on in this part of Ed's story where he is talking with God about how he had spent so much time with Him every single day. That's what made the difference in Ed's Heaven encounter. He was already in a deep, intimate, daily relationship with God, and that simply continued during his time in Heaven. May Ed's story give us the courage and momentum to pursue God each day with a reckless abandon.

44

YOUNG MAN SEES HOW OMNIPRESENT GOD HAS BEEN IN HIS LIFE AND JUST HOW MUCH GOD LOVES HIM

When we last encountered **Joe Joe Morris**, he was coming to the end of his out-of-body experience and had agreed to accompany an angel who told him it was time for judgment. Below, we step into a moment later in his heavenly journey when an angel is telling God about Joe Joe's life.

I was assigned a woman angel, and I realized that the angel that took me from earth was my guardian angel because he was telling God about when I hit puberty and all those developing years. He told God all these personal things about me. And God was fascinated, locked in on all this information. And God's like, "Okay, so what happened next?" And the guardian angel would tell him I was discovering myself, and God's like, "Yep, that's how I made it. That's perfect. That was My perfect timeline. That's exactly what was supposed to happen at that moment."

I'm thinking to myself that everything is in the open. God sees everything and He's unashamed to rejoice in His creation. And I remember thinking, "Who is this?" At that moment, I realized that God is truly omnipresent and He takes a personal, vested interest in every single one of our lives, and we're going to find out in great detail when we are with the Lord for eternity.

Reflections on Joe Joe Morris's Experience

This connects back to the story that Jim Woodford shared earlier of an angel showing Jesus the book of his life. Joe Joe witnesses God giving the angel all of His attention, fully engaged and excited about everything that had unfolded in Joe Joe's life. For Joe Joe, this experience illustrated the theological truth that God is truly omnipresent and also that He takes an interest in every single part of His creation.

Joe Joe's testimony flies in the face of the lie that we are simply meat bags of chemicals here on the earth and nothing more. The reality is that each of us is a treasured part of God's creation that He watches over and rejoices in.

45

MAN DESCRIBES HOW EVERY PART OF HIS BEING GRAVITATED TOWARD THE PRESENCE OF JESUS IN HEAVEN

When we last encountered **Alwyn Matthews**, he was sharing about how enhanced his five senses were in Heaven. Below, we move into the time in Heaven that he spent with Jesus.

Suddenly, I sensed the presence of Jesus, and He was standing next to me. This is a moment that I'll never forget. The best way I can explain this is every human being has felt their heart beat and every human being has felt their stomach growl. I doubt if most human beings have felt their kidney express itself. I felt my kidney, my liver, my lungs, my skin, and even the hair follicles on my skin gravitate to the presence of Jesus. This is my engineer, this is my creator, this is who I was designed for.

I was literally drenched and immersed in the love of Jesus. This is the thing, there was a connection to my body, and I could feel my body feel that. I could feel my body cry out. I could feel my body heat up, all while this experience was happening. I'm feeling like I'm in two places at one time. That's the truth of what was happening. So I'm with Jesus and there's a moment when Jesus looks at me and for whatever reason, I'm embarrassed. The reason I'm embarrassed is that I feel I'm a big preacher of stewardship. You've got to be faithful with what you've been given. You've been given a vineyard; be faithful with it. And for whatever reason, when we experienced the loss that we had as a church, I felt I squandered what was given to me. There was a part of me that was embarrassed just for a fleeting moment to even look at Jesus.

This is when Jesus just said, "Look at Me, Alwyn, look at Me." His look did not want to penetrate my successes, did not want to penetrate my achievements, did not want to penetrate the places in the spaces that I love about myself. His love wanted to penetrate my weaknesses, wanted to penetrate my failures, and wanted to penetrate the deep crevices of my heart that in some way, in some form were hidden from His presence because of my own personal insecurity. Wherever I preach now, that's what I want to share with people, because there are so many in the church who have let the love of Jesus touch some places, but they don't let it permeate and penetrate other spaces that they're embarrassed about.

Reflections on Alwyn Matthews's Experience

Don't forget Alwyn Matthews's story is one of a spiritual transformative experience (STE) and not an NDE, so it's not all that surprising that Alwyn describes a connection to his body where his entire physical being is reacting when he comes into the presence of Jesus. Although Alwyn didn't describe this, many have shared stories of sensing or seeing a cord that kept their spirit tethered to their physical body during the entirety of their experience.

Alwyn's description of being drenched and immersed in the love of Jesus is in line with what numerous NDEers have shared with us about their encounters with Jesus in Heaven. In fact, that love immersion seems to be a defining factor in how profoundly the experiencer's character and personality is shifted after they return to their body.

The most beautiful part of Alwyn's time with Jesus is when Jesus called him out of his shame and told Alwyn to look at Him so His love could penetrate all of the things that were weighing Alwyn down in his heart. It's a beautiful picture of Jesus's great love healing the wounds Alwyn was carrying from the difficult season he had just walked through.

46

MAN ENCOUNTERS SATAN IN HELL AND DESCRIBES HIM AS THE MOST BEAUTIFUL CREATED HE'D EVER SEEN

When we last encountered Ivan Tuttle, he was sharing about the many types of angels he learned about in Heaven. Below we're going to jump to a time earlier in his NDE journey when he encountered satan in hell.

This is the thing, satan or lucifer, he's not this big scary guy with horns popping out of his head and a long tail. That's something that his demons helped create in order to put fear into people. What lucifer or satan looks like, he is probably the most beautiful creature you've ever seen on earth. He is so handsome and so good-looking and so beautiful. And there's this light that still emits from him. He hasn't lost that, that light still emits from him.

Let me tell you what, he could talk anybody into doing anything. He has a lot of power—as long as you don't have Christ in you, he's got a lot of power. And when he comes around, if you're important enough for him to come around, that's a really powerful thing because his beauty is second to none. You've never seen it. Even men will sit there and look at him and go, "Wow, I wish I looked like that," because it's just how you would feel. And even when I was in hell, I'm thinking, wow. You know, if I had a look like that, I would have had the world by the tail, so to speak. Those are the thoughts that run through your head, even when you're in hell and you're seeing it. So I see him for who he is.

Reflections on Ivan Tuttle's Experience

Due to popular media, we have a caricature idea of what satan looks like—the devil with pointy ears and a pitchfork. Since he is a fallen angel, it's not surprising that satan would still appear as a beautiful creature with a light still emitting from him. If you've done any amount of research about people who were immersed in satan worship, they'll often describe satan manifesting and appearing as an alluring Romanian prince or something similar during their rituals.

It's interesting to note that even though Ivan was experiencing and seeing horrors in hell, the allure of satan's beauty was so strong that he was still attracted to it and in awe, even in that darkest of moments and places.

47

MAN WHO LOST HIS MOM AND LITTLE BROTHER IN A HOUSE FIRE SEES THEM IN HEAVEN

When we last encountered **Mark McDonough**, he was sharing about the NDE he experienced during surgery to repair the burns he had sustained during a house fire. Below, we jump into a different part of his story in which he's sharing about seeing his mom and brother in Heaven who had both died as a result of the fire.

Other people's NDE experiences have included very accurate descriptions of loved ones and their features. I don't remember seeing Mom or my brother the way I saw them here on earth, but I saw them and I was comfortable in the dynamic and the relationship. It's like they're there and they're with me in every decision I'm making and they're equally present and I had no problem with it. It wasn't like I'm sitting there going, "Wait, I don't see them like I did yesterday in the swimming pool." That just wasn't an issue. I kind of liken it to how my wife often wonders if those close to us who claim to be atheists, will they have the opportunity to change their mind at a certain time, or will we miss them if they're not in Heaven?

I know that won't be a concern. I feel that those things that we think we will miss here on earth just won't be issues. That's kind of the way it felt. Whether I see my mom again, ever face to face. In Randy Kay's book, he talks about playing golf in Heaven. Will my golf clubs look the same? I don't know if they will, but I won't have a problem if they're not Titleist or if they're not Arnie Palmer. It's just those kinds of issues weren't there. But the overwhelming feeling and sense was that everything is the way it's always been, and it is just the way it's supposed to be, and it's always going to be the way it's supposed to be. God has it all covered, and yet everything's so simple. As He said, it's just as we've been told from day one. And I've also said it felt as if every question that could possibly come to mind, I didn't even have to ask. The answers came as fast as I could think.

It's so hard to put into words—just the security, the secure, safe, certain, nurturing, loving, forgiving. It's all there in one, but a euphoria that I can't put into words. When John Burke interviewed me, he pointed out a quote, and I must have said somewhere in another interview, "It's really difficult to put into words." And then right after that, "Almost indescribable"—as if it wasn't redundant, but I can't be redundant enough on that one.

Reflections on Mark McDonough's Experience

While Mark McDonough didn't see his mom and brother face to face in Heaven, he is confident that they were there with him while he was in Heaven. He goes on to talk about how our worries over whether we'll see this family member or that friend in Heaven will not be an issue. That fits perfectly with what so many of our Heaven experiencers have shared. You're so overwhelmed by God's presence and love and the sheer awe of what you're experiencing, all the questions and worries simply fade away.

Mark also touches briefly on being able to get answers to every question that came to his mind while he was in Heaven. These answers sound like they came instantaneously and fit with the spirit-to-spirit communication many others have described throughout this book.

Similar to pretty much all of NDEers we've interviewed, Mark notes that what he experienced is so indescribable, it's difficult to put into words. Although it's difficult, we're so glad our friends who've been to the other side give it their best shot, because their stories give us so much hope and insight into the future that waits for each of us in the afterlife.

48

MAN SEES FAMOUS PREACHERS AND EVANGELISTS IN HELL

When we last encountered **Ivan Tuttle**, he was describing how alluring satan appeared when he saw him in hell. Below, he shares about seeing famous preachers and evangelists in hell and how God revealed to him why they deserved to be there.

I even saw pastors in hell, former pastors, former evangelists who were in there. Now I'm not going to name names. God will not allow me. He won't release me to do that for various reasons. But I can tell you that some of them were people we knew, famous people, but they're in hell for various reasons. Some because they did things they shouldn't have done sexually with children and with other adults and things.

There are some there because they stole and robbed people. I mean, literally, there are some there because they were very vicious toward their family, and these are people who never asked for forgiveness. They justified what they did. They tried to justify it and say, "Hey, it's okay. God still loves me. I still have my anointing, so it's still okay that I'm doing this." No, it's not. I saw that, and that's what took me into hell.

Reflections on Ivan Tuttle's Experience

What Ivan describes above is one of the more sobering parts of his time in hell. He saw famous pastors and evangelists in this place of eternal torment. As others have described, when you're in your spirit body, there's a knowing and an understanding about the things you're experiencing. This seems to apply whether an experiencer is in Heaven or hell. Ivan understood why these "professional Christians" deserved to be there—that they had justified their egregious sins and didn't ask for forgiveness.

Our prayer is that this part of Ivan's story will drive every person who encounters it to their knees into a posture of deep self-reflection and repentance.

49

WOMAN GIVES EXTREMELY DETAILED ACCOUNT OF JESUS'S APPEARANCE IN HEAVEN

When we last encountered **Heidi Barr,** she was recounting how even the blades of grass sing God's praises in Heaven. Below, she shares one of the most detailed accounts of Jesus's physical appearance that's ever come up in an interview.

Jesus is perfection. His hair was about my length. It was a chestnut brown and had some streaks in it. It was wavy. He had a lean face with some scruff, you know, a beard and mustache, but not too long. He had a beautiful mouth, a gorgeous smile. I couldn't look away from His smile. It was infectious. His eyes radiated all the joy in the universe. This was hard for me to tell anyone at first, but His eyes are blue. They are the most beautiful blue eyes I have ever seen. I did not want to say anything about that because even though people in my family have hazel eyes and my father has green eyes, most Jewish people I know have brown eyes, but Jesus had blue eyes. I thought nobody was going to believe me if I said Jesus had blue eyes.

In terms of build, he was between 5 foot 9 and 5 foot 11, slender, and around 160 pounds. He was wearing a white robe. His hands were slender and His fingers were long and tapered. He had beautiful nails. His feet were like mine, long slender feet, with long toes, which I thought was cool. The only thing I will say, which may sound like an imperfection, but it was not: I really appreciated His nose because it was crooked. I thought, "Wow, He has a crooked nose. That is so great." It gave His face so much character. He was the most real person I have ever met. His face was the most real face I have ever looked at in my life.

Reflections on Heidi Barr's Experience

So many of the people we've interviewed had more to say about how they felt when they were with Jesus in Heaven rather than talking about His physical appearance. Heidi, on the other hand, had a lot to say about how Jesus looked. She was a teenager when her NDE took place, so that may have influenced the sorts of things she focused on or noticed during her time in Heaven.

You just finished reading her description of Jesus's physical characteristics, so we won't repeat that again here. It's worth noting that she says that Jesus was perfection, the most real person she'd ever met. This shouldn't really surprise us since He is the perfect mingling of divinity and humanity.

50

MAN ENCOUNTERS JESUS IN HEAVEN AND GETS A GLIMPSE OF THE NEW HEAVENS AND NEW EARTH

When we last encountered Ian McCormack, he was in the midst of his out-of-body experience. Below, we move into his encounter with Jesus.

Next, I watched the light get brighter and brighter. And suddenly the veils of light that were surrounding Him began to part and I looked up. I was overwhelmed. Here was someone, arms outstretched, twenty to thirty feet away from me. And I immediately knew that was God. The robes He was wearing were robes of light made up of this incredible cloud of glory. He had shimmering garments of light, but they were white like monks' robes. And when I looked at His face, I saw His hair was pure white. That is what shook me. I did not know what to think. Is that Jesus? I had never seen Jesus with white hair, but His hair was shoulder-length, pure white.

When I looked at His face, that was where the source of all the light in the universe was coming from. It was His countenance. It was so bright. It eclipsed every light I had seen to this point. It was seven to ten times brighter. When I looked directly at it, the light did not hurt my face. But I could sense that if He spoke, He could speak into existence galaxies and constellations. It was like looking into eternity within eternity within His countenance. So the fall of man, the face of God. I remember when a messianic Jewish friend gave me a Bible to read, I treasured it. I got to the end and read Revelation 1:13-18: His head and His hair were white like wool, like snow. He said, "I was dead but behold I am alive forevermore. I hold the keys of death and hades. I am the Alpha and the Omega." And it says His face shone like the sun at full strength.

When I read that, I just fell out. I thought, *That was written 2,000 years ago.* This is John, the beloved, to whom Jesus said, "Look after my mum, Mary." You know what I mean? Here, he sees Jesus in His supernatural, glorified, resurrected form. And I have the privilege to be standing before the Son of God with arms of love reaching out. So I walked closer to Him, captivated by the beauty of it, and I experienced light emanating from His face and instant purity. My entire being felt the innocence of childhood restored as though His purity had been imparted into me. You cannot make yourself pure or forgive yourself. Only God can cleanse you of all your sins with His blood. As I got closer, more light emanated out holiness—a very, very abstract word. I had never met anyone holy. Here the holiness of God filled me and I felt pure, holy, forgiven, loved, full of peace, full of joy, full of comfort, and a broken heart healed. I came right up to experience His presence, and He began to move as though He wanted to show me more. But why couldn't I see His face? Why hadn't He unveiled His face to me? I did not know that no man looks upon the face of God and lives. Even Moses could not see it. But He moved like He was a door of radiance and light. As He moved, directly behind Him I could see a whole new dimension opening of grass and fields. I could see flowers. The radiance that was emanating across Jesus's countenance and entire being was emanating across this entire planet.

It was like a new Earth in front of me. I was getting words: Garden of Eden, paradise. Why hadn't I been born there in the first place? It was like I was looking at a parallel universe in time and space. It was like *The Matrix*, like there was a totally new Earth. I was thinking that Heaven was supposed to be full of clouds with people wearing robes and walking around with little fat Italian babies firing arrows, and Morgan Freeman swinging the pearly gates. No one had told me that God created a new Earth. And then I saw a crystal-clear river and heard the Lord saying, "I have a new Heaven, a new Earth, and a river of life." I could see trees—not just one tree, but trees of life. I looked up and I could see the new heavens. I was amazed. And I was assuming that above that was the new Jerusalem, the city of God, the bride of Christ. I was looking at the new Earth and was captivated by it.

I knew I was home. And Jesus came right back in front of me. The door into eternity closed. I had just had a glimpse.

Reflections on Ian McCormack's Experience

Ian's encounter with Jesus seems to be focused on expressing key aspects of Jesus's character, namely His purity and holiness, expressed through His hair of pure white, robes of light made up of an incredible cloud of glory, and His face that appeared to be the source of all light in the universe.

What Ian experienced of Jesus seems to be directly related to his personal transformation in Heaven. He said his entire being felt the innocence of childhood restored as though Jesus's purity had been imparted into Ian. So many of our NDEers have noted a transformation in personality and character after they were immersed in the love of Jesus in Heaven. What Ian describes above gives some helpful verbiage to describe what God is doing on the inside of the experiencer.

51

MAN ENCOUNTERS A WHOLE GROUP OF PEOPLE WELCOMING HIM AT THE GATES OF HEAVEN

When we last encountered **Captain Dale Black**, he was in **the** latter part of his out-of-body experience following his body **in** the ambulance as it went from the crash site to the emergency room. Below, we fast forward to Dale's experience at the gates of Heaven.

When I got the near the wall around the city of gold, there **was a** welcoming committee that was just congregating there to **meet** me. It looked like they had been assigned to meet me at the exact **time** I was arriving. And this group came to meet me and greet me, **and I** could see their smiles and the brilliance in their eyes and what appeared to be love exuding from every pore of their being. They loved me. They absolutely loved me unconditionally. And I could feel it and sense it and know it, yet not one of these people was a blood relative on **earth.** Not one of these people was anyone I had known personally on **earth.**

That may frustrate a lot of people, because I've had a lot of **emails** come back and people have been relatively unkind about that. **They** said, "That's not possible. That's not right. Your story is not **true** because you're going to meet your family."

Okay, now, wait a minute, time out. You know, my family is **on** the inside. Listen to what God taught me, because maybe there's some value in learning what God taught me here. What do you mean they're not my blood family? They're more my blood family than anything else because we have the same blood flowing through our veins. It's the blood of Jesus that binds us together.

Even though I didn't know these people, they were my blood family. These were my brothers and my sisters in Christ. And nothing could possibly be more wonderful or more bonding than the blood of Jesus. So yes, they were my family. They are my family. And I would say this to anybody: If you know Jesus as your Savior, if you're on your way to Heaven, you're going to love it. If for no other reason than you are going to be surrounded with the most loving people, your brothers and sisters, by the millions. They love you unconditionally for who you truly are. Not who you want them to think you are, but who you truly are. That was mind-boggling to me.

When I woke up in the hospital and I sat in my wheelchair, I thought about this a bit, and I sort of meditated on the event. I started realizing the Lord was talking to me: "Dale, did you notice any skin color differences in that family that I sent to you?"

And I thought, "Yes. Yeah, there would be what we'd call white and black and Asian."

"Dale, did you notice any gender differences there?"

"Well, yes I did."

"But did you notice it when you were there?"

"Absolutely not." And then silence.

I connected the dots in the silence, as God was talking to me, and I realized there is no racism in Heaven. There's no racism in the body of Christ. There is no room for racism or gender identity. We are brothers and sisters and our bond is unbreakable. It's complete. It's thorough. It's fulfilling. This is what I learned in Heaven—love is absolutely unconditional. And it's hard to describe because it does not exist on the earth.

Reflections on Captain Dale Black's Experience

Captain Dale Black recounts what is a common experience amongst many NDEers—that they are greeted by what he described as a welcoming committee. This is often comprised of friends and family, but uniquely in Dale's experience, he doesn't know any of the people who are there to greet him.

God taught Dale an amazing truth through this group of people who were there to greet him. Even though none of them were a part of his blood family on earth, in Heaven everybody there is connected to one another through the bloodline of Jesus. Furthermore, Dale suggests that all of the terms we use to group and categorize people on the earth are irrelevant in Heaven. As he just shared, there is no room for racism or gender identity in Heaven. The big takeaway is the things that have been used to separate and divide people on earth are stripped away in Heaven. We're all simply brothers and sisters in the bloodline of Jesus!

CONCLUSION

Step into the afterlife and you'll be amazed at the beings you're going to meet!

As you've seen across the stories throughout this section of the book, most of these afterlife experiences involve at a minimum a touchpoint with one divine or supernatural being. Be it a member of the Trinity, an angel, a demon, or occasionally satan himself, every experiencer returns with an amazing story to tell.

Many experiencers report encountering other departed souls in both Heaven in hell. In Heaven, they are either there to greet the NDEer who is newly arrived or visible in the distance going about their heavenly business. In hell, these departed souls are seen as they're experiencing a state of ongoing torture and torment. Those former souls are there to bring comfort and the latter souls often serve as a cautionary tale to those of us still here on earth as we're hearing or reading these stories.

Moving beyond the divine and supernatural beings and departed souls, the most controversial of the beings you heard about in these stories are the animals in Heaven. Theologically, many of us were taught that animals do not have souls, therefore they do not go to Heaven. The sheer number of accounts in which we hear about people encountering all sorts of animals (horses, lions, butterflies, etc.) as well as their own personal pets that have already passed on should be enough to at least keep us open to the possibility that there may be animals in Heaven. If there are, it shouldn't in any way detract from the wonder and grandeur of our life there on the other side.

Discussion Questions

1. In this section of the book, you encountered a number of stories in which NDEers said they saw their long-lost beloved pets in Heaven. Are you okay with these experiences, or do they make you theologically uncomfortable? If so, why?

2. You've read stories of encounters with all three members of the Trinity. Which story stood out to you the most? Why was it highlighted to you?

3. Quite a few of our experiencers shared about encounters with angels. Have you ever had an angel encounter? If so, share it with the group.

4. A number of the NDEers talked about encountering both famous and everyday people experiencing the torments of hell. What did these stories bring to mind about your own future eternal destination?

SECTION 5

LIFE REVIEW

Many near-death experiencers report a time during their NDE when they see their life passing before their eyes. Some describe it as a movie of their life that is playing in their head. This can include the good things you've done in life as well as the bad things. Some people say that in the midst of the life review, they're able to sense and experience how other people were impacted by the choices and actions that are replaying in front of them. It is not uncommon for people to express feeling overwhelmed by the many things that God has forgiven them for.

52

MAN GOES THROUGH LIFE REVIEW AND SEES VISION OF CANCER-STRICKEN BOY WHO PROPHESIED HE'D BE IN HEAVEN ONE DAY

When we last encountered **Randy Kay,** he had a wonderful reunion with his beloved childhood dog, Casey. Below, we step into Randy's life review.

Jesus reached down, pulled me up, and wrapped His arms around me. Then He revealed to me this series of vignettes in my life, both good and bad. The good times were the times when I had served Him. I taught in the church; I prayed with my dad, who wasn't a believer, to receive Christ. So there was that series of things, but then there were the bad things that, surprisingly, weren't condemning. They actually were comforting in a strange way. I realized what Jesus was doing. He wasn't showing me these things to condemn me. He was showing me to reflect His grace. I kept thinking, *Lord, really, You forgave that?* And I was looking at these things and later I'd forgotten all of those. I remember all of the vignettes that were the good times, the positive times. And I realized that the Lord had removed those bad times as far as the east is from the west. The only reason he showed those to me was to reflect His grace.

One of the striking times was a boy in a hospital bed. I'd been an orderly at the time, but I'd forgotten this instance from when I was a teenager. I walked into this boy's room. He was emaciated and was dying of cancer. He had veins showing through his skin. His eyes were hollowed out. We had this conversation that I was seeing, even though I'd forgotten it in my lifetime because it seemed like a small event in the scheme of things at the time. I was seeing this playing out as though I was there, and he said, "I'm going to Heaven." I was an agnostic at the time because most of my youth, I was an agnostic. And I said, "Well, that's great. I don't really believe in those things, but I'm sure if there is one, you're going to go."

Then he said, "I'm going to pray for you, and someday you'll be there." I was seeing that very time that he was praying for me in the past while I was in Heaven. The Lord was showing me that his prayer was answered many years later, so that he was prophetically speaking into my life that I would be in Heaven. I was in Heaven at the very moment, and I was seeing this vision of my encounter with this young boy.

Reflections on Randy Kay's Experience

It is very common for NDEers to share about having a life review, but one thing to note about Randy's experience is that while he knows Jesus talked to him about both good and bad things from his life, he is unable to remember the bad things. It's as if they've been erased because he's been forgiven. Of all of the experiencers we've crossed paths with, Randy is the only one who has expressed this biblical reality so concretely.

Randy also recounts an experience God reminded him of from when he was a teenager and a dying boy prayed for him and revealed to him that one day he'd be in Heaven as well. Randy had completely forgotten about that encounter, and here God was purposefully bringing it back to mind. That's such a great illustration of how purposeful God is in establishing our paths and the encounters we have on a day-to-day basis. Things are often more purposeful than we realize.

53

TEENAGER HAS LIFE REVIEW IN HEAVEN AND COULD LITERALLY FEEL HOW SHE HAD HURT OTHERS

When we last encountered **Heidi Barr,** she was sharing about how Jesus looked in Heaven. Below, we move into what Jesus revealed to her during her life review.

I was a rather good kid. I was having some issues at that time. I had experienced a great deal of abuse in my 16 years. At that point I was fighting back and rebelling. I was using drugs and hanging out with kids I should not have been. When I had my life review, Jesus did not focus on that. He did not give me any lectures or point an accusatory finger at me. He did not tell me to stop doing drugs and hanging out with those kids. What I received was a life review that was short because, as I said, I was a good kid. I was nice to people, even if I was hurting myself. What He showed me was that I was judging myself.

Jesus was pointing things out. He was there saying, "Well, why don't we look at this? Why don't we consider this? What do you think about that?" But He was not judging me. I was judging me. The one thing I saw and felt was, if I hurt someone, if my words hurt someone, I felt what they felt. I understood the impact my words and actions had on other people, and it changed me. I am not perfect, believe me. I can cuss with the best of them and I can yell at my kids and my husband. This changed me in that I am very aware of what I do. I am aware of how my actions impact others and I pay attention to myself. But as I said, my life review was short because the only person I was really hurting was me. The things I saw in my life review impacted me when I came back to life.

Reflections on Heidi Barr's Experience

Heidi Barr was only 16 years old when she had her near-death experience. Given her young age, her life review was rather short. Her life review was little different from most because, as she says above, God revealed to her how much she was both hurting and judging herself.

Like other NDEers, she reported that she was able to feel what the other people she had hurt felt in the midst of a specific inter-action. This part of her experience profoundly impacted her understanding of how her words and actions affect other people.

54

YOUNG MAN NERVOUSLY WAITS TO FIND OUT IF HIS NAME IS WRITTEN IN THE BOOK OF LIFE

When we last encountered Joe Joe Morris, an angel was telling Jesus all about Joe Joe's life. Below, we're with Joe Joe in the throne room of Heaven as he's receiving his life review.

looked to my left and to my shock, I saw God. I knew in my spirit it was God because the space shone brighter than the sun. Like it says in Revelation, the space shone brighter than the sun. But He was sitting on His throne, and He was drinking out of a coffee mug. In my religious mind, I was thinking, *Why is the Creator of earth sitting on a throne doing nothing?* And I raged against Him. That anger boiled back up again, and I'm ashamed. That's how much pride I had in my heart at that time. Moments later, a surround-sound voice boomed and it said, "Let judgment begin." And that sent chills through my body. Right after that, that surround-sound voice came out of everywhere and three big hologram screens popped up and I saw my life playing from the very beginning.

When I was born in Lake Dallas, Texas, my parents were holding this little infant, this little Joe Joe. That was about the only good memory because what I saw in my life was only the religious spirit that I had participated in all those years and it was not good. I saw how I mistreated my siblings. I saw all these bad things that were happening. Growing up in my 12-, 13-, and 14-year-old years, I saw how angry I was and then my life kept speeding up when we were moving around a lot. We moved to Minnesota, and I saw myself working long hours in the shop. We had a huge farm accident that burned down one of our shops. I watched all that happen and I remember thinking to myself, *I can't believe this was my life*, and it was not good.

I saw myself go take that nap. And inside I was like, *No, no, do not lay down.* Because I knew that was the end. And the moment I heard my neck snap, all of a sudden the screens folded up and went away. And that was it.

By the way, the whole entire time I was watching my life, it felt like a day or two had passed. I saw so many details that would take me hours to explain. Then that surround-sound voice boomed again and said, "Is his name in the Book of Life?" And I'm thinking, *Oh no.* Because in Revelation it says if your name is not in the Book of Life, you are cast out. I knew very clearly that the word of God was ringing within me. I'm a student of the word, so everything I'm seeing is lining up with Scripture.

An angel next to me was holding this huge book of names. And he started reading through them all, and I didn't hear my name. And it went on and on and on and on—names like Daniel, Kalin, Jessica, Hannah, Rebecca, all these different names, some people I knew, some people I didn't. I was thinking about claiming a name, but I knew I could not be dishonest. In that same surrender I had when I left the earth, I had to do it again in the throne room. And all of a sudden, in that moment of surrender, I heard the name Joe Joe, and my hair stood up on the edge of my arms. God jumped off His throne and He stood right in front of me. He said, "Joe Joe, I am here to show you who I truly am. This whole time you thought I was a judgmental, hateful, fearful God, but that is not who I am."

He basically stripped everything from my old thinking, just took it away. And He said, "This is how I see you." He started my life from the very beginning, showing me that when I was born in Texas, how my parents held me, that's how he viewed my life. The lenses by which He saw me were good. And He showed me when I gave my sibling a glass of water, one time when I helped our neighbor harvest their peach trees, and when I helped another person with their cherry trees. He also showed me all the times I had shared the love of God with people. He showed me all the moments He adored and took personal interest in. I remember thinking to myself, *Who is this God that He would take this much time to look into my life?*

Reflections on Joe Joe Morris's Experience

Many NDEers describe their life playing out like a movie during their life review, but Joe Joe's story takes it to the next level when he talks about his life playing out on three screens in the throne room of Heaven. When it's all said and done, the big takeaway for Joe Joe as his life review experience comes to a close is that God cares enough to be aware of and involved in every minute detail of our lives.

Joe Joe shared with us earlier that he was out of his body for approximately 30 minutes, but given the volume of things that came up in his life review, it seemed as if one or two days had passed. This is very common among experiencers, many of whom share complex and expansive stories even if they're only gone for a few minutes.

It's worth noting that one very unique facet of Joe Joe's time in Heaven is the Book of Life. He is on pins and needles waiting to find out if his name is written there. These life review stories are quite common, but a life review story with a reading of names from the Book of Life is a bit more rare.

55

MAN'S EVIL DEEDS ARE LAID BARE DURING LIFE REVIEW

When we last encountered **Bryan Melvin**, he was sharing about encountering Hitler in hell. Below, we get into Bryan's life review.

I was facing a reckoning, because what was being revealed to me at that moment was how I had gained everything that God had given me.

He loves us unconditionally. He makes the rain fall on the unjust. He makes sure the animals are fed. He takes care of things. He nurtures. He builds up. So what did I do with it? I took advantage of everything. He gave me good parents. I lied to and betrayed them. He gave me friends. I lied to them, betraying and stabbing them in the back. I stole from people. I sold drugs to the church youth group. I was a corrupter of youth. I could see how the people who were at the skating party were getting whacked out on what I had sold them. I became one of the biggest drug pushers in the entire school, and I knew nothing about drugs.

I had to make an image change really quickly and get involved in that scene just to cover myself. That was how I lied to myself and betrayed people. It was all revealed to me. The Lord showed me how I made life ugly, and when you make life ugly in a biblical sense, you transgress God's law. Most people do not understand that it is a royal law of love. It is loving God with all of your heart, mind, and soul and loving your neighbor as yourself.

God revealed to me how I took advantage of people, so I could not go up to the Lord and say, "You know, Lord, I had a crazy sign hit me on the head and that is why I acted crazy. I am just a victim of circumstance." There was nothing like that. I could not say anything. I saw how ugly I was on the inside. No matter my excuses, no matter how many good things I did, they did not cover up what I was like on the inside.

It was more of a sensation of feeling what they felt. I could feel my parents' pain seeing me strung out on drugs and talking nonsensically. They knew it and they loved me, but they still knew I was stealing their money and doing this stuff. I saw how I made God feel too. It says that after you die comes judgment; well, this is a judgment. You must face yourself. The real you is exposed. Whether you are a Christian or not, nobody is going to stand before Him thinking they are hot stuff and all justified. That will all be flushed down the proverbial commode. You are going to see what you are really like.

It was not pleasant. I never really answered the Lord. I wanted to, but I could not. I was flummoxed, like a deer in the headlights. You realize this is real and you wonder why you did not listen. I saw how good the Lord had been to me. He witnessed to me, He spared my life through multiple car wrecks, He saved me from being shot two times, and so much more.

Reflections on Bryan Melvin's Experience

Bryan Melvin's life review was focused on helping him to see that despite all the bad things he had done, God had still blessed him with many wonderful things in his life that he took for granted. This experience seems to have had a profound humbling effect on Bryan that helped him to grasp the goodness of God and see his own depth of need for a Savior.

56

MAN DECLARES, "WHEN I RETURN TO HEAVEN, THEY'RE GOING TO NEED THREE ANGELS AND A FORKLIFT TO GET MY BOOK OF LIFE OPEN"

When we last encountered **Jim Woodford,** he was rejoicing that there are horses in Heaven. If this account seems familiar, you are correct. You already encountered parts of this account back in Section 4. However, it bears a second look as an out-of-the-box sort of life review.

Anyway, getting right to the main event—after showing me much more, we came back to the ground of paradise, which I learned was outside the walls. I was looking once again at the horses and I realized I hadn't seen my guardian for a while. So I turned to look for him and I saw him, and he was about 40 to 50 feet away on a small rise. When I looked, he was bent over almost in the kneeling position and was holding up a book, and facing him was a more magnificent figure than even the angels. But I couldn't see the face; it was in profile to me.

You know how you drive down a hot road on a warm summer day and there's a shimmer on the pavement? There was this kind of shimmer covering the features of this magnificent being, but clearly He was reading what the guardian was holding up. And I took note of the book that the guardian had taken out of his sleeve. It was as thin as a cheap roadside diner menu. And suddenly the awareness came over me that what the guardian was holding was the book of my life. Instead of it being a book filled with good deeds and kindness, all I had to show for a life that I thought was the epitome of success was this tiny, thin book. Charles Dickens wrote a wonderful line when he wrote, "Mankind should have been my business," Instead, it was all about the pursuit of wealth. And all I had to show for it, although I thought myself a kind person, all I had to show for my life was this little thin book. I am determined to live my life now so that when I go back, when they open the book of my life for this chapter, they're going to need three angels and a forklift to get it open.

Anyway, I was watching and this figure was leaning forward, clearly intent on the little bit that was written in there. Suddenly, the figure straightened up and the angel folded up the book, put it in his sleeve, and disappeared. And then this magnificent figure turned toward me. As He turned from profile to direct-on, suddenly the shimmer that had covered His features vanished. And I found myself face to face with none other than Jesus Christ, the Son of God—someone I thought was just some old Jewish legend that people had made up.

Reflections on Jim Woodford's Experience

While Jim did not have the traditional life review experience, this part of his time in Heaven seems to have had the same effect as one would get in a life review. Jim watched an angel show Jesus a pitifully tiny book, which he realized was the book of his life. Jim's money and worldly successes did not amount to anything significant in Heaven.

This was a critical turning point in Jim's journey when he vowed that he would now live a life serving Jesus and when he returns to Heaven it'll take three angels and a forklift to show Jesus the book he's written with this latter part of his life on earth.

57

PASTOR RECEIVES A CORPORATE LIFE REVIEW OF THE HIS CHURCH'S MINISTRY IMPACT IN HEAVEN

When we last encountered Alwyn Matthews, he was sharing about how every part of his body reacted to the presence of Jesus. Below, we step into another part of his heavenly journey in which he experiences what you could term as a sort of corporate life review in the mansion that was built by the works and deeds of Downpour Church.

He takes me to Downpour mansion. He starts showing me the things that we've seen happen over the years, things that we've seen, but things I thought we lost. But they were all remembered and they were all established as a sign and an act of worship and a reminder of the things that God has done.

I was given the opportunity to walk through ministry moments in the life of our church, and we will experience that in Heaven. And this is the thing people say, "How are we going to worship all the time?" You're going to walk through moments when you've seen God move and you are able to—how do I explain this? I was able to walk through ministry moments and experience even in a greater magnitude what God did and what God was doing and even see angelic activities that my earthly eyes could not see here on earth during those ministry moments while I was in Heaven.

Reflections on Alwyn Matthews's Experience

What Alwyn shares here is another experience that's a bit out of the box in terms of the traditional life review. However, if individuals will receive a life review, is it all that much of a stretch for a church or a ministry to receive a life review as well?

The important insight to note from what Alwyn describes is that as the ministry moments were replaying before him, he was able to see more fully what God was doing in the midst of each of those circumstances and see the angelic activity that was a part of those moments as well.

Even though this is a corporate life review, the insight that divine and angelic activity was taking place in each ministry moment should give us hope that God is equally active in every moment of our individual lives as well. We simply don't always have the eyes to see it.

CONCLUSION

O ne thing is crystal clear in the stories you read in this section: there is a lot of variety in terms of what people experience with their life's work and deeds being laid bare and fully revealed in Heaven.

Whether it's playing on three literal screens as Joe Joe described or playing out in your mind's eye as others have said, the life review is a truly humbling experience that shows the experiencer that in spite of our actions and choices God has been with us and for us along the whole journey of our life, even if we didn't sense or see Him. The grace and forgiveness of God that manifests in the midst of the life review is one of the key transformative moments in Heaven, second only in impact to being fully immersed in the love of God.

Some of the stories in this section had some unconventional elements. Joe Joe waited to see if his name was in the Lamb's Book of Life, Jim Woodford saw that pathetic tiny book that contained his life's work and deeds, and Alwyn walked through a life review for his church. While these particular experiences deviate from the norm, they deserve to be mentioned under this section because these stories relate to the life's work and deeds of the NDEer, and the transformative impact that results is in line with that of a traditional life review.

Discussion Questions

1.   Of these six life review experiences, which one resonated with you most? Why?

2. Did any of these life reviews make you uncomfortable? What about that story gave you cause for concern?

3. When you think of your own future life review, are you excited or nervous? Why?

SECTION 6

ENCOUNTERING OTHERWORLDLY ("HEAVENLY" OR "HELLISH") REALMS

When NDEers cross over to the other side, not only do they meet other beings, they can also encounter entire cities, structures like houses, other buildings, roads, etc., and vast landscapes filled with all of the things we'd expect to encounter in nature, all very much like what we might encounter down here on earth.

Sometimes these things are simply a part of the scenery in Heaven or hell that don't have a significant meaning and other times they reveal profound truths. As you read through these stories, keep an eye out for the hidden truths that might be revealed in these structures and landscapes.

58

MAN SEES NURSERY WITH ALL OF THE LOST CHILDREN AND ABORTED BABIES IN HEAVEN

When we last encountered **Jim Woodford**, he had resolved that going forward the book of his life deeds would be so big at the end of his life it would take a forklift and three angels to open it. Below, we step into one of those most beautiful structures he encountered in Heaven.

One thing I do want to talk about, because this is a comfort to so many parents. There was one building that stood out among all the rest, and the buildings are made, not of stone, not of wood, but of a material that has a light in it. Now I don't want it to sound too Las Vegas-y, but it was a gentle, welcoming light. This particular building glowed with a light that had a warmth to it. I asked what building that was, and I was stunned when they said, "That is the nursery."

I responded, "A nursery in Heaven?"

They said, "Yes, James, the souls of aborted children or children who die in their innocence from disease come back here." Each soul is so precious to God that they're cared for. They grow at a different rate because they're not growing in a physical body. So they grow at about three times the rate that a child does on earth. This is where they take care of the little souls that were unwanted or died. I had no idea how this part of the story would have such an effect on women who have lost children or who had an abortion at a time in their life when they had no other option. It's been a blessing to explain to these parents that their child lives.

Reflections on Jim Woodford's Experience

Jim Woodford is one of several NDEers we've encountered who saw a nursery in Heaven that receives the souls of children who are aborted or are lost early. We've seen these nursery stories shared live in a church setting and I can vouch for the impact on men and women who have lost children. In terms of all the things we've encountered in NDE stories, the account of a nursery in Heaven seems to inspire the biggest amount of hope and comfort.

Compared to the lost children, this next thing seems like a minor point, but do take note of what Jim says about the building materials of the nursery. Literally everything reflects the light of God in Heaven.

59

MAN SEES PARENTS BEING REUNITED WITH THEIR ABORTED BABIES AND LOST CHILDREN IN HEAVEN

When we last encountered **Ivan Tuttle**, he was still in hell, seeing well-known preachers and evangelists undergoing endless torment. Below, we step into a beautiful part of his Heaven experience in which parents are being reunited with their lost children in Heaven.

I didn't put this in the book, but I need to tell you a little something here. One of the things that I did see was I had a sister who was stillborn and I got to see her. She was there in Heaven. I got to see my great-grandfather on my father's side. He was in Heaven. I had no idea, you know, that he was a Christian. He was a strong Christian man. He was in Heaven. I got to see other people.

Now here's the remarkable thing. If you don't mind me getting into this, it has to do with little babies. Here's the thing that I saw—I saw all the aborted babies in Heaven, waiting. They're in an area waiting for their mothers to show up. They're waiting for their fathers to show up. They're waiting because every single one of them is in Heaven. There isn't a single one who didn't make it into Heaven. And they're waiting.

We know that people make mistakes in their life. And if they just ask God to forgive them for their mistakes, just like with me, when they get to Heaven they get to see their little ones. And God does this strange thing and I haven't talked about this much before, but God does this thing. If that parent needs to see what it's like to have that little baby, God allows that child to become a little baby so they can hold it, just to see what that's like. And then He lets the baby kind of grow up real quick, but God allows that to happen so that the parent can get that feeling that they didn't get, that they lost.

That to me was still the most lasting thing in my mind. Everything was beautiful and great, but seeing those little babies. Miscarried babies, stillborn babies, or children who died at a very young age—they're there. They're waiting. When you see a mother who was going through something in her life and she did something wrong that she thought, oh no, and then she's reunited with her child and that child greets her. Oh man, that's so powerful!

Reflections on Ivan Tuttle's Experience

It's amazing how much Jim and Ivan's accounts about the lost children in Heaven are so similar. The thing to take note of from what Ivan talks about above is the parents being reunited with their lost child. It's hard to think of anything in life that is much harder than the loss of a child, so it's the absolute grace and mercy of God on full display when He allows parents to be reunited with their lost children in Heaven.

Also, note what Ivan said about parents being able to experience the child at whatever age or stage they need so they can both experience and receive healing and comfort for those ages and stages with the child that they most feel they missed out on.

60

MAN RECOUNTS SEEING VAST CITY IN HEAVEN

When we last encountered **Ivan Tuttle**, he was witnessing parents being united with their lost children in Heaven. Below, he explains the things he saw in a vast heavenly city.

The first thing I saw was a huge city and these huge white buildings I've never seen. It was like white marble stone that sparkled. And it was just gloriously white. I can only think it was like a marble, but it looked like it was studded with diamonds through it. It was just glorious and beautiful. I saw lots of trees, mountains, everything, but I saw these two big trees by the river that ran right down to the city, right down the middle of the street. Now this river was beautiful. It was crystal clear. In fact, you look at it and you're like, "Is there really water in there?" It was so clear. But then it got to an area where it was bubbling and it sounded like little babies laughing. Have you ever heard little babies laughing when they think something is really funny? It almost sounded like that. And I watched that.

Then there were streets that looked like gold, but it was soft when you stepped on it. And it was like, "Oh, this is amazing." You can step on it and move around and do things. And it's really an amazing feeling that you get when you do that. And it's so beautiful. And you look at the trees, now—there were 12 different fruits to come out on this tree. And they come out at different times and you can see it. And sometimes God will say, "Hey, let Me show you this." Boom, boom, boom. All 12 different fruits will come out. That was the experience I was allowed to see at the time. And it was very, very unique. So that's just some of what I saw.

Reflections on Ivan Tuttle's Experience

Similar to what Jim Woodford shared earlier about the building material of the nursery he saw in Heaven reflecting or emitting a light, Ivan Tuttle also recounts buildings made of materials that sparkled.

Ivan recounts seeing streets of gold in Heaven but notes that they were not hard like we'd expect based on our experience with gold and other metals down here on earth. He says the streets of gold in Heaven were soft when you stepped on them and felt amazing to walk on.

Since the book of Genesis begins with man and woman in a garden, it should come as no surprise that we often hear stories about people encountering trees and rivers in Heaven. Ivan even notes that he saw a tree that produces 12 different kinds of fruit. Perhaps there is a hidden meaning there. We'll let you, the reader, be the judge of that.

MAN EXPERIENCES THE FORMLESS VOID OF DARKNESS AND CHAOS IN HELL

When we last encountered Ivan Tuttle, he was experiencing a vast heavenly city. You've already seen part of this encounter in Section 3, but below we step into an expanded and full context of Ivan's experience in hell.

This demon has me. And I'm hearing all these screams. I'm hearing people yelling, you know, people screaming. It's pitch black there, but in the spirit you can see through that blackness and you can see the people. And here's the remarkable thing. When you see people, when you're in the spirit only, you see people instantly. When you look at them, you know absolutely everything about their life. You know every little detail in their life, every little thing that goes on in their life; there's not a thing that you don't know.

As I looked at these people, so many were wondering, "Why am I in hell? What am I doing here? What did I do wrong? Get me outta here. I need to get out of here somehow." But they all knew, even those who were Christians at one time in their life, they knew that they were in hell. All their prayers, when they try to pray from hell, it's like an iron dome is over it. They're not going anywhere. It's like it just hits something and it stops. And these people were screaming. The smell, the stench was horrible.

Now I never saw flames, but I felt this intense heat all the time. It was an intense heat. These demons would sit there and I'd watch them with other people. They did the same thing to me. They stab you with things. They pull on you. They jerk on you. They stick you with great big, long thorns or something. They stick them into you. It's the most horrible feeling. On earth, when you get a splinter, you know that that little dinky splinter hurts so bad in that finger. Can you imagine that same pain from a little splinter through your whole body? That's what it's like—your whole being, your whole spirit being, it feels every ounce of the pain. So intense. But the difference is when you're in the flesh, you can pass out. In the spirit, you live with that pain. And here's the thing to remember—that pain lasts forever. It never stops. It keeps going and going. Listen, a hundred million years, we can think, "Okay, a hundred million years," our mind can kind of grasp that. But a hundred million years isn't even a tenth of a second in eternity. It's like nothing.

I think the thing that was the worst of all was knowing there's no hope. When you are in hell, all those people in there, they know there's no hope. I mean, they want to get out, but they know it's over. It's over, man. Once that happens, there's no getting out of it. You know, I'm one in like 500 billion. I don't know if there's anybody else that's ever gone through what I went through. I just know that when I was in hell, I knew this was it. It was final. And I didn't think I was ever going to get out of this. It was the most horrible, horrible feeling. Even when I talk about it today, my eyes are tearing up. I'm trying not to, here, but my eyes tear up because of the hopelessness that you feel, the horrible feeling that you have because the pain is so intense, the smell is so gross, and it never stops.

It's like it penetrates all of your being. The smell just comes through you and it's so gross. And in the laughter of them laughing at you—you're not laughing, but the demons are laughing. They're making fun of you. You fell for it, buddy. You're the stupid idiot who didn't listen to God. You're the one who turned your back on Him, especially people who have been Christians. The demons love it.

Reflections on Ivan Tuttle's Experience

While it may seem a bit odd to include this part of Ivan's hell experience in a part of the book where we've been focusing on structures and landscapes, there is a purpose for including it here. What is striking about what Ivan shares is even though he's in hell, it comes across in this instance as both formless and void, a chaos of sorts. This seems like the exact opposite of the order God put into things during creation.

Lack of structures and landscapes aside, it's hard to think of anything more horrible than what Ivan describes. Remember that in your spirit body, all of your senses are turned up to the max, so everything that hits your senses is infinitely beyond anything you experience back on earth.

62

DEMON SHOWS MAN SOULS IMPRISONED AND TORTURED IN JAIL CELLS IN THE PIT OF HELL

When we last encountered **Bryan Melvin**, he was experiencing his life review. Below, we step back to another part of his experience in which a demon is taking him down into the pit of hell.

The Bible talks about chambers of death and it describes hell as a pit with a dungeon and cells. I was seeing the pit of hell, but at the time I did not fully grasp what I was seeing. I was scared, but at the same time I also knew I deserved this place. I wanted to wake up but could not.

So I was standing there trying to process all of this and all I could do was follow this creature. He started pointing toward the road and all the things that were going on. I could see tornado vortexes dropping people off into the cells just like I had been. I also saw this wide, dusty road with these gaggles of hideous-looking creatures. These demonic entities were escorting people along this road and delivering them to these cells. It was extremely hot, dry, and dusty. As Bill Wiese says, it is so hot, your eyeballs are going to melt out of their sockets. The dirt of the place felt like I was walking on rotted flesh, but it was dusty. Very strange. I could see hot glowing rocks in various places and I could hear a roar of flame too. It all stank. It smelled so bad I could taste it.

I kept following this creature, and he took me to the center of the road to a circular pit. The best way I can describe it would be a spiral staircase. The bricks were the cells and the cells were stacked six high and layered as a bricklayer does in a circle. Behind the first few cells, it opened into little V-shaped formations and little rooms the farther it went back. We walked over there and when I looked down, I saw a bottomless pit that went as far as I could see.

The creature told me this was a grand place. He motioned to me and I followed him back toward the cubes. When we got back over to the cubes, all I could do was just stare. We looked inside two of these cubes and I could see people inside of these cells. Somehow I was instantly granted knowledge of their life history. I knew how and when they got there.

I could see what was going on in the cell from my perspective, but I also could see from the perspective of the person inside the cell and what they were experiencing. This is exceedingly difficult to explain, but I could see it from both perspectives at the same time. So I was looking at this stuff transpiring and the people were experiencing just degrees of recompense just like the Bible says, payback for how they gamed the system, gamed God, and made life ugly. It all comes back to you. You are dwelling in a never-ending nightmare. That is what these people were experiencing and I saw a lot of people there.

Reflections on Bryan Melvin's Experience

In the story above, Bryan is recounting a travel narrative in hell in which he goes on a journey with a demon who is leading him down to the pit of hell. Bryan recounts seeing a road and at one point a staircase that seemed to lead to a place that had no bottom or end.

As we might expect, Bryan also recounts hell being a place that is hot, dry, and dusty. The big thing to note structure-wise from this part of Bryan's account is that he saw cells everywhere. These were like jail cells or prison cells where souls would be placed to endure their eternal punishment. These cells are a common feature of many of the hell experiences people have shared with us.

63

JESUS INVITES RABBI TO EXPERIENCE THE SECOND HEAVEN

When we last encountered Rabbi Felix Halpern, he had died from an unintended drug overdose and was having an out-of-body experience. Below, we step much further down the road in his Heaven experience in which Jesus invites him to experience the second Heaven.

In the period of time—and it has not closed completely—that followed my return, the envelope was, I can only say, pretty wide open. Sid Roth put it this way: "It's like living in an eggshell, cracked with a light, always coming in from the other side." That is a better picture of it all.

The Lord invited me to see the second heaven where the demons were. When I was standing above the second heaven, I could see a clear separation, not like a firmament between Heaven and earth, but there was a definite separation that I was standing on. There was a particular demon, and there were many in there, but this one demon tried to climb up and grab hold of my ankle, but it could not. It was pitiful. I can have pity on them because I realize that we go from glory to glory in Yeshua; we go from beauty to beauty. Who we are is always coming to a greater reflection of the glory of God, the majesty of Yeshua. But they are going from decay to decay.

They were horrible and pitiful looking in that they did not even know that they had no authority to come to me. They had no ability to grab hold of my ankle, and the Lord showed me why: because I am covered by the blood of Yeshua. I came back with an understanding of the kind of authority that we live in daily. It is both a passive and an aggressive authority. It is aggressive in that we can use it against the kingdom of darkness, but it is also passive in nature. We live in a constant state of victory and power to such a degree that I realized that from our feet, the ground on which we walk and all the way up to the heavens, those airways, we have complete authority. For that reason, I can raise my hand to the Lord to worship Him and the worship and everything that is innocent, the spirit, extend all the way up into the heavens. We have complete authority by the blood of Yeshua.

What we have done in the church world is replace soul problems with devil problems. Catch that for a minute. People have fewer problems with the devil than they realize. What they really have are soul issues. We have upset something that is great for the enemy. We have inadvertently given him authority or have let him think that he has authority that he just does not have. And of course I can do a teaching on this in the Scriptures to back this up. There is no demonic attack and no demonic principality that can come against the blood of Yeshua—just like the blood that protected the Israelites from the angel of death coming through Egypt, just like the 144,000 are sealed by the Holy Spirit. The blood of Yeshua is profoundly authoritative and powerful over every demonic principality, over every sickness and disease, and I think that we have lost the reality of the power of the blood of Yeshua.

Now that is a tough topic for Jewish people to understand, because the Jewish people are 2,000 years away from sacrifice and the shedding of blood, and it has become a Christian term and a Christian concept, but it is a very Jewish concept obviously— through the shed blood of the Lamb, through the blood on the lintel posts, on and on. And part of Leviticus is about atoning and shedding blood. I think back to your question: that was transformative to such a degree that everywhere I go, I wear python boots when I minister. My python boots are an immediate lesson that the devil, the serpent, has been cast to the ground. He is under my feet and that is where he is going to stay.

Reflections on Rabbi Felix Halpern's Experience

Rabbi Felix recounts Jesus inviting him to stand above the second heaven. He notes seeing a distinct separation between Heaven and earth and a ton of demonic activity in the second heaven. This is one of those parts of an NDE account that has a profound spiritual lesson for the Christian believer.

Felix notes how pitiful the demons were and that they had no authority to come to him because he is covered by the blood of Jesus. If we are followers of Jesus and covered by His blood, we operate from a place of profound authority and power over demonic principalities, sickness, and disease. Felix ironically wearing python skin boots to remind him that the devil is always under his feet is a reality Christians need to get hold of so we can stop giving the devil and demons more power in our lives than they actually have.

64

MAN FINDS HIMSELF AT THE BORDER BETWEEN HEAVEN AND HELL

When we last encountered **Jim Woodford,** he was being shown a nursery in Heaven that receives the souls of all the lost children and aborted babies. Below, we step into an earlier part of his journey in which he comes to a sort of border between Heaven and hell.

I swung my vision to the left. As I left that beautiful vista on the right, the grass went from green to brown to black to scorched. I was really taken by looking for the technical reason. Why would there be this dichotomy between these two vistas? The darkness continued to the left and into what seemed to be a crevasse. I guess I'm just naturally inquisitive. I made a few tentative steps to the left to see what was beyond this chasm. As I looked down, it was as though the walls of this chasm were covered with a shiny black anthracite coal. The first thing I saw at the very pit of the bottom of this abyss was a fire, a red fire, like a glimpse of a campfire in a distant valley.

But I was caught by the difference. Not only that, there was a sense of gloom, a miasma, a sense of dread. I think ever since we crawled out of caves, we've always feared the darkness. I started to turn away from this, but then something happened—the fire became greater at the bottom. As I was looking down, two things happened. The brightness of the fire increased, and I realized that down and looking sideways, it was as though a large door had opened and I could hear a sound for the first time. The sound was the sound of two large doors being forced open on hinges that had not been oiled. You could hear them screeching and so on, just rusty. That flooded the view with more light, and I realized the light was coming from the side to the bottom.

Then, to my utter amazement, something shuffled out of that doorway. The doorway was huge and so was the creature that came out. I looked down on it, and it appeared to have a form—large, round. It was on fire. Its body was on fire. Its head was squat on the shoulders and it seemed to be searching around the bottom of this pit for something. Suddenly it was as though it became aware of me, and it swiveled its head around and looked up at me. And I can tell you something—the look of hatred that I saw in its glowing eyes, not just for me but for all of mankind, will stay with me forever. On top of that, there was an odor that came out of that pit, a sense of decay, a sense of all things bad. As I said, a miasma.

Reflections on Jim Woodford's Experience

Many NDEers report coming to a gate or a threshold, often one they're unable to cross. Jim Woodford had an experience early in his journey in which he came to a place that you could almost describe as the border between Heaven and hell. When he looked to the right it was lush and beautiful, and when he looked to the left the ground was scorched and the darkness increased. This may have indeed been a liminal space where Jim's journey could have gone in one direction or another, depending on what he did or whom he called out to.

To his left Jim also saw a pit with a door at the bottom, out of which emerged a demonic creature. This creature knew Jim's name and would be a part of what I suspect was the most terrifying part of his experience.

65

MAN DECEIVED INTO THINKING HE HAD ARRIVED IN HEAVEN, BUT IT WAS ACTUALLY THE GATEWAY TO HELL

When we last encountered **Bryan Melvin**, he was seeing souls imprisoned in cells in the pit of hell. Below, we step into an earlier part of his experience when he arrived at a place that he would soon find out was not at all what it seemed.

I was cast into a tunnel-like vortex moving toward a yellowish dim light, a different type of light. I fell out of the sky and bounced on the ground. I stood up and thought I must be in hell. I remember when I was a kid, everyone talked about hell having fire and brimstone, devils, and the guy wearing tights with the pitchfork and wings and stuff. There was none of that.

I was sitting on a hill and there was a little valley with a house on the other side of it. Everything was brownish and dead-looking because it was so hot. The house was oddly like the house that I used to live in with my parents back in Virginia, but not quite; there was a difference. There was a dilapidated tree in the wrong place in the yard. It was where our driveway would have been. It was not the same house, but it was. I saw all that and then all these people came out of the house. Then more people came up out of the valley. It looked to me like they were coming to welcome me to paradise, slapping me on the back and everything. However, things just did not feel right.

I kept thinking that some of these people could not really be here because they were not dead. The people began to morph into other creatures right in front of me, trying to distract me. One even tried to appear as my mom, and I said, "You are not my mom. My mom's not dead. You are not dead." Then they all changed. I could see that their eyes were like alligator eyes with yellow irises. And suddenly I could see what they really looked like. That was when they all surrounded me and I started saying Jesus's name and title nonstop. I had permission. He gave me permission to say His name and title. That is the first thing that people need to realize.

He gave me permission to say His name in this place. When I said His name, they could not grab hold of me. They could not bite me, but they could push me and touch me. Being poked and prodded by these creatures was an odd sensation. The good news is that they were unable to do what they had originally been planning to do. One creature, whom I nicknamed lizard breath, came forward out of the crowd.

In fact, I found a statue of this creature that was made near Loveland, Colorado. I saw it from a distance and told my brother-in-law, "That looks like the creature I saw." It is the best representation I ever saw of lizard breath. So we walked over to it. When I saw the statue, it was opening day for this place. This statue was in the African art section, and it said, "This is the traveler who escorts people into the underworld." Talk about creepy. This was a total *Twilight Zone* moment for me.

Lizard breath had a dinosaur or alligator-like tail, like it was reptilian, but his mouth was bigger. I could not tell you how many eyes he had because his breath was so foul that it would distort his face. He took me and he said, "Come, follow me, and I will give you half of my kingdom." I started following him and we took a few steps toward the horizon. He stuck his hands into the horizon and ripped it open. He stepped up and out of this place and motioned for me to come. I did not know what to do, so I just followed him, because I did not want to stay there with those creatures.

Reflections on Bryan Melvin's Experience

We've already talked about experiencers sometimes having a welcome committee of sorts when they arrive in Heaven. Bryan Melvin was taken to a place that looked like his childhood home and saw a group of people who seemed to be coming to welcome him to paradise. However, he had a sense that something was off, especially when he realized some of the people he recognized in his welcoming committee were not actually dead. Things took a turn quickly when all of those people revealed their true form of reptile-like creatures.

Bryan often says that if he had been resuscitated before his welcoming committee revealed their true form, he would have thought he had gone to Heaven and wouldn't have experienced the life-altering results of the whole rest of his NDE journey.

This part of Bryan's story is the only one of its kind we've encountered thus far in which an experiencer was taken to a false Heaven before being taken into hell.

66

JESUS TAKES MAN TO A HEAVENLY CITY FILLED WITH MANSIONS

When we last encountered **Alwyn Matthews,** he was receiving a sort of life review for the ministry of Downpour Church. Below, we get into an expanded telling of that part of Alwyn's journey in which Jesus brings him to a city filled with mansions.

In a sense, with this whole experience, I think because of my pursuit, God was healing me. He was literally restoring me. Then Jesus takes me on this journey. We are traveling, we are moving, and He's excited to show me this memorial city. That was the word. It was not a word that was said, it was a word that came up in my spirit—*memorial city.* The mansions in the city are dedicated to ministries and churches and whatever we've done unto the Lord. It could be something big, something small, whatever. It's all significant in the eyes of the Lord. And He takes me to the city, and when I say city, it's probably an inferior word; it's literally a country.

It's magnanimous, it's massive, it's huge. The city itself carries a presence; again, it's something you perceive in your own Heaven that "Wow, I know what the city is" even though you've never been there. I know what the city is. And with that, I want to say this one thing: we will travel in Heaven, we'll be going to places and all of that is an act of worship. And so He takes me to the city, and He starts showing me this mansion and that mansion. And then he takes me to Downpour mansion. He starts showing me the things that we've seen happen over the years, things that we've seen, but things I thought we lost. But they were all remembered and they were all established as a sign and an act of worship and a reminder of the things that God has done.

I was given the opportunity to walk through ministry moments in the life of our church, and we will experience that in Heaven. And this is the thing people say, "How are we going to worship all the time?" You're going to walk through moments when you've seen God move and you are able to—how do I explain this? I was able to walk through ministry moments and experience even in a greater magnitude what God did and what God was doing and even see angelic activities that my earthly eyes could not see here on earth during those ministry moments while I was in Heaven.

All of a sudden, the deep appreciation, the deep sense of wonder that comes forth was unbelievable. And in all this, the reason I felt Jesus was showing me this was because He was telling me, "Don't give up. Tell My church not to give up." The thing was, Jesus was building these mansions based on the materials that we have here on earth. When I use the word *materials*, it's not bricks and cement and steel and all that. The materials of our sacrifice, the materials of our ministry, the materials of our hard work. He has a way of using those materials to be the infrastructure of these mansions in Heaven. And I literally felt Jesus saying, "There are mansions that are complete and there are mansions that are incomplete." It was almost like He was saying, "I am the architect. I am the cornerstone. I will build My church, but I need you to partner with Me and I need you to join with Me. Don't give up. Don't lose your hope, because what you're doing here on earth matters."

The excitement that Jesus had in building those mansions was not because He was wanting to build a beautiful mansion. It was because He wanted to use the materials of His precious children.

He showed me mansions that were beautiful, and He showed me mansions that were *beautified*. That's the best way I can explain it. Mansions that were beautiful were mansions that fulfilled the mandate on the ministry and stuck it out. Mansions that needed to be beautified were ministries that suffered pain, loss, grief, suffering, sorrow, bitterness betrayal, bankruptcy, whatever could be. Whatever the situation is, we're here to step in and beautify them. That was reflective of the redemptive nature of Jesus.

He was saying that there are so many in their lowest moments, questioning, "Is what I'm doing worth it? Is anybody listening to these podcasts? Is anybody watching these things? Is anybody getting anything out of my sermon? Are any of these kids even hearing me when I'm teaching in Sunday school? Is anybody receiving the love of Jesus through this feeding program that I'm doing downtown?"

He is saying, "Keep going, because I'm using every little thing that you're doing to build this incredible thing. But when you feel I've given up and when you feel it's too much for you to handle, come to Me, those who are weary, and I will give you rest." He's saying, "Rest in Me and I will complete what could never be completed. I will beautify it." Now, that's not an excuse for us to say, "Well, I guess Jesus will take care of it. He's our insurance." That should be a motivation and encouragement for us to know how much we've been invited to co-labor with Him.

Reflections on Alwyn Matthews's Experience

The idea of mansions in Heaven is quite commonplace on an individual level, but what Alwyn encounters in this heavenly city are mansions that are a result of the work of churches and ministries. On the one hand, it feels like Jesus showed Alwyn this to encourage him to keep pushing forward in his own ministry, which had endured a prolonged rough patch. On the other hand, it seems plausible that God sent Alwyn back with this story to encourage pastors and leaders that their work, no matter how small or seemingly unnoticed and insignificant, is seen by God and contributes to the expansion of the Kingdom. The memorial city is a beautiful illustration of God taking notice of all the ministry we do for Him, big and small.

67

MAN SEES A MASSIVE PARTY ERUPT IN HEAVEN'S THRONE ROOM OVER ONE LOST SINNER COMING HOME

When we last encountered **Joe Joe Morris,** he was waiting to find out if his name was written in the Lamb's Book of Life. Below, we step into a later part of his throne room experience in which the whole room erupts into a celebration over another lost soul being saved.

In that moment of glory, I look up and as this is happening, I'm seeing all the angels around me sing, "Glory, glory and honor to Your name. Praise be the Lamb that was slain. May He reign forever and ever for all eternity." And they were just praising the King of kings and they were praising the Father. And I remember thinking to myself, *This is nuts. This Heaven is a roaring party.*

They were shooting rocket launchers off and it was crazy. And I'm like, *This is uncool.* I was getting uncomfortable with how crazy they were celebrating because this booming music was sweeping across the whole entire room. The throne room was about the size of, perhaps a bit bigger than a stadium. I could not count the angels. There were too many to count, but they were all celebrating over one lost sinner who had come home, and that was me. I remember thinking it felt so good to be forgiven. I knew God loved me unconditionally at this point.

Reflections on Joe Joe Morris's Experience

Joe Joe Morris had a prolonged time in what he understood to be Heaven's throne room. While he was there, a celebration erupted over a lost sinner who had come home. Based on his Mennonite background, the celebration made him very uncomfortable.

Joe Joe does give us some insight into the size of the throne room, saying it's slightly larger than a stadium.

He saw more angels than he could count celebrating over that lost sinner, and then we come to find out that the lost sinner was Joe Joe. This was the point at which Joe Joe accepted that God loved him unconditionally.

68

ANGELS GIVE MAN AN AERIAL TOUR OF HEAVEN

When we last encountered Jim Woodford, he was standing at a sort of border between Heaven and hell. Below, we fast-forward to a point later in his journey when the angels were showing him a heavenly city.

From there, they showed me more things. Suddenly, I was conscious of one of the guardians standing next to me. He said, "Hold my cloak." So I reached over and held on and suddenly we were above looking down and I thought I was looking at a reflecting pool, but it opened up and I realized I was having an aerial tour of Heaven. I hate using that term because you hear people talk about our experiences and they call it heavenly tourism. You know what a lack of faith is in that term of derision. I believe with all my heart and know this is real. I wasn't imagining it. I wasn't hallucinating.

I didn't know at that time that I wasn't being allowed to stay—you have to remember that. People have asked me, "Did you see your family?" No, I did not. It was explained to me later that I could not set foot in the heavenly city, but they would show me the heavenly city. I didn't connect it with the fact that I wasn't staying. I did see the halls of knowledge, the halls of wisdom, how Heaven is laid out, and yes, the streets are gold, but it's not the brassy gold that we come to think of on earth. It's a different shimmer of gold. It's not the Fort Knox kind of gold. I saw many things and had the opportunity to ask many questions.

Reflections on Jim Woodford's Experience

Since Jim Woodford is a pilot, it seems fitting that the angels would take him on an aerial tour of Heaven. Although he didn't make the connection at the time, he was unable to set foot in the city because he was not staying.

In terms of the many things Jim saw, he specifically recounts about seeing a hall of knowledge and a hall of wisdom. Jim is the only experiencer who has referenced those heavenly structures when recounting his experience. Jim also mentions seeing streets of gold, which is a common description amongst NDEers.

While there is always a bit of predictable overlap between these Heaven and hell experiences, each story has its own unique elements that often seem to have been tailored for the experiencer.

69

MAN FINDS HIMSELF FACE DOWN BEFORE GOD'S THRONE SURROUNDED BY A RING OF IMPENETRABLE FIRE

When we last encountered Rabbi Felix Halpern, Jesus had invited him to experience the second Heaven. Below, we step into his time in the throne room of Heaven.

In no time, I was before the throne of God. When I share about the life and death aspect of it, it is hard for me to talk about it because I feel, in that moment, the fragility of my physical life, the tearing between the mortal and the immortal. I feel like my chest can just collapse inside because I can relive that moment of when it happened and now understand what it really meant. So the Lord brought me into the heavenlies. I was before the throne and it was surrounded by a ring of impenetrable fire ripples, like ripples of fire that were inconceivable in terms of their depth. It could not be penetrated really. And I was on my face at that point.

One of the lingering effects is that when I worship in the presence, I have to cover my eyes when I think about it because of the brightness. I share in my book, *A Rabbi's Journey to Heaven*, that I was incapable of handling the brightness of the glory of the fire of God and God's presence. In my opinion, it was because I was not meant to stay there. For the redeemed who are staying there, it is different. However, my eyes were not able to absorb the fullness of the fire. My eyes felt heat and I was down prostrate before the Lord. My mind had no other thoughts. The only thing I could think about was that I was in the presence of God Himself, in the presence of the glory.

Reflections on Rabbi Felix Halpern's Experience

Rabbi Felix's throne room experience definitely has a bit of a different vibe than Joe Joe's experience a few pages earlier in the book. Felix found himself in Heaven's throne room, face down before God's throne. The throne was surrounded by a ring of impenetrable fire.

Felix describes having a lasting effect from his experience. When he worships in the presence back here on earth, he has to cover his eyes when he thinks about the brightness in the throne room. Felix seems to be forever marked by his time in the presence of God and His glory.

70

MAN IS INSTANTLY TRANSLATED FROM THE PIT OF HELL TO THE GATES OF HEAVEN

When we last encountered Ivan Tuttle, he was facing a void of darkness and chaos in hell. Below, we step into a pivotal moment during the latter part of his hell experience when he was suddenly ushered to the gates of Heaven.

This demon was taking me and putting me in my final place. What I mean by your final place is when you go to hell, you're put in a place that you're going to be in forever. You're not moving around. You're not walking around. You're not partying down there. Get that out of your head. That shouldn't be a part of your speech anyway. But you know, people say, "Oh, I'm going to party down there, dude." That's not a party. It's almost like there's a chain, but you don't see it. There's a chain around your waist and you get put in your final place. Your feet move around, but you don't go anywhere. Your feet just kind of dangle and you can move your arms around, but you're locked in a place as these demons start in. And this demon was getting ready to put me in my final place.

As he was doing that, a voice rang out and this voice said, "It's not his time. I made a promise to his mother. You must let him go." This voice was so powerful that this demon, which I was still trying to fight with, this demon was hitting me and he was poking me and stabbing me. All of a sudden he cowered down. He was like, "Oh no!" and he let go of me. Thank God. And instantly I was translated right to the gates of Heaven. And there I was greeted by this great big angel. Now this angel could be seven or eight feet tall. I didn't go around with a measuring stick, but I can just tell you he was tall. I had to really look up at him. He was tall and he was a good-looking guy. He had this powerful, gentle voice when he'd speak.

It's kind of hard to explain how we communicated, but you could hear his voice. It kind of just went through you and you knew it was an angel. And he said, "Hey, you need to take my hand. You're not ready for this. You're going to have to go back to earth and straighten out your life, but God wants me to show you some things." So he took me by the hand and he brought me into the gates of Heaven. And we walked into the gates of Heaven.

Reflections on Ivan Tuttle's Experience

Ivan Tuttle was facing the horrifying reality that a demon was about to place him in his final resting place in hell where he was sure to endure endless torment. In that moment when all seemed lost and hopeless, a voice rang out declaring, "It's not his time. I made a promise to his mother. You must let him go." This is another NDE story where the prayers and intercession of a mother had an impact on the experiencer's eternal destiny. Because of the promise God made to Ivan's mother, he was instantly translated from the depths of hell to the gates of Heaven.

At the gates of Heaven, Ivan encounters a large angel who takes his hand and ushers him through the gate so he can see some things in Heaven before he returns to his body. It's very intriguing that Ivan had the opportunity to actually go through the gate. Many people who are not staying in Heaven report being prevented from entering the gate or going into the heavenly city.

CONCLUSION

As you've seen throughout the stories in this section of the book, both Heaven and hell have structures and landscapes just like we do back here on earth.

Experiencers report that pretty much anything they saw in Heaven reflected the light and glory of God. Often the actual structures and landscapes themselves are secondary and it's what's happening in the midst of that space and the truths that are being revealed that are the most important.

For instance, the nursery in Heaven as recounted by both Jim Woodford and Ivan Tuttle—it's not the building that's important, it's what's happening with the lost children having a chance to grow up and eventually be reunited with their parents that is most important.

With the throne room encounters, Rabbi Felix Halpern and Joe Joe Morris's experiences couldn't have been more different, but the thing to note in each of those cases is how each of those men were profoundly transformed by what they experienced in God's presence.

In the hell experiences, regardless of the structures or landscapes encountered along the journey, hell is a place of intense heat and torment. The things hitting any or all of your senses that are cranked up to maximum sensitivity are both horrendous and overwhelming. These hell encounters should really make us introspective as we ponder our final eternal destination.

Discussion Questions

1. We had two NDEers share about nurseries in Heaven for all of the souls of lost children and aborted babies. What does this tell you about God's heart for children and for parents who have had to endure the loss of a child?

2. Ivan Tuttle shared about being put into his final resting place in hell, but that was suddenly interrupted because God said He had made a promise to Ivan's mother. Is that fair? How does that square up with your theological understanding about why somebody deserves to go to hell?

3. NDEers share about structures and landscapes in both Heaven and hell. Do you think these are literal structures or are they something else altogether because people are experiencing all of this in the spirit?

4. In terms of making a change in your life, which stories have had a bigger impact on you, Heaven or hell?

SECTION 7

LEARNING SPECIAL KNOWLEDGE

During their time on the other side of the veil, many experiencers receive special knowledge. This may come through something they saw, something they experienced, or a special impartation of knowledge or information from a being they encountered.

71

GOD SHOWS MAN THAT THE DEMONS HATE IT WHEN WE PLAY WORSHIP MUSIC

When we last encountered Ivan Tuttle, he had been instantly translated from the pit of hell to the gates of Heaven. Below, Ivan recounts special knowledge he acquired in Heaven about the ways music impacts the spirit.

I'm going to let you know something—here's a secret from Heaven. When music is played, it ignites the spirit and activates the spirit before the flesh ever hears it, because the spirit is more in tune. Music came from Heaven. Music wasn't something that we invented on earth. Music came from Heaven. So music was made for the spirit, not for the flesh. So be careful what you listen to. Music in Heaven, when it hits you, it penetrates your body. You taste it. It's like, mm, that tastes good.

You feel the music. You see the music. You hear the music. It goes through you and you can feel the melodies. You can feel the different things, the notes. I mean, literally you feel like you want to rise on something and your spirit is doing it. Your spirit reacts to it. And oh, there's nothing like it. And when you hear them singing holy, holy, holy—oh, it's so deep. Everything inside of you is like, yes, holy, worshiping God. Oh, I'm a lover of music now, way beyond those people. I'm not musically talented. I can carry a tune, but I don't have the best tone in the world to sing. I can sing "This Little Light of Mine," I can do good on that. Other than that, I'm kind of out of it. But you know, I love to sing.

This past week I happened to be around some very musical people. I was listening. I was like, oh, I was just lost in it. The music in Heaven. When you understand what it does to your spirit, listen, folks. If you're having problems at home, put worship music on. I'm going to be blunt—I'm not talking about rap music. Okay? Worship music. I'm talking about worship music that is pleasant to the ears and pleasant to the spirit and the soul. Nothing's wrong with the Christian rap music. It's for a generation, but you want to have something you can soak in the Word of God and just let it soak into you. You turn that on. You know what? Demons hate it.

This is what I saw from Heaven. The demons hate it when you have worship music. Why, when they start worshiping in church and they start doing the music, they should just let the music go for a lot longer because the demons are like, "Ah, I can't stand it!" They're covering up their ears. They can't handle it because it's not worshiping lucifer. It's worshiping God. It's giving praises to Jesus, giving praises to God. It's not giving praises to lucifer. So they hate it. The worldly music—every kind of worldly music, I don't care what it is—it's not worshiping God, even though God gave them that talent to do what they do. Unfortunately, they use it for the wrong reason. And so that activates another thing in your spirit. So just think about that. Music is awesome. Do you know that people with Alzheimer's, if you play music, they can sing a song when they can't even talk to somebody? But you play music, they can sing a song. Where does that come from?

Reflections on Ivan Tuttle's Experience

Ivan Tuttle learned several profound truths about music during his time in Heaven. First, music activates and ignites our spirit. Second, the demons hate it when we play and sing worship music.

The big takeaway from Ivan's experience is that whether we're actively singing or simply soaking, we should make worship music a part of our life 24/7 as much as possible to attract the hosts of Heaven and repel the hordes of hell.

72

MAN SEES VISION OF CREATION IN HEAVEN AND REALIZES GOD'S GLORY IS ON ALL THE WATER OF THE EARTH

When we last encountered **Ivan Tuttle**, he shared the profound truths he learned about music in Heaven. Below, we get into what he learned about God's glory touching the water.

One of the experiences that I had when I was in Heaven is I got to see how the earth was formed and I got to watch how God came down. The Spirit of God came down and hovered over the waters of the deep. And I watched this happen and one of the things that people don't realize is that God's glory was all over this water. And when God's glory gets on something, it never leaves. All of the water that we have here on the earth now was here back then. So one of the most amazing things that people don't realize is God's glory is on every drop of water that's here because God's glory never leaves. It never goes away. I mean, you could ask Moses, who had to wear a veil over his face after he just barely glimpsed God.

So when you start thinking about this, every ounce of water here on this earth has had the glory of God on it, has had the presence of God on it. So when you have that, you start understanding things. We can look at different things about water. We can look at the living water, Jesus's living water. We can look at the fact that we baptized people in water. We can see the pool of Bethesda when the water was stirred. We have seen people who have been baptized. When we go to baptize people now, people get healed. I mean, people with stage four cancer come up out of the water, and a week later they go to their doctors and the doctor says, "Hey, your cancer's cured." We've seen people who were demon possessed come up out of the water no longer demon possessed. Their lives are changed.

We're watching these things happen on a continual basis every place I go when we do the baptisms. But what I try to get people to understand is that God's glory is on the water. Most people, when they're taking a shower is when they start realizing things about God. They start having experiences with God when they're in the water. This is happening all over the world. People are starting to report these things that are coming in. It's not that there's anything special about the water except for the fact that God came down and He made our water different from any water that's out there anyplace else in the universe. That's why scientists are always trying to find out, is there water on the planet? There's water on the planet, there's got to be life. And they'll go there and they'll find some drops of water someplace and they bring it back. There's zero life in it because it didn't have God's Spirit, the glory of God on it. Water reflects, water absorbs, and water has memory, and every ounce of water we have today is super special. Think about it the next time you have a drink of water.

Reflections on Ivan Tuttle's Experience

During his time in Heaven, Ivan Tuttle saw the creation of the earth unfold before his eyes. Imagine having a front row seat to what is described in the early part of the book of Genesis! One thing that really stood out to Ivan was the spirit of God hovering over the waters and how the glory of God was all over the water.

If God's glory is still on every drop of water here on the earth, that has quite a bearing on what we can expect to happen in the baptismal waters, where we see people healed and delivered, not unlike what people were expecting in the pool of Bethesda in Jesus's day. The best parallel we can make today is what God has been doing for over five years at Todd Smith's church in Dawsonville, Georgia, where they've had innumerable cases of total healing and deliverance through the waters of baptism.

73

YOUNG MAN SEES PEOPLE'S PRAYERS BUILD A BRIDGE IN HEAVEN THAT ALLOWED HIM TO RETURN TO HIS BODY BACK ON EARTH

When we last encountered Gabe Poirot, he was talking about all of the amazing colors that were hitting his senses in Heaven. Below, he describes how the prayers of faith constructed the bridge that brought him back to his body on earth.

One of the things that Jesus showed me when I was in Heaven was how these children of God, family of God, were praying in faith. They were praying the words of God and they were joining in agreement. And there were these bridges He showed me. I saw the earth and I saw these bridges that kept rising. As people stayed persistent—as people stayed praying the word of God, not praying just feelings or emotions or just things that they were thinking, but praying the word of God—the bridge formed; it went high and higher and higher. That was the bridge. That was the road that I went back to the earth on.

God showed me how He still has a destiny for me, how He has a plan for my life. He showed me how His plan is for me to share the gospel of His power to this world and bring the good news of Jesus Christ to this world so that they can know Him for who He truly is. He showed me that, but He wanted me to come back down to earth also. He has tools to accomplish things. Just because God wills something to happen doesn't mean it automatically happens. There's a way in which He goes about things, and it's His word— that is His way, His word. He's just shown me how when people pray His word, He can move on the earth.

It so marked me and I'm so thankful to everyone who prayed. You might not know of me, but I just want to say to anyone who was praying for me, thank you so much. I can't ever stop saying thank you to whoever it was that did pray. I know people in my local Fort Worth, but it was all over the world that I saw people praying. I just want to say thank you, because prior to this in my life, I had said thank you to people for praying for me. But after this I meant it and I understood it. I really saw how prayer is not just some nice-feeling, people-pleasing thing to do for people. It's not some backdoor, indirect, passive thing to do. It's accomplishing God's will.

The spiritual realm is much more real than the earth realm. It's much more real. When I came back down to the hospital, there were some things that my family was still kind of worried about. I only had half my hair when I first came back. It took me a little bit for my eye to open. And there were some things that they were just kind of worried about. But I knew that all is well. I just knew. I knew that whatever it is that the doctors told me to worry about or whatever it is that the hospital is worried about—so temporary; it's a blink of an eye. I knew my spirit man is whole and healthy, and I knew my body would reflect what I really am.

I'd heard about Heaven before. I'd heard about Jesus before and about eternity before and spiritual things, to be honest. A lot of times when I heard about spiritual things, they kind of weirded me out. I was like, "That's weird," but this was just so real. You can't say something's weird after you experience it. Well, you can, but it's a good weird.

Reflections on Gabe Poirot's Experience

Gabe Poirot shouldn't have woken up. If he did, he should've been a vegetable, but that's not at all what happened. When he was in Heaven, Jesus showed Gabe that it was people praying God's word that built the bridge, the road that led him back to his body on earth.

The big takeaway from this part of Gabe's story is that your prayers are powerful. When you tell somebody you'll pray for them, follow through. Your prayer and intercession may be the proverbial straw that brings the breakthrough.

74

WOMAN DYING OF CANCER ASKS YOUNG MAN WHO'D RETURNED FROM HEAVEN, "HOW DO YOU DIE?"

When we last encountered **Retah McPherson** and her son **Aldo**, we learned of Aldo's encounter with a boy in Heaven and the message he asked Aldo to deliver to his parents. Below, we step into Aldo's conversation with a woman dying of cancer and how she called on Aldo to teach her from his firsthand experience of dying and crossing the veil to the other side.

One day a lady came to my home who was dying from cancer, and she said, "I want to ask Aldo, how do you die?" I thought, *Wow, we can't ask someone that.* In those years, we hadn't even fully dealt with our own trauma yet. All the trauma that he went through, and the spiritual hurt.

I helped him come down and he said, "I want to show you how you die." I thought, *No, what do you mean you want to show her?* And she was really done. And he says, "Ma'am, just close your eyes." And she closed her eyes and he said, "You can open them. You can open them now." He says, "Just like that and you stand before the throne."

Jesus says, "I will never leave you and never forsake you." He takes you from here to there. You'll never be alone.

Reflections on Retah McPherson and Aldo's Experience

Spend a little bit of time in NDE circles and you'll soon realize that people regularly ask people who've had Heaven and hell experiences very difficult questions. They usually have something rather specific they want the experiencer to weigh in on using their special knowledge and experience.

The encounter Retah describes is a woman who was close to death, asking the only person she could find who had already died about what it was like to cross over to the other side.

Truthfully, this lady's question is much easier than many of the crazy and far-fetched questions NDEers are often asked.

75

YOUNG MAN IS INSTANTLY TAUGHT MUSIC THEORY IN HEAVEN

When we last encountered **Joe Joe Morris,** he had just encountered a massive party in Heaven celebrating a lost sinner who had finally come home. Below, he shares what God showed him about music in Heaven.

We were not allowed to listen to contemporary Christian worship, because we were told it was demonically inspired. So I would write music that I would teach to the choir. I was a youth pastor at that time, helping co-lead among some other leaders and being groomed to become an elder in the church because I was very zealous like Saul in the Bible. Again, I would teach the choir this music. And then a couple weeks later, the elders would pull me into the meeting and say, "Why did you teach this music to the choir? It's demonically inspired. Stop writing this music." I was writing hymns, so this just did not make sense to me. Every time I would write something that I knew God wanted me to write, I'd get slapped in the face with it. I felt like God was playing with me.

Not only did He judge me by punching me in the face with a hockey puck, now He's judging me by having my home life be so chaotic. Plus, I'm getting slapped on the wrist for every single song I produce and write. This time was my dark night of this soul, and I spiraled into dark, dark depression. I did not want to live. I did not want to exist anymore. I was forcing myself to eat. I was smiling and cheering everybody else up on the outside, but on the inside I was lifeless and just going through the motions. Moments later, after walking into the Kingdom of God, there were these lessons that were popping up and I was learning music theory. It was the most insane thing because I was learning the beginning concepts of five-part harmony. God showed me that we have an indefinite range to compose with, which was mind blowing—10-part harmony, even a bigger range to compose with instead of our usual four-part harmony here on earth.

Reflections on Joe Joe Morris's Experience

Joe Joe Morris loved writing and teaching worship music, but his work was rejected by the Mennonite community he was a part of at that time in his life. When he went to Heaven, God gave him a special impartation of music theory, which was both an acknowledgment of his gifting and a way to heal the wounds he had received at the hands of others who had wrongly attacked and discounted his gift.

76

GOD SENDS MAN BACK FROM HEAVEN WITH THE SECRET THAT WILL CHANGE YOUR PRAYERS FROM TRANSACTIONAL TO TRANSFORMATIONAL

When we last encountered Rabbi Felix Halpern, he was face down worshiping in Heaven's throne room. Below, we step into a profound truth God revealed to him about prayer.

I refer to this as "the gift" in my book *A Rabbi's Journey to Heaven*, because it is a gift that was given to me. And I asked the Lord, "Is this only for me because I went to Heaven and had this experience, or is this transferable?" I know that what I went through is not transferrable, but my life and lessons and who I am today is transferrable and can help imprint people for greater glory for the Lord. Remember when the Lord told me I would be in the book of Psalms for 30 days? Well, 30 days turned into 60 days and 90 days turned out to be 18 months. When I came back, I could no longer accept the world of typical Christian church culture as it was when I left. I just could not see myself going back into certain things.

One of them was prayer. The Lord revealed the difference between transformational prayer and transactional prayer that is changing people's lives. And the only reason I talk about this is because I am back. I was given my life back to talk about it. Otherwise, I would not even know about it. And the Heaven soul cleanse that comes in the book that people are going through now turns convention on its head. Because if we think about it, let's say that 80 percent of our prayer life is consumed with transacting something with God, right? We are asking God to heal, to bless, to move, to touch our ministries, et cetera. It is always asking God for something; that in itself is not wrong. Yet what I am about to say relates to that other 20 percent of our prayer life that is in what I call the transformational space.

Transactional prayer is always dominated by I, me, and mine. Transformational prayer is always dominated by the Father, by talking about the Lord God. I began to realize that transactional prayer is a needs-based prayer life because we live on a needs-based planet. Heaven is easy, but earth is hard. I have known the Lord for 45 years. I do not think I have ever been without an area that I did not need prayer for. And I think as long as I stay here, I will always have areas of prayer that I need. One prayer is answered today and a new one comes up tomorrow. You can pray for your children, your grandchildren, your wife, your family, your health, and on and on. It keeps going and never stops.

A cycle of needs-based prayer reproduces. It can breed a needy spirit, which I believe hinders the abundant life. The Lord showed me that transformational prayer is rooted in sufficiency. It is a sufficiency mindset. Transactional prayer that is needs based is an insufficiency mindset. We are always needy. The Lord showed me when I went on this 30-day soul cleanse that we can reboot our system. For those 30 days we begin to starve our soul of the natural order of needs and give all of our needs to the Lord: Father, I give You my needs for 30 days. In those 30 days, every morning do the psalms that we have put together. Do no praying. Other than that, it is like a liver cleanse or any other cleanse of the body where you abstain from something to recharge the organs. I do not believe my results have anything to do with my Heaven experience. My soul and my brain are imprinted with the glory of God, the majesty of God, the things of God's nature. His handprint is everywhere.

Reflections on Rabbi Felix Halpern's Experience

So much of the Christian prayer life is dominated by needs-based transactional prayers. God showed Felix how to pray transformational prayers that will produce an abundant life. This gift wasn't just for Felix; it's a prayer strategy that is readily transferrable to anybody who is ready to take hold of these truths Felix learned in Heaven.

CONCLUSION

In this section you encountered stories about special knowledge related to music, water, prayer bridges, transformational prayer, and even a question about what happens when we die. While Joe Joe's story of learning music theory in Heaven seems to have most likely come from a direct impartation of knowledge, the other stories in this section represent conclusions the experiencers came to based on what they saw happening and how they best understood it.

NDEers must wrestle with what special knowledge is actually okay for them to share. Sometimes the knowledge is merely for the experiencer. Other times God will ask the experiencer to hold on to something until He gives them the green light to share.

Discussion Questions

1. Of the stories you encountered in this section about special knowledge brought back from Heaven, which one impacted you the most? Why?

2. Did Aldo's answer to the lady dying of terminal cancer give you some comfort about what you'll experience on your dying day?

3. Do you agree with Ivan Tuttle's explanation of how worship music transforms the atmosphere of a place, igniting the soul of the believer and repelling demons?

SECTION 8

RETURNING TO YOUR EARTH-BOUND BODY

All journeys must eventually come to an end. Some NDEers know they're returning to their body very early in their experience, while others don't know up until the moment they're about to return to their body. Some people's re-entry accounts are just as dramatic as the circumstances that started the experiencer down their whole NDE journey in the first place, while others are about as exciting as waking up from a nap.

77

MAN RETURNS FROM THE DEAD AND TELLS HIS WIFE, "JESUS HAS HORSES IN HEAVEN!"

When we last encountered **Jim Woodford**, angels had given him an aerial tour of Heaven. Below we step into Jim's account of returning to his earthly body.

Two guardians appeared beside me and lifted me from the ground and turned me around and were carrying me back down the path. I wrenched my shoulder away to turn to beg one more time to be allowed to stay. Jesus was gone, but standing exactly in the place where He had stood was this magnificent warrior angel that had greeted me. All of a sudden he began to expand. He grew even taller than 15 feet, and he put his wings out to their full magnificence and they spread out and upward in this beautiful gold, and he was surrounded with light and the message was clear that he was barring the way forward for me.

Suddenly, I felt the angels hold me again. Everything went dark. I was in a black tunnel and I could hear water and it was cold and painful. I felt like I was descending at a tremendous speed, but unlike the tunnel of light there was no beauty, just darkness. I was going down this steep descent.

They tell me that I scared the daylights out of the nurses because I had been triaged. They told my wife that there was no hope of me coming back—there was no brain activity, no sign of dreaming, no sign of hallucinating, nothing, and brain activity of course is the measure of death, not heartbeat. They had me hooked up to everything. There was complete failure of all my organs. The doctors had said to Lorraine that they would keep me hooked up until our children arrived to say goodbye. Then they would recommend that she pull the plug on the machinery that was pumping blood through my organs.

Suddenly I sat upright and scared the daylights out of the nurse, as she told me later. I was screaming around all the tubes because I was intubated. They ran and got my wife and said, "Mrs. Woodford, come quickly." Lorraine's a nurse. She ran into the room and she couldn't believe it. She said my eyes were as big as saucers. I was trying to reorient from the beauty of Heaven to lying on a gurney. She climbed up on the bed with me and started to cry. They were slowly watching my blood pressure come back to normal. All my organs started to operate again. Eventually they pulled the tube out so I could speak clearly. My throat was terribly sore and raw. I looked into my wife's pretty face, and I said, "Lorraine, I saw Jesus, and Jesus has horses." Of all the things I could have said to her: "Jesus has horses and I'm back."

Reflections on Jim Woodford's Experience

When it was time for Jim Woodford to return to his body, he began to descend at a great speed into a dark, black tunnel. When Jim had fully returned to his body, he sat upright in bed and scared the nurse who was caring for him.

As he described above, his body was in complete failure. He was being kept alive on life support until his children arrived to say goodbye. There is no medical reason Jim's body should've had this spontaneous turnaround. The only explanation is that it was a verifiable miracle.

78

MAN SCARES PARAMEDIC HALF TO DEATH WHEN HIS BODY SUDDENLY COMES BACK TO LIFE

When we last encountered Ivan Tuttle, he was sharing about how he saw God's glory hovering over the water during his time in Heaven. Below, we step into the story of his dramatic return to his body.

Here's what I saw. I watched as I was kicked out of Heaven. Talk about rejection, but I had to go back and I knew I had to go back so I can go back to Heaven for good. And I knew I was on a mission when I got back. So I was coming back into my body and I was in the room seeing these two paramedics—one kind of tall, thin guy, and then another shorter, stockier man. The shorter, stockier man had already come over and checked me. He turned around and looked at the other guy and he was shaking his head, "No, man, this guy's dead." The blood was starting to coagulate in my wrist and in my elbow. When he went to move it just a little bit, it wasn't real stiff, but it was stiffening up. Rigor mortis was already beginning to set in just a little bit, and I was dead. I was so far gone, they just walked out of the room. They were calling the morgue, and the radio wouldn't work in that apartment. So he went to use my phone and the taller guy said, "Hey, there's a girl in the apartment so you might want to just kind of check him to make sure he's not bleeding someplace, that she hasn't committed some crime or something."

So he came walking back in there and he went to put his hand down underneath my side to just check to see if there was any blood any place. When that happened, I came back to life. I came into my body. Well, when I came into my body, I couldn't breathe. My whole body started vibrating like it got shocked with 240 volts and I couldn't talk. And this guy jumped back. I keep joking and say I scared him to death and he scared me to life.

But he kind of jumped back and he was just kind of looking at me, you know? And I was trying to talk, and my jaws didn't want to work. My tongue was not working. My eyes were real dry, because my eyes were open. It was just a weird feeling. And nothing wanted to work right. For quite a little while, you know, I was trying to talk and to say things and to breathe. They were trying to say, "We need to take you to a hospital." No. That was the first word I could get out was no, no, no. I was trying to move and I couldn't really move. Finally, I struggled with it and they got me up out of the bed.

I told him, "I need to stand up, need to stand up," and they're trying to check me; they're putting a blood pressure thing on me. They're trying to do whatever they can and I'm going, "No, no." I could say "no." Then I was saying, "Leave, leave, leave." I could get the word *leave* out. Finally, I just told him to get out of there—I started being able to speak. Not clearly. It was weird. Even my voice sounded strange and it was kind of hoarse sounding. And I got them over to the front door. I walked enough to get there, but it was a shaky walk. Believe me, it was a weird walk because my bones were all stiffened up or something. They didn't move correctly. My brain was telling them to move, but my legs were like, "I ain't moving." Finally, they started moving.

So everything started working again just right, and they left. I kicked the girl out too. I grabbed her purse and her jacket and gave it to her and she left. It was cold out there. I wasn't going to make her leave without her jacket. And so everybody left. I have to be honest with you. I had a lot of drugs in my apartment and the cocaine was easy to flush, but marijuana does not flush. When you put it in the commode, you have to put tons of toilet paper on it and wet it, because it just won't go down. So I was trying to get rid of all of this stuff because I wanted nothing to do with it. I knew that I was never going to go back to that lifestyle.

So after I got rid of the drugs, I dumped the booze I had there—I had a little bit of alcohol there in the house and the beer that she brought over, and I dumped all that down the kitchen sink. I had an avocado green rocking chair from the seventies. If you're too young to remember those, I had one of those and it was a low back and it didn't have a real high back on it. That thing would rock back and forth and swivel around. I sat in that thing and I rocked and I cried. Brother, I cried so hard because I had a second chance. I wasn't going to stay in hell, I had a second chance, and I was thinking of all these things and just crying out to God, "Forgive me, God, forgive me, forgive me."

How could I have been so foolish? How could I have been so stupid? I mean, I'm being blunt, but to me, that's stupid and so foolish to just walk away from God. And I cried and wept and I sat in that rocking chair for hours. I cried until 6:30 in the morning, and this was around midnight when it started, a little after midnight. I cried. I mean, I went through a whole box of Kleenex.

Reflections on Ivan Tuttle's Experience

When Ivan Tuttle returned to his body, he was stone cold dead. The paramedics were in the process of calling the morgue, when all of a sudden Ivan's body began to vibrate and he was back. In short order, Ivan kicked the paramedics and the girl out of his apartment and his body slowly began to return to normal functioning.

Ivan immediately got rid of all the drugs and alcohol in his apartment and spent the rest of the night weeping and asking God to forgive him.

Ivan's story of reentering his body is definitely dramatic, but all drama aside, note how he immediately rids his apartment of drugs and booze and spends the rest of the night asking God for forgiveness. Both of these actions are an indication of the genuine transformation that had taken place in Ivan during his time on the other side of the veil.

79

YOUNG MAN COMES OUT OF THREE-WEEK COMA WONDERING WHY HE'S EVEN IN THE HOSPITAL

When we last encountered **Gabe Poirot**, he recounted seeing a sort of bridge built by people's prayers that allowed him to come back into his body. Below, he shares about what happened when he woke up in the hospital.

On November 14th, I fully woke up and my memory came back. My personality came back and I was healed, so much so that I didn't have any pain. But I looked around and I said, "What am I doing in a hospital right now?" I thought that everyone else around me had gone insane. I was like, "Y'all are crazy. I'm fine." And the calendar said November 14th. And I was like, wait a minute. What? It really felt like I just went to bed on the night of October 24th, and then I woke up and it was November 14th. I'm like, what in the world?

This nurse comes running in, "Sir, you had a traumatic brain injury. You should have died, but now you're coming back." And I'm like, yeah, I'm back. And people were coming in and I could tell that they had been saddened, but they were so happy to see me. And I was asking them, "Why are y'all sad? Can't you see me now? I'm healed." I said, "Get me out of this hospital. I'm going back home. We have to get back to this ministry. I've got to keep preaching the gospel."

So I got out of the hospital. It took a while because they did not want to release me. They were doing all these tests on me every single day and looking at every part of my body and all these things. The biggest thing I was just frustrated about was they shaved half my head. But I eventually got out. I am 110 percent back and life is even better. They thought I was probably going to be a vegetable for the rest of my life. They thought I was going to be nothing. It was either I was going to be nothing or I was going to be dead, and praise God, He raised me back to life.

Reflections on Gabe Poirot's Experience

Gabe Poirot has one of the less dramatic re-entry stories—all of a sudden he just wakes up back in his body. At first, Gabe is a bit disoriented, wondering why he's been in the hospital for three weeks and why they shaved off half of his hair.

The amazing part of the story of Gabe returning to his body is that he was healed. Doctors were convinced he was going to die once they took him off of life support, and even if he did survive he was going to be a vegetable. As Gabe shared above, he was healed and able to go back to his normal life.

This is yet another verifiable miracle. When there was no hope medically, God brought about complete and total restoration.

80

MAN SAYS THE DAY HE RETURNED TO HIS BODY WAS BOTH THE BEST AND WORST DAY OF HIS LIFE

When we last encountered **Randy Kay**, he was experiencing his life review. Below, we step into the part of his story in which he is returning to his body.

I'd heard this song in Heaven, this singing. There was a couple singing that same song at my bedside, and I thought, "Was this You, Lord, was this them, or was it Your angels that I was hearing?"

The first thing I sensed was the acrid smell of the hospital, the disinfectant. I was in paradise, and now I was in this stark room with people around me and this couple singing at my bedside this beautiful song of praise. I realized that somehow God had enjoined the prayers and the praises, the song of those people. It was the same exact song that I heard in Heaven. I realized to some extent that the prayers of the saints were joined in the hallways of Heaven, if you will, such that they were enjoined by those in Heaven and by the Lord to enact His will here on earth. It will be done on earth as it is in Heaven.

That was the best day of my life and one of the worst days. Little did I know that ahead of me would be some even worse days of my life, ironically. But I had that relationship and solid belief, and I could always go to the Lord. We were friends. We were friends. It was wonderful.

Reflections on Randy Kay's Experience

One of the things that is really intriguing about Randy Kay's return to his body is as he comes back to life he hears music being sung in his hospital room. It's the exact same music he had just been hearing in Heaven. You'll have to decide whether you believe it was the worshipers in the room influencing Heaven or Heaven influencing the worshipers in the room. Either way, there was a connection in the spirit between what was happening in that hospital room and what Randy was experiencing on the other side of the veil.

Randy says that the day he returned to his body was both the best and worst day of his life. Many NDEers report being depressed and longing for Heaven in the weeks and months after they return to their body. It is very difficult for experiencers to come to terms with all that they experienced on the other side of the veil, a process that can take as long as seven years.

81

MAN SAYS IT WAS LIKE THERE WAS A HUGE BOARD MEETING TO DECIDE WHETHER OR NOT HE SHOULD RETURN FROM HEAVEN

When we last encountered **Mark McDonough**, he was recounting his time in Heaven. Below, he shares the circumstances surrounding his return to his body.

Many have asked if it was my decision. Did God say, "This isn't your time yet" or did I decide there were still things I want to do? "Wait a minute, God, I haven't seen my grandchildren yet, let alone my children at age 16." It was more like, for me, there had been a huge board meeting where everyone who mattered was present and every issue related to this decision or this answer was discussed and beaten like a dead horse. I understood now that it wasn't my time. It wasn't like I decided, God decided, or my mom. I knew my dad needed me, and I remember a strong sense that it was going to be difficult. Recovery would not be easy, but there were other things I needed to do in life still, good things, so it wouldn't be all work and sadness.

Later, I found out that when I started losing massive amounts of blood, the doctors went out to talk with my dad and said, "We're losing blood from his rectum. It's probably a Curling ulcer," which is where the stomach lining ulcerates from the trauma and the surge of adrenaline.

Dad said, "Full court press. I cannot lose my son, my wife, and now my oldest son. You've got to save him."

I had this sense that he and I were both going to have some challenges ahead for sure, without Mom. That was an awareness. I was not going to Heaven yet. I was not dying yet. I was going to be back here on this earth without Mom and I was going to be helping Dad and my brothers in some way. And that's kind of what I shared with Dad later that night. It was 11:00 or something before I got back into the burn unit, a long day.

Reflections on Mark McDonough's Experience

The story of Mark's return to his body is interesting because it's not like God or some angel specifically told him he was going to return. What Mark experienced was a sense that there was this general consensus reached, as if there was a board meeting in which the decision was made that he still has important things to do with his life.

You also have to take note of the grace of God in allowing Mark to return. His father had already lost Mark's mother and little brother and he would need his oldest son to help navigate the difficult days ahead.

82

WOMAN SAYS WHEN HER SPIRIT RETURNED FROM HEAVEN IT WAS SO FAT IT ALMOST DIDN'T FIT IN HER BODY

When we last encountered **Karina Ferrigno Martinez**, angels were taking her on a tour of Heaven. Below, she shares her dramatic journey back to her body.

just heard the voice: "Do you want to go back?" Without thinking, *Well, if I go back, I'm going to go through this*, I just said, "Yes." And he said, "So be it."

So I turned to go, but I went back and I said, "Can I tell everybody?"

His is not a voice that speaks fast. The voice is just gentle. And His sweet voice said, "They will think you are crazy."

And I said, "I don't care. I want everybody to know what I just saw." So I promised Him that I would tell everybody and bring as many people as possible to the Kingdom.

When I turned around, He said, "You were seeking Me everywhere, but you couldn't find me." I never understood that until now. Then He said, "You are awesome." Then all of a sudden I fell into this glass floor.

This floor was all glass, but it was bright. It's so bright. I was on my hands and my knees and I couldn't get up because whatever it was, it was just pushing me. But it was just so intense to the point I felt that power coming toward me. All of a sudden, I got a little bit of my head up and I looked and it was this white gown with gold and purple coming toward me. I couldn't see His face clearly. It was all white, this light. I could barely see His hair. And then He asked me again, "Are you sure you want to go back?"

I said, "Yes." I could feel something like He was not content with that. But He understood. I could just feel what He was feeling. But I was okay because I felt like I needed to come back. And He was the one who brought me down.

When I got to the place I passed, I was on top of the lake and then I was going back to the same position that my body was. I looked and I said, "Wow. We don't take anything." I had my Apple watch. We don't take anything to this place. And I said, "Is it going to hurt to get in there?"

He said, "It's not going to be the same." So when I went in, I tell people now I almost felt like now I see more. It's like my spirit was so fat that it was not able to fit in my body. But when I got in, it was just horrible. I just took a deep breath, and I grabbed my husband, I yelled at him, and I said, "I just came back from Him!"

My husband was looking at me. "What happened?" So I got up—nothing. I had no problems breathing, no pain, nothing, nothing, nothing. I got up and I grabbed my kids. I sat down and I started telling them everything I saw as much as possible. I could hear this darkness talking to me as soon as I came here. I felt everything that I felt in the past, but I was able to identify it and able to fight it.

Reflections on Karina Ferrigno Martinez's Experience

Karina Ferrigno Martinez was asked a couple of times if she wanted to go back. She recounts being brought back down and describes a unique experience when her spirit was coming back into her body. After being in Heaven, her spirit was so fat, it was almost as if it was too big to fit back into her physical body.

Based on what she describes, her physical body had also received a level of divine healing as she said she no longer had any pain or breathing problems.

83

MAN RETURNS FROM HEAVEN AND WAKES UP IN THE MORGUE

When we last encountered Ian McCormack, he was with Jesus in Heaven and had been given a glimpse of the new heavens and new earth. Below, we step into the story of his dramatic return to his body.

When Jesus comes into you, Christ in you, you cannot help but be changed. That exchange—you give your heart to Him because you love Him. He gives His heart to you and He gives you His perspective on life. And it is an eternal perspective. I looked back and next to my mom appeared my dad, my brother, my sister, and millions of other people, a sea of humanity. I said, "God, why do You show me all these other people? I only know my immediate family."

He said, "Ian, because most will not step foot inside a church any longer to hear My name. I want you to go back, tell them what you have seen."

I said, "But, God, they will not believe me. They will not believe what I have seen. And I do not even know if I love these people."

He said, "Ian, I love them. I desire all of them to come to know Me."

I said, "Well, I do not understand that kind of love. I can say I love my mom. I can go back for her. How do I go back down the tunnel into darkness and back into my physical body?"

He said, "Ian, tilt your head, open your eye, and see." And in a second I was back in my body, tilting my head, opening my eye to find that I was no longer in the emergency room. I was in the mortuary on a slab with a different doctor holding my foot with a scalpel, freaking out as this corpse came alive right in front of him. Both of us were terrified. God then spoke, saying, "I have just given your life back."

I said, "God, if that's true, can I look out the other eye?" So I rolled my head to the right and to the left and that doctor was spinning out of his tree.

Three of the nurses had followed me from the emergency room down to the morgue, and as my corpse moved, they freaked out and bashed into each other. I thought, *Well, this is not someone coming out of a coma. This is not someone coming out of a near-death experience. They are treating me like I am a dead piece of meat.* I potentially could have been dead. I looked back at the doctor. He dropped my foot and wanted to run. He said, "You have been dead for 20 minutes, son. We have done nothing to bring you back." I could see him almost urging me to tell him what I had seen. I thought, *My God, if I tell him I have seen the Lord, they will fill me up with Prozac and send me off to a mental asylum.*

My next thought was, *God, please heal me. I can feel nothing from the neck down. I have been dead for 20 minutes. I could be on a machine for the rest of my life. Please heal me or take me back to Heaven.* Power went through me like electricity, and within three or four hours, my entire body was supernaturally healed. I believe in the resurrection power of Christ and His healing presence. The next day I walked out of the hospital completely healed.

Reflections on Ian McCormack's Experience

Ian McCormack's transition back into his body was instantaneous. God told him to tilt his head and open his eye and he was back. Ian quickly realized that he was no longer in the ER. He was now in the morgue. It's fair to say that his unexpected return gave the doctors and nurses an experience they would not soon forget. Ian had been dead for 20 minutes, and the medical staff hadn't done anything to try to bring him back.

Although Ian was back in his body, he could not feel anything from the neck down. He boldly asked God to either heal him or take him back to Heaven. Ian felt something like electricity run through his body, and within a few hours he was completely healed and he left the hospital the next day.

As we talked about earlier with Ian's story, a sting from one box jellyfish can kill you, let alone five. The only explanation for Ian's healing is a miracle from Heaven.

84

WOMAN EXPERIENCES THE WORST PANIC YOU CAN IMAGINE WHEN HER SPIRIT RETURNED TO HER PHYSICAL BODY

When we last encountered **Heidi Barr,** she had just received her life review. Below, we get into the story of the traumatic experience of returning to her broken body.

saw, as I looked farther, that there was a meadow and I could see a misty pathway that was shrouded in clouds. It was as if there was a veil between what was coming down the pathway and myself. I could see people were coming. I could hear singing, but I could not make anything out clearly. I just saw people were coming toward me on that pathway.

This was all far away, but I could see every detail. And it was at that moment, as I was staring at this, that Jesus came and stood right next to me. And He said, "You did not die. You must go back."

I buried my face back in God's chest, and I said, "I am not going back."

He said in a clear voice, "You did not die. You must go back." His voice was clear as a bell.

I said, "No, I do not. I am not going back. I am not going back." He took my hand and I kept screaming at Him, "I am not going back. I am not going back. You cannot make me go back." I was having this huge argument with Him.

As He pulled me off God's lap, I remember screaming, "I will feel pain." And the next thing I knew, there was no surfing, no tunnel, nothing. Bam!

We were right above my body and I did not want to get in my body, but He shoved me in. I call it hoovering. I was hoovered in, vacuumed into my body from underneath and hit my face. Think about being shoved into a box and hitting the inside of the box. I hit the inside of my skull and I panicked. I had the worst panic attack you can imagine. I felt trapped in this body, but the next thing I knew Jesus was in my body with me. The only way I can describe it is to say that He smoothed my arms into my arms and He smoothed my legs into my legs. He made me one person again. And He said one last thing before He left me, which was, "Your life is in good hands." That was something that haunted me for years. It took me a while to remember how to open an eye, how to talk. I was gravely injured, but I did eventually manage to crack open an eye. I saw the ranch owner kneeling next to me, crying. I croaked out his name and the rest is history.

Reflections on Heidi Barr's Experience

Heidi Barr was sitting in God the Father's lap when Jesus came to her and revealed that she had, in fact, not died and it was time for her to go back. She screamed and pleaded with Him to not take her back, yet He took her back to her body. This is by no means a scientifically derived number, but it seems about half of the people we've talked to about their Heaven experiences are eager to return to their body and the other half are completely content to stay with Jesus in Heaven. In Heidi's case, it simply was not her time. She had more to do in this life.

She described her spirit being sucked back into her body from underneath and feeling like her spirit hit the inside of her skull. This sent her into a panic—she felt trapped in her body. When you consider the euphoria people describe when their spirit is no longer hindered by the limitations of their physical body, it's not all that surprising that you would feel confined and compressed when you reenter your body.

While some of our NDEers experience healing when they return to their body, that was not the immediate case for Heidi. While her healing is truly a marvel and a miracle, it did not happen immediately; it was a journey, to say the least.

85

MAN RETURNS TO HIS BODY AFTER FOUR DAYS IN A COMA AND ASKS HIS NURSE, "DO YOU KNOW GOD?"

When we last encountered **Captain Dale Black**, he was encountering an entire group of people welcoming him at the gates of Heaven. Below, we jump to the part of Dale's story when he woke up in the hospital four days after the plane crash.

I woke up four days later after having this experience in Heaven and back. I woke up, and when my eyes opened on the morning of the fourth day in a coma, I was like a completely different person. Nothing looked the same. Nothing seemed the same. A ridiculous example might be, if you remember the movie *The Wizard of Oz*, you went from black and white and then all of a sudden it's color and dimensional—that's ridiculous. But in a way I felt like someone gave me new eyes when I woke up from the coma.

I tried to talk to the nurse and I couldn't. I was trying to talk and I had all these stitches in my face, and I felt like I was ripping my face apart. But I was trying to tell her—and I think the noise she could hear came out just muffled and garbled. But I was trying to say this: "Nurse, do you know God? Do you know Jesus, His Son? You've got to know Him. You got to know Him. He's real. Heaven is real." That's what I was trying to say.

And all she would say is, "Dale, are you awake? Doctor! Doctor! Dale?" And then they came in. I couldn't talk. All I wanted to do was tell them about God, tell them that Heaven is real and that Jesus is the way to God. His Word is the framework. Everything we see around us, this is all just a test. This is basic boot camp, in a military training sense. This is a proving ground, a testing ground to get us ready for eternity with God in Heaven. We have thousands of choices all day long. And what are we going to do with those choices?

So I came back completely changed—human, frail still, but my life has never been the same. I've never beat on the same drum. And I'm not trying to indicate that I've arrived and I'm some kind of a spiritual guru. That's not what I'm trying to say. What I'm trying to say is that all I want to do is please God. I'm human. I make mistakes. But all I want to do is please Him and do what He wants me to do and go where He wants me to go and say what He wants me to say when He wants me to say it.

Reflections on Captain Dale Black's Experience

When Captain Dale Black returned to his body after his coma and his time in Heaven, he immediately knew he was a changed man. His description of the world going from black and white to color, as we've all seen in *The Wizard of Oz*, is a great word picture of how things looked as he saw the world through new eyes. Many of the NDEers we've talked to suggest that it's like they now see the world and more specifically other people through the eyes of Jesus.

Dale's immediate burden was to tell the nurses and doctors about Jesus and the realities of Heaven. That's the calling and destiny that still drives his work and ministry to this day.

CONCLUSION

As you no doubt already realize after reading these accounts, the spirit returning to the physical body can be both a dramatic and traumatic experience.

For the friends, family, and medical staff who are around the NDEer when they suddenly come back, it's a great shock. The only rational conclusion to reach in each of the accounts you just read is that it was God's miraculous intervention that brought each of these people back.

Many experiencers report always feeling like they have a foot in Heaven, a feeling of longing to go back. This may be especially stronger in those who did not want to return but were not given the choice to stay in Heaven.

In some of the stories you just read, the experiencer had dramatic healing when they returned to their body. Others had to endure a long healing journey, many with physical and medical issues that still plague them to this day. It's a mystery why God allows some experiencers to have complete healing and restoration while others are burdened with ongoing medical problems.

Discussion Questions

1. Why are some people given the opportunity to choose whether or not they want to stay in Heaven, while others are simply told they're going back?

2. Is it fair that some of the experiencers did not receive full healing when they returned to their body? Why?

3. What do you make of Heidi Barr's dramatic experience of her spirit coming back into her body? Are you surprised God didn't make it less traumatizing for her?

SECTION 9

POST-NDE LINGERING EFFECTS

Whether somebody has a Heaven experience, hell experience, or the afterlife combination platter of the two, it's impossible to not be profoundly marked by it. People report having dramatic shifts in their personality, new direction in their journey of faith, and some are now fully awakened to the supernatural activity that is taking place here on the earth.

While the majority of the people we've encountered have been dramatically changed for the better, we've also met experiencers who still carry a certain amount of trauma and PTSD from some especially disturbing experiences with hell and the demonic.

86

IN THE DAYS FOLLOWING HIS NDE, MAN IS CONFRONTED BY SEVEN DEMONS WHO SAY THEY'RE READY TO COME BACK HOME

When we last encountered **Ian McCormack**, he had just woken up in the morgue and experienced a miraculous healing that allowed him to walk out of the hospital the next day. Below, we step into the first of several supernatural experiences Ian had in the days immediately following his NDE.

We went back into the village that night. I went to sleep and woke up as though something had spooked me. Something was freaking me out. I was deeply at peace, but my body was shivering. I rolled over and looked out the window and saw seven people gawking at me. I thought, *Why have we got people coming to see the blinking jellyfish, whatever, and why are they staring and lurking outside my bedroom?* But then as I looked, I realized that they had a human form but they were shadowed, dark, spiritual beings. When I looked at their eyes, I could see their eyes did not have round pupils. They were slits like you would see on a serpent.

And I was thinking, *What the heck is that?* And then as I looked at them, they spoke to me and said, "You are out and we are coming home." I was thinking, *You must be flipping joking, coming home?* I had no point of reference for when Jesus said an unclean spirit goes out of a man and finds six or seven worse in a dry barren place and tries to come back into the house that has been swept clean so they can try to inhabit it. At that moment I was having a firsthand introduction to spiritual warfare 501, you know, instantly. I was seeing with my eyes that were now open to the supernatural and the spiritual realm. I was in a village that was full of voodoo. I had been places where they do evil things; I could sometimes feel it, but I had never seen it. It is much scarier when you think that you potentially had one of those evil things inside of you.

But of course, when you die, your spirit leaves. Why hang around the corpse? Go find some other poor soul. The Scriptures say they seek a place of rest. I turned the lights on and started freaking out. I wondered if I was going mental. Was I seeing the bogeyman? This seemed so *Loony Tunes*. I got to the point where I was sitting on the ground, thinking I had nearly snapped, when God said, "Son, pray the Lord's Prayer."

I could not fully remember it, so I walked through my previous experience and I said the only thing in the Lord's Prayer where it says *deliver us from evil*. God said, "Pray, *deliver us from evil*."

So I said, "Now wait, God, I have a bunch of evil. I do not know where the heck they came from, but they are certainly attentive toward me. I do not know what I have done or what I have said, but God, can You deliver me from the evil that is outside my window? That is just ominous."

I finished praying the whole Lord's Prayer. I walked through the entire testimony. I remembered the whole thing, and God said, "Okay, son, now you have prayed. Turn the lights out and go to sleep."

I responded, "God, that is easy for You to say; You are up there. I am down here. And I have a pack of whatever they are outside my window. You must be joking." I sat there and contemplated. I thought, *Well, the prayer worked last night. I mean, I went to Heaven. I saw God. Well, why not? Why not? God's got power over evil.* I decided to turn the lights out and wait to see if they would come back. They did not come back. I realized there was power in the Lord's Prayer.

Reflections on Ian McCormack's Experience

Immediately following his NDE, Ian McCormack started seeing in the spirit. His first encounter was with seven demons who manifested outside his bedroom window. Surprisingly, they told him they were ready to come back home.

Having limited experience with prayer and deliverance ministry, Ian did the only thing he knew to do—pray the Lord's Prayer. After all, it worked during his NDE. He said the Lord's Prayer, turned out the light, and the demons did not come back that night.

As Ian recounted, he had no experience in spiritual warfare, so this was like being pushed into the graduate level ministry, spiritual warfare 501.

87

MAN CONTINUES HAVING DEMONS HARASS HIM FOLLOWING HIS NDE

When we last encountered **Ian McCormack**, seven demons had manifested outside his bedroom window. Below, he recounts the other demonic attacks that continued until he left the country.

Later that evening, I woke up in the middle of the night. There were three spiritual entities, which I can only understand to be demons from the Bible, standing in the shape of a human form. If you think they were once angels, I am sure they had some angelic body. Now God had destroyed it. I think Ezekiel 28:18 says that God consumed lucifer and the angelic bodies with fire. So that's spiritual darkness because we do not fight against flesh and blood. So I was now seeing spiritual beings of darkness trying to assail me. That freaked me out, so I turned the lights on.

For some reason, they hated the light. I sat down and went through the same experience, and God said, "The Lord's Prayer saved your life. *Deliver us from evil*—pray it again." Bam! I prayed and they were gone. So the next night I woke up. There was a girl I had been trying to move on, a beautiful young Creole girl. She said, "Hey, I want to talk to you." I was thinking, *No, I am not interested in girls. Just leave me alone*. She said, "I have got to talk to you. It's so important." I walked around the side of the house and opened the door. And here was this young girl and the red spiritual entities that I had seen out of their physical bodies. One of them was inside her.

I could see it inside her eyes. She held the door. I could not shut it. Her voice had changed.

So I had this woman speaking with a man's voice, and I was thinking, *That is the thing that is in her. What the heck?* And it said, "You are coming with us tonight." I could not physically shut the door. I could not budge it. I could hear someone or something crawling on the edge of the house. And I went, *God, help me!* The next minute my hand lifted and I said, "In Jesus's name." I thought, *Did I just say that?* And then an invisible fist hit this girl on the chest. Her physical body was thrown through the air and onto the ground. I was going, *This is madness!* "Jesus" had been a swear word. Now that word had power. I wondered what the heck was going on. That woman had some evil thing in her. She was demonized. I had heard about demonized people going into trances, walking on fire, and hanging from meat hooks. I had seen some of that stuff.

I was beginning to connect the dots and realized this woman must be involved in voodoo. Who knew what she was involved in or what spirit she had gotten involved with. Her body moved like a snake, trying to lunge toward me. I slammed the door shut and was freaking out. I wondered what I had done to cause these spiritual beings to want to take me out. God said, "Well, your sin will find you out—you were willing to try to sleep with that girl. And in this world, if you sleep with one of the local girls, you either marry them or the brothers will kill you."

That must have been right. I had seen that happen in Thailand. I had seen that in various parts of the world. You touch the locals and you are in trouble, but normally you get away with it when you are a sinner like me. Now, I had just seen God. I was praying every day. The Bible says let there be no foothold, no sin. That puts the fear of God in most Christians. Do not muck around, you know? So I was standing there thinking I needed to get out of this country.

The next night I saw a spear come through the window. Her boyfriend and brothers were trying to kill me where I slept. I shone the torchlight at them and their eyes were red. And now I had three men with red eyes and the girl whose eyes were red outside my house. I realized that was where some of those flipping demons must have gone. For some reason, they were trying to kill me. And of course, I had the name of Jesus and the power of the Lord's Prayer. I also had a bit of Irish in me, being called McCormack—a family name that means "no fear."

I now understood that the demons cowered back from the light and the prayers.

Reflections on Ian McCormack's Experience

Ian's demonic harassment continued after that first night. The second occurrence was three entities manifesting in a human-like form. Next, a girl he had been trying to get with showed up asking to speak with him. Ian could see in her eyes that she was being demonically influenced, speaking with a man's voice and wielding superhuman strength. What must have been under the influence of the Holy Spirit, Ian raised his hand and said, "In Jesus's name." The girl was thrown back on the ground and began to writhe like a snake.

The next night a spear came through Ian's window. He realized that the girl's boyfriend and brothers were trying to kill him. Ian would soon decide to leave the country.

Ian likely had many questions, but based on his handful of demonic encounters in those few days, he did understand that the demons cowered back from the light and from his prayers. It wasn't much, but it was something he could work with.

88

MAN ENCOUNTERS WHITE-EYED DEMONS COMING OUT OF AN IDOL STATUE

When we last encountered **Ian McCormack**, he was continually being harassed by demons, so he decided it was best to leave the country. Below, we step into another demonic encounter he had when he visited his brother in Perth.

The Lord had shown me the kingdom of darkness and now I was realizing that the kingdom of darkness rules much of this world. By God's grace, I was able to get out and make it to Perth; I flew out of there. I met up with my brother and shared my testimony with him and it freaked him out. I slept in his best friend's bedroom, who was away in Nepal. In the middle of the night, I was attacked by these white-eyed spiritual entities. As I walked around, God showed me that they came out of a Buddha statue that was sitting on the fireplace. I wondered why the white-eyed demons had come out of that idol. It turned out his roommate was studying to be a Nepalese monk and was talking to some guru up in the mountains of Nepal. Previously I had thought Buddhism was quite harmless, but here I was finding that the idols have spiritual entities inside of them and the Bible calls them demons.

Next, I flew home to New Zealand. When I got home, I got a sense of another demonic attack. I said, "God, how do I get rid of them?"

Do you know what He said? He told me to read the Bible. He had already told me in the plane; when I asked Him what had happened to me, He said, "You are a reborn Christian."

I said, "I have heard of Catholics, I have heard of Baptists, but what is reborn?"

He said, "When you prayed the Lord's Prayer in the ambulance, you were born again."

I said, "I do not understand all this."

He said, "If you want to know, read a Bible."

I said, "I do not have one. I have never read one."

He said, "Your dad's got one." So I walked into the bedroom and asked my dad. Within six weeks I had read the entire Bible.

Reflections on Ian McCormack's Experience

After leaving the island, Ian went to visit his brother in Perth, Australia. While he was staying at his brother's house he was attacked by several white-eyed spiritual beings. As Ian looked around his brother's house, God showed him that these demons were coming out of an idol statue in the living room.

When he returned home to New Zealand, Ian asked God how to get rid of demons. God told him to read the Bible. Six weeks later he had read the Bible from cover to cover.

Of all the NDEers we've interviewed, Ian's story of multiple demonic encounters following his time on the other side is definitely the most severe we've found to date.

89

MAN SEES ANGELS WATCHING OVER HIM AFTER HE RETURNS FROM HEAVEN

When we last encountered **Mike Olsen**, he had just met his organ donor in Heaven. Below, we step into a time following his NDE when angels were watching over him.

After my transplant, I got home and was lying in bed recuperating after 64 stitches across my chest. You know they break the rib cage open to go in and get the lungs. So anyway, I was in my bedroom and my wife was at work and I was just lying there trying to recuperate. All of a sudden, I opened my eyes and an angel was standing in my room, tall as the ceiling to the floor, and just staring at me. So I said out loud, "What is this, Lord?"

And the Lord said, "They're just watching you. They're just there. They keep watching you. They haven't left you since Heaven."

I thought that was amazing. I mean, it is amazing that we read about these stories in the Bible and we just think, "Well, that's a nice story." Even angels appearing to Joseph in a dream, we think, "That happened then, but will it happen now?" Yeah, it will, and God continues to do things like that. We just need to believe that He is much bigger than our problems, much bigger than what we go through. It's just been an incredible journey.

Reflections on Mike Olsen's Experience

While Ian McCormack began having encounters with the demonic following his NDE, Mike Olsen began having encounters with the angelic. You can imagine his surprise when he woke up from a nap to see an eight-foot angel standing in his bedroom staring at him. When Mike asked the Lord for an explanation, He told Mike they'd been watching over him since he left Heaven.

This is yet another example of how following an NDE, for the experiencer, the veil between Heaven and earth is quite thin. They are often able to see in the spirit or operate in giftings they didn't have before their time in Heaven.

90

GOD TELLS MAN IT'S TIME TO BEGIN SHARING THE STORY OF HIS TIME IN HEAVEN

When we last encountered **Mike Olsen**, he realized that angels had been watching over him since he returned from Heaven. Below, we step into the part of Mike's post-Heaven journey where God told him it's time to begin sharing his story.

Just telling my story to you, I mean, I didn't go out and tell my story. I'm not that type of person who wants everyone to look to me. I just want them to see the Lord in my life. But one day the Lord said, "You need to start sharing your Heaven testimony." And I said, "Okay, Lord." I began sharing it with nurses because I went to the hospital every month to do blood work and things. I've also been sharing it with, I don't know, people on the street, you know. It's kind of weird, but I just started sharing and people would just break down and weep.

I met this one lady at a hotel. My sister-in-law was in the hospital and we were visiting her, and I was at the hotel. The lady said, "I see you have a service dog with you."

I said, "Yeah, I just had a double lung transplant, but I died and went to Heaven."

And she said, "Tell me more." So I did, and she just started weeping.

She goes, "You know what? I was struggling with Heaven. Is it real? Is God real? Man, you coming to see me today at the front desk here and tell me that story. I am so at peace now. It's not going to bother me anymore."

You know, we overcome the enemy by the word of our testimony and by the blood of the Lamb. And I just believe that's what I've been doing—just sharing the testimony.

Every one of us has a story. And of course, people with NDEs have a story, and it might seem strange to people and almost unbelievable that these things happen. But you know what? I'm still engaged in Heaven. I mean, every time I tell the story it's almost like I relive it and I have the same feelings as when I was in Heaven. It just shows what an awesome God—that He allows these things to happen to us to assure us, assure everybody that there's a place called Heaven. And He wants you to go there.

I tell people I was brought up in a religious household, so we kind of knew all the stories of Jesus. I was raised Catholic, so I knew all about Jesus in my head, but He hadn't reached my heart. When I was a young man, I think 19, I just simply said, "God, if You're real, show me who You are." And believe me, He did. I asked Him to come into my heart, change my life, do whatever He needed to do. And man, I was radically changed from the person I used to be, and it was all His doing. And He's shown Himself faithful throughout all these years. He knew that I was going to have trouble with my lungs down the road and that I was going to have a terminal illness. He knew that already. And He already kind of went before me and lined things up.

Reflections on Mike Olsen's Experience

Many people do not share about their afterlife experience because, as you've seen throughout the stories in this book, they're afraid people are going to think they're nuts. Sometimes God tells a person they are specifically not to share about what they saw or experienced until He tells them it's the right time.

One day the Lord simply told Mike that it was time for him to begin telling his Heaven testimony. Mike was obedient and has been amazed by the numerous ways God has used his story to impact people who are in desperate need of hope and a touch from Heaven.

91

AFTER RETURNING FROM HEAVEN, MAN HAS ENDLESS PASSION AND DRIVE TO INTRODUCE THE LOST TO JESUS

When we last encountered **Captain Dale Black**, he had just come out of a four-day coma following his plane crash. Below, he shares about the passion that has driven him since he returned from Heaven.

A lot of the people say, "Oh, Dale, I bet you just can't wait until you get to Heaven. I'm sure you're ready to go right now, aren't you?" And on one side, yes. Sure. Of course. But you know, all of us—you're already in eternity right now. You're already in eternity because you are a spirit. You are a soul. Those are going to live forever. Now the only question is, where will you go? But your body will die, unless the Lord returns. And He very well may in our lifetime. If we live to a normal lifespan, we may very well see the return of Jesus. And we can talk about that someday. But this is just the way it is. We have eternal life guaranteed, eternity guaranteed. In the meantime, you're touching lives. You're reaching people who would never be reached. And every day that you're doing this, every time you've touched someone, you're changing eternity for that person. So keep going, keep doing the great work that you're doing.

For myself, I'm going to just keep doing the same thing on a small scale. I'm not a big-name ministry. Probably never will be, but I love God. And I want to have every breath matter for Him. And I want to help people find that Jesus really is the Son of God. He really was the Messiah; the promised Messiah was in Jesus. And you can trust Him. You can trust His Word. Follow Him with your life. You have nothing to lose and everything to gain. That's just one thing that I learned in Heaven.

Reflections on Captain Dale Black's Experience

One of the lasting effects of Captain Dale Black's time in Heaven is he's all about making Jesus famous. Regardless of the size or scale of his ministry, he'll be helping people meet Jesus until he returns to Heaven.

We've seen this over and over from so many of our friends who've had near-death experiences. The things that drove them and literally consumed their lives before their time on the other side of the veil lost appeal after they returned to their body. They're simply passionate about Jesus.

92

MAN RETURNS FROM HEAVEN INFUSED WITH AN ENTIRELY NEW DEPTH OF LOVE AND EMPATHY FOR OTHERS

When we last encountered **Randy Kay,** he had just returned to his body after his time in Heaven. Below, Randy shares about the profound change to his personality after his time with Jesus.

It's interesting, I've never shared this before, but I've been in the training and human development arena, right in the corporate arena and the like. There's a test you can take, an assessment, psychometrics we call it, to determine your versatility, to measure the degree of empathy that you have. So I had taken it years before, and for my versatility factor I was on the left side of the spectrum, which is not good. I didn't empathize very well with people.

When I took the test after my time in Heaven, I was on the other end of the spectrum. I hope that doesn't sound boastful, it just means the transition, from an empathy standpoint, from where I was before Heaven to the place where I am today post-Heaven was not because of anything that I did. It was because of the impartation of God and the Holy Spirit during my experience with Him. Now I feel things deeply because I know the love of God. So when I look at someone, I have a deep love for you, not because that's who I am, but because of who God is through me. I saw the love, the consummate love that God has for other people. It was all consuming to the point where I believe that if anyone had even a small fraction of understanding of the degree of that love, they could not help but be believers because they would know the true God, the God of Jesus Christ.

Empathy is something that we talk about oftentimes, but it is different from sympathy. Sympathy is realizing or understanding the feelings of other people. Empathy is really feeling as the other person feels. The only one, certainly in my lifetime, in my experience, who had consummate empathy, who understood our feelings and thoughts was Jesus.

And that's the model for us, isn't it?

Reflections on Randy Kay's Experience

I've only known Randy on this side of his Heaven experience, and I can vouch for him being one of the kindest and most empathetic guys I've ever had the pleasure of meeting. The first time I ever heard him share the story of how his results had changed on the psychometrics assessment, I was like, "Randy, you now have verifiable data that your character and personality measurably shifted when you were in Heaven!"

While Randy and I have had numerous NDEers share about how they are vastly different on the other side of their afterlife journey, Randy is the only one with a data-driven assessment to back up his story.

93

MAN SAYS HE'S MUCH MORE PURPOSEFUL WITH HOW HE SPENDS HIS DAYS AFTER TIME IN HEAVEN

When we last encountered Gabe Poirot, he had just woken up in the hospital after being in a coma for three weeks. Below, Gabe shares about the lingering effects of his time in Heaven, which we were able to capture around a year after his skateboard accident and near-death experience.

would definitely say I've always taken what I do very seriously. There'd be some days when I would wake up at 11:00 am because I would stay up till 3:00 am just going the whole day, making as many videos as possible, editing as much as I could, live-streaming, talking, going on zoom baptisms, and just whatever it took. Now I'm even more passionate and also very cautious with how I spend my time because I know I have eternity. I have the rest of my life to live. And when I say life, I mean the rest of me to live, which will be forever. But I only have a little bit on earth. And some people may say, "Gabe, you're 21. You have a lot of time left on earth."

No, no, no. I have a tiny amount. And I'm much more purposeful with it. I'm on earth with a purpose to bring the gospel I have now. I might have fun and enjoy stuff too, and watch football games. Those things are great. I'm going to enjoy what God gives me. I'm going to freely receive. But my main purpose on this earth is to do what He called me to do. I think about His Kingdom differently too. It's not just an aspect of my life, it's not just college or it's not just the time that I'm spending doing it, it's the team that I'm on. It's the family that I'm in. It's my ultimate family. And I just so care about them.

Reflections on Gabe Poirot's Experience

Gabe Poirot was always passionate and purposeful about sharing the gospel with others, but on the other side of his Heaven journey, he realized how truly short his time on earth is. He's now even more intentional with his time, working to maximize his Kingdom impact.

This is truly an amazing truth for Gabe to have gotten hold of at 21 years old. Many of us don't catch this until well into our latter years. The earlier each of us can get hold of this Kingdom-driven purpose and intentionality, the better.

94

NEAR-DEATH EXPERIENCER SAYS HE'S CONFIDENT JESUS IS THE ONE TRUE WAY TO HEAVEN

When we last encountered **Mark McDonough**, he was sharing about the circumstances that led up to him returning to his body after his time in Heaven. Below, he shares about the lingering impact of his near-death experience.

I frequently speak of it like a double-edged sword because I right away returned to the same mortal that I've always been with the same kinds of confusion, but yet had a certainty that He has the answers even if I don't know what they are. And that is the one truth that we can all rely on—that certain knowledge that His is the one true story. Jesus is the one true Savior, and He's the one true way to Heaven. That's absolutely certain. Whereas on the other side of the sword is the want or desire to scream, "God, why this shoelace too? In the same day, really?" I'm still that same guy who can get just as angry and escalate a molehill into a mountain, but I'm also the guy who is 100 percent sure that God is with me. He's just not giving me any advantages to skate through any more easily just because of that experience.

But He has given me a certainty that I can share and I think that's reassuring. I know it has been for my loved ones and my kids. My appreciation for the more important things in life is without a doubt greater than it ever could have been otherwise. Certain things just don't matter, and our time here is so finite and so minuscule and so relatively microscopic compared to eternity that I can't worry about those little things. That doesn't make me any less human, though, because it's a process, as we know. It changed me in the sense that as soon as I start thinking that my will and God's are in sync, I'm playing God again. I'm starting to think I know and I don't. I thank God for that ignorance going through medical school and residence because it was so hard. I thought, "Okay, God, but You're with me and this is Your will too. Right?" And whether I heard an answer or not, in my mind it was enough to keep me pushing forward or persevering.

My big soapbox these days is we don't know why. Even when we think we do, that's just our ego trying to remind us to keep moving forward, persevere, take the next step. And He's always been there. And I also don't say that you can't be in fear and faith at the same time. A lot of people in recovery circles like to say that. I think they both reside in very close proximity because I do know from past experiences that this next lesson could be a struggle. It could be painful, and I have some reasonable fear about it. At the same time, though, I can also be comforted and chill, certain in the knowledge that God will provide whatever I need. And Romans 8:28 tells me, and my wife constantly reminds me, He can even make good from this too on a bad day. That's just me defining something as "bad," because tomorrow I'm going to see yesterday as, wow, that was a really positive thing. But if I can stay open-minded to that, that's the true plus that came from the experience. Whether that's a handicap or an asset, I'm not sure.

Reflections on Mark McDonough's Experience

Mark McDonough exudes a confidence that we've seen from many men and women who've been to Heaven. Mark is confident that Jesus is the one way to Heaven. He knows that in his life back here on earth, no matter the struggle, God will provide what he needs.

Having the privilege to come back to earth after time in Heaven often results in, as Mark shared, a focus on what's important, an ability to filter out the things that simply don't matter.

We have noticed sometimes that people put our friends who have been to Heaven up on a pedestal like they're living the perfect Christian life and they have all the answers. It's reassuring to hear Mark say that he's still human and he must go to God for perspective when things are hard. Yet Romans 8:28 gives him reassurance that whatever it is, God can make good from that too.

95

AFTER 35 YEARS OF WAITING, GOD RELEASES MAN TO SHARE ABOUT HIS NDE IN A BOOK

When we last encountered Ivan Tuttle, he had just reentered his body and nearly scared the life out of the paramedic who was in his bedroom. Below, he shares about God finally releasing him after 35 years to share his powerful NDE story.

After 35 years, I was getting a little discouraged. After seven years, I kind of quit asking Him, because I'd be like, "Okay, Lord, now can I?" and He'd be like, "Not yet. Not yet, soon." And I'm thinking, "Oh, well, His soon and my soon are like two different things." I've learned that. And then finally, it was August 17, 2013, and it's just like a voice spoke to me and said, "I want you to write a book. I want you to write your testimony now. You're going to write a book."

Now, I don't know if anybody else out there has ever heard of ADHD. I am a perfect candidate. I've been diagnosed with that for many years. Of course, back when I was diagnosed it was just diagnosed with "you're a bad kid." Back in the fifties, they had no idea what that was. So in the fifties and sixties, nobody had ever heard of it hardly at all, but that's what I have. And it was amazing because I'm thinking, "Okay, God, now don't get me wrong. I can write a TV commercial." 'Cause that's, you know, 30, 60 seconds. And I can have a lot of fun with that. But you know, when you have to write a book, I'm like, "God, I don't know what to do." And He said, "Just sit down."

So I pulled up my laptop. I sat down on the end of the sofa, and I started typing and I thought an hour went by. I had eight pages. Okay. Now I've never typed eight pages in my life. And I had eight pages typed out. I was so proud of myself. I thought, "Well, there we go. There's my testimony." You know? And I printed it off and I thought, "Wow, man, this is good. I got my testimony." And of course I gave it to a few people and everybody's going, "Well, where's the details on this?"

"What do you mean? Look at what happened! I'm alive and God did this." And they still wanted the details. So I took those eight pages and I just sat there and I said, "God, what's going on here?"

And He said, "That's your outline. Start writing, just take the first part that you have and just add to it."

And I'm like, "Well, God, I don't know how to write a book."

He says, "Don't worry. I know the Author of the best-selling book in the world. It's called the Bible. I'll help you."

So that's how it happened. And it was like, ah, I was so relieved to finally talk about it and all this stuff just started flooding my mind.

Now I would never read any books about anybody else dying, going to hell, or going to Heaven or anything like that. I didn't want to read anything that anybody else had written because I didn't want to taint my mind. I wanted my experience to be 100 percent mine. People knew what I was writing. They were trying to send me books, "Read this book, read that."

I'm like, "No, this is something between God and me," you know? And so that's how it happened. And it was such a release to have that happen. And then finally in April of 2014, I published the first part of my book.

Reflections on Ivan Tuttle's Experience

Ivan Tuttle is one of many near-death experiencers we've met whom God did not allow to share his story for a certain amount of time. As to why God does this, it's hard to be certain, but it's likely that the fame and attention would crush some before they had the character to handle it; for others it's likely that there's a divine timing aspect to when the story is shared with world.

Note that Ivan says that he avoided reading books about other people's afterlife experiences because he didn't want to taint how he told his own story. We've heard from a number of NDEers who wanted to have integrity in the way they shared their story, and avoiding these other books was a way to not conflate elements of somebody else's story with theirs.

96

WOMAN WALKS IN A LIFESTYLE OF DEEP CONSECRATION AFTER HER TIME WITH JESUS IN HEAVEN

When we last encountered Karina Ferrigno Martinez, she had just squeezed back into to her body back on earth following her time in Heaven. Below, she shares the many ways she was transformed following her afterlife experience.

People need to understand that everybody has their own walk, right? And what I mean by that is in the end it's all through His glory. On the second day following my NDE, I could see and hear spirits. I would be walking and going along and all of a sudden I'd be like, "Oh, what am I seeing?" I just didn't know. At that point in time, I didn't know the Bible. I didn't know that there was a tree and a river like glass called the sea. I'm still studying and learning, but there are many things that were shown to me in Heaven that I didn't know were in the Bible.

I began to pray all day every day because I didn't want to let go of my experience. I knew that I had to let go of some of it to be able to focus on my own family, so I would get in the shower and pray and receive. I didn't know what *shalom* was or who Caleb was. I heard Jesus and I knew that it was Him because it was the same voice.

When I was in prayer, just crying, "Please take me home," I heard, "You have the spirit of Caleb." And I go, "What, who's Caleb?" So I wrote down Caleb in my journal. I texted a friend of mine who does a lot of research asking him to help me find out who or what Caleb is. He texted me back while I was driving, and I grabbed my phone and read a little bit of his response. Immediately the Holy Spirit came in to give me confirmation. When I got the confirmation, I cried hard. I'm sure the lady who was walking her dog near my car wondered what was going on with this crazy woman.

I had so many health issues. I was losing my hair, my brain, and other things might have been damaged beyond repair. God fixed my heart. He gave me a new one.

Reflections on Karina Ferrigno Martinez's Experience

Immediately following her time in Heaven, Karina was able to see and hear spirits. Like Ian, she seemed to still have a foot in Heaven, walking close to a thinned veil between Heaven and earth, allowing her to see what was happening in the spirit realm.

Karina became a woman of prayer and intercession, praying and seeking God as often as she could. She also became a woman of the Word. One of the very eye-opening parts of this season of her journey is she began to discover so many of the things she saw and experienced in Heaven are actually mentioned in the Bible. This is truly one of the most beautiful things we hear about from people who have an NDE before they were following Jesus or before they had much exposure to the Bible. Their minds are absolutely blown when they find what they saw in Heaven in the pages of Scripture.

Although it's not mentioned specifically, it's worth noting the total transformation that Karina experienced. Following her time in Heaven she no longer wore sexy clothes. She even had her breast implants removed. Everything about her life is a striking 180 compared to her former life before she went to Haven.

97

MAN SAYS, "PEOPLE LIKE ME A LOT BETTER AFTER I DIED AND WENT TO HEAVEN"

When we last encountered **Ed Loughran**, he was sharing about encountering the Father, Son, and Holy Spirit in Heaven. Below, he shares about the lasting effects following his time in Heaven.

I feel inadequate. I've used words as a pastor, as an attorney, as a trial attorney for my profession, and this is the area where I often come to the very end of my ability to express it, other than I feel like I have butterflies in my chest talking about Heaven.

When I finish talking about it, I'll probably feel sad. I don't tell my Heaven story a lot because there's sadness and loss when I'm reminded of it, just like I lost my mom. It's like, oh, it's Thanksgiving and I lost my mom six years ago. Oh yeah, I lost my mom. I feel that even though I know she's with Jesus, even though I'm very confident of that, even though God has given me revelation and prophetic vision of those things, I still feel loss and grief.

I've had encounters with Holy Spirit here after that that have been the most empowering encounters I've had in my entire life. I can say indirectly that people like me a lot better after I died. I think there's a thinness there. I think my heart is very tender.

Reflections on Ed Loughran's Experience

Ed Loughran reflects the feelings of so many of the NDEers we've interviewed. While on the one hand, he's glad to be back here on earth with his friends and family, there is a sadness and a loss that comes from not being in Heaven. In Heaven the soul is completely unburdened and unhindered, not only in the sense that it's not held back by a physical body, but it's no longer carrying the weight of this life and the world.

Note that Ed talks about a thinness. The easiest way that we've found to describe this is that the veil between earth and Heaven often remains very thin once the experiencer returns to their body here on earth. It's almost as if they always have one foot in Heaven and one foot here on the earth.

Lastly, note that Ed said that people seem to like him better following his Heaven experience, that his heart is now very tender. As Randy Kay and so many of our other friends have recounted, you can't help but being changed by Heaven, and there's a tenderness and a love you receive for other people. It's as if you're now able to see people through the eyes of Jesus.

98

YOUNG MAN HEALED OF ANGER, DEPRESSION, CELIAC DISEASE, AND BED-WETTING AFTER HE RETURNS FROM HEAVEN

When we last encountered **Joe Joe Morris**, he was sharing about God giving him a major download on music theory during his time in Heaven. Below, he shares lasting effects and transformation that resulted from his time on the other side of the veil.

I wake up and I'm on my pillow and the alarm is going off—29 minutes have passed. I remember just screaming, no, no, no, no, no, no, no, this can't be true. I was just in the most glorious, most real experience. I felt more emotions, more alive in Heaven than I did on earth. As I was waking up, I began to realize I no longer had a darkness within me. I didn't feel hollow anymore. There was a new spark in me. After a few weeks passed, I realized I was fully healed of bedwetting and fully healed of Celiac disease.

When I woke up I was a changed man. Some of the religious people I knew thought I had a demon. They truly thought I was demon-possessed. But the enemy cannot make you fall in love with reading the word of God. The devil cannot make you want to bring other people to repentance. The enemy cannot make you want to pursue a holy lifestyle. From that moment forward everything changed. A couple of months later, I decided to leave. It was very painful because I'd been raised to stay in those Mennonite circles. I loved the people group I was with, but God called me to move on. I pray for the Hutterite and Mennonite groups that they would accept the Holy Spirit and follow the design and the desire of God's heart for their life, because I realize that our desires are placed there by God. My message now is to activate people's dreams and desires so they can make that their full-time, lifelong calling.

Reflections on Joe Joe Morris's Experience

Joe Joe experienced both spiritual, emotional, and physical transformations upon his return from Heaven. On the spiritual and emotional front, he no longer had the darkness, the depression, and the anger that had previously been weighing him down. He had a renewed desire for God's word and for telling others about Jesus. On the physical front, he was healed of Celiac disease and no longer wet his bed.

While Joe Joe could be bitter and angry with the communities he grew up in, God has given him a heart for the Hutterites and Mennonites. He longs to see them filled with the Spirit and activated in their God-given calling just like he was.

99

MAN SAYS HE CRIED FOR TWO TO THREE WEEKS ANY TIME HE SAID THE WORD "HEAVEN"

When we last encountered **Alwyn Matthews,** he was with Jesus in a heavenly city filled with mansions. Below, he shares about the many ways his life is dramatically different following his time in Heaven.

tried to keep things normal. I didn't want to make a big deal of it. I sat on my couch and called my wife, Leah. She says to this day that when I called her name, she knew I had been with Jesus. She sat next to me on one side and my seven-year-old sat next to me on the other. Again, I'm just trying to be normal. I said, "I don't know how to say this." And then my voice started breaking. I said, "Leah, I went to—" and I couldn't even say the word *Heaven*. For two to three weeks after my experience, when I would say the word *Heaven*, I'd start crying.

There's a video of me sharing my experience with my church. When I would say the word *Heaven*, every essence, every feeling, all the emotions that I had in my experience would come back on me. I've never been hung over, but for 48 hours after my experience, that's what it felt like. I was just in between here and there. I would be driving the roads of Brisbane, which is a beautiful city, and I'd be like, "Man, I'm in a third world nation. I'm missing planet Heaven. I'm missing my home." I'm feeling all these feelings and that went on for about four months. I hardly prepared a sermon because I was just downloading all these truths from Heaven that were reverberating within me and I would share them with our church.

The biggest change in me is probably my nature, the way I see people. I've always loved people, but just the depth of love that I have for people, the depth of how desperate I am for them to experience what I experienced, for them to experience at least a facet of the depth of love that I experienced. That's become a lifelong mission. That's why we are traveling the world.

This gave us a reset in pretty much everything. It changed how we lead our church. We've handed a lot of our responsibilities to other leaders and pastors so we can actually be out there and be a blessing. It's completely changed our lives, how we do family. It's changed how I relate with my kids. It's changed every part of me. I don't think there's an area that was not changed in me.

Reflections on Alwyn Matthews Experience

Although Alwyn Matthews experienced a spiritual transformative experience (STE), the long-lasting effects are similar to those of a traditional NDE. He recounts strong feelings of missing Heaven for about four months. This is not uncommon with these sorts of experiences. People often report having to overcome an initial period of shock and even feelings of depression because of how much life on earth pales in comparison to what they encountered in Heaven.

Similar to what we saw earlier in this section from Randy Kay and Ed Loughran, Alwyn also talks about having a whole new depth of love for other people that manifests as what Alwyn describes as a desperation for others to experience even a fraction of what he was touched by in Heaven. Perhaps this will be Alwyn's lifelong mission until he returns to Heaven again.

Alwyn closes his story stating that every part of him has been changed. From how he leads and does ministry to how he lives out his roles of husband and father, it's all informed by Alwyn's time in Heaven.

100

MAN HAS PROOF GOD LITERALLY HEALED HIS HEREDITARY HEART DEFECT AFTER HE RETURNED FROM HEAVEN

When we last encountered **Ivan Tuttle**, he was sharing about the moment God finally released him to share his story as a book 35 years after his NDE. Below, Ivan shares how God literally repaired his hereditary heart defect when he returned from Heaven.

There was a miracle that happened to me. I had something called hypertrophic cardiomyopathy. Hypertrophic cardiomyopathy is something that you cannot get rid of without a heart transplant. You have to have a heart transplant to get rid of it. There's no other way to get rid of it. It's a thickening of the muscles of the heart, because your heart is nothing but a big muscle. And the walls of the heart are thick, especially on the left side, and it's hereditary.

My father died at 56. My oldest sister died at 56. I have a sister who is 71 right now. She has it. I have a brother who's in his fifties. He has it real bad, and all their children have it. The grandchildren have it. Everybody's got it. It doesn't skip a generation. It doesn't skip a person. I had it. Everything was set up there. We had some blood drawn from way back when, and there was a genetic marker for it. I had it, I had been tested for it. I had it. I don't have it. God took care of that. It's gone. It was a generational curse. It was broken. I don't have it anymore. I mean, I really don't. I just had another exam. In fact, I gave it to Sid Roth and I said, "Here here's my exam. I don't have it, it's gone."

My sister, Carolyn—her last name is Biro—she started the first cardiomyopathy foundation and you can probably look her up online. You can see Carolyn Biro. Of course, she died, but she still had that. That's still going on. She started that up and she educated doctors on it. So that'll just give you an idea. God healed me through all of that. Instead of coming back and having my heart, my lungs, my kidneys damaged—and my brain might be damaged—but all these things should have been damaged beyond repair. God fixed my heart. He gave me a new one.

Reflections on Ivan Tuttle's Experience

Ivan Tuttle's family is plagued with a hereditary heart defect. It was documented that he had the genetic marker for this before he had his NDE. Following his time in Heaven, he no longer has this. The generational curse was finally broken!

Ivan got the two-for-one special during his time on the other side. Not only did God transform his figurative heart (mind, will, emotions, character, etc.), He even healed Ivan's physical heart. Many times when people tell you they were miraculously healed of this or that, they often don't have medical documentation to prove it. Ivan's is one of those rare cases where he has the paperwork to show that this literally changed after his time in Heaven.

101

MAN SAYS THAT AFTER HEAVEN, GOD GAVE HIM A LOVE FOR OTHER PEOPLE THAT COMPLETELY ENRAPTURES HIS SOUL

When we last encountered Rabbi Felix Halpern, he was sharing about the prayer secrets God revealed to him in Heaven. Below, he shares about the ways his love for other people is at an entirely different level following his time Heaven.

I have always had a love for people. That is why I started serving the Lord. I love people, have a heart for the lost, and want to see people healed. However, the love that I returned with from Heaven is on an entirely different level. It is the love of God. It is a love that when I see someone I could weep. I had love for people and ministered in that regard, but now I flow in a love that completely enraptures my soul in a way that I must touch them, because it is not me but God touching people through me. That supernatural love has had a profound effect on both my ministry and my personal life. I do not think you could come back from Heaven without it.

I do not know how you can come back from Heaven unchanged. The Lord gave me a choice. He said, "This will be transformational or it will be transactional. And if it is transformational, it is going to come at a price." Transactional, I knew that meant that this would eventually wear off. I told the Lord I was willing to pay the price because I was not about to go back and lose what He did. The reality in our lives is that anyone who goes through this, the enormity of Him giving you your life back never leaves you.

Reflections on Rabbi Felix Halpern's Experience

Rabbi Felix has always loved people; in fact, that's why he got into ministry in the first place. However, after he came back from Heaven, the love that flowed out of him for others was at an entirely different level. He notes that this new level of love is not on account of anything he's doing; it's God touching people through him in such a way that his ministry life and personal life are totally transformed.

In the latter part of what Felix shares, he talks about God giving him the choice of whether his time in Heaven would be transactional or transformational, but the latter would come at a price. Felix was willing to pay the price so the effect of the transformation would be permanent.

While not all of us have had the opportunity to go to Heaven, Jesus does offer that same choice of whether or not our relationship, our journey with Him will be merely transactional or wholly transformational. As it did in Felix's case, for us the latter will come with a great cost. May we all be brave enough to choose that less traveled path and never look back.

CONCLUSION

A s Rabbi Felix Halpern intimated so well in the final story of the book, you can't come back from Heaven (or hell for that matter) without being profoundly changed.

Some of the experiencers in this section of the book reported being awakened to the supernatural realm, seeing both angels and demons at work in our world. Big picture: when God awakens that level of spiritual discernment in a believer, logically it would seem to follow that He's giving the believer an opportunity to partner with Him in prayer and intercession to impact the situation at hand.

Many of our friends who have been to the other side received dramatic healing in their physical bodies. Quite often the circumstances that led to them having a near-death experience in the first place should have left them debilitated at some level for the rest of their life. There are also those who either had a long healing journey following their NDE or had some things that were never fully healed. In these circumstances, it's a mystery why healing manifests in the former situations and not the latter. However, don't think that those who aren't fully healed after their NDE aren't thankful for what they experienced on the other side of the veil. There are often so many other things that have been transformed in their life for which they give God all the praise and glory.

One of the most common things we've heard from our friends with Heaven experiences is that they have a new capacity for love and empathy. This change runs so deep that they often don't care about the things that seemed so big prior to their afterlife encounter. Bigger than just being nice to people, this love has with it an insatiable burden to tell others about Jesus. Alwyn captured this so well when he said he is desperate for people to experience at least a facet of the depth of the love that he experienced.

By and large, these changes from time on the other side are ongoing and, as Rabbi Felix says, transformational, often setting the experiencer on a lifelong mission and trajectory that they'll likely stay on until they return to Heaven again, for good this time.

Discussion Questions

1. What is it about the love experiencers encounter in Heaven that seems to permanently transform them?

2. Why do you think some of the NDEers experience full physical healing, while others only experience partial healing?

3. Why do you think God holds some NDEers back from sharing their stories?

4. If you had an NDE, how do you think your life would be different when you returned from your afterlife experience?

AFTERWORD

IS GOD TRYING TO GET MY ATTENTION WITH THESE NEAR-DEATH EXPERIENCES?

Many people have asked us if we think near-death experiences are on the rise. Well, let us tell you something straight up—yes, absolutely! With medical advancements reaching new heights, people who were once on the brink of death are coming back to life like it's just another day at the office. Plus, society's gotten less judge-y about NDEs, and folks are speaking up about what they've been through. And with the Internet, it's easier than ever to spread the word about these paradigm-shifting Heaven and hell stories—they're everywhere, from books to podcasts, YouTube videos to TV shows. We all need to buckle up, because the near-death experience train is picking up speed, and it's not slowing down anytime soon.

When we read and listen to these afterlife narratives, it's easy to get caught up in the enchantment and thrill of it all. The spine-tingling encounters with Jesus, otherworldly beings, and even animals in the celestial realm are absolutely mind-boggling. But let's not forget that God didn't bestow these experiences simply to entertain us with a captivating story. No, these visions and encounters are far more consequential than that. They serve a purpose that is both profound and powerful, and the primary focus of this book has been to give you the framework and vocabulary to process and make sense of these encounters.

Let's be real here for a moment—things are pretty dark these days, all across the world. Fear, despair, and depression are everywhere, and no amount of Netflix binges or happy-hour cocktails can fill that gaping void inside. The only real cure for all that ails us is Jesus Christ Himself. He's the only one who can offer us true hope, deep healing, and the kind of transformation that lasts a lifetime. And as we alluded to earlier in this book, Randy and I have been getting bombarded with messages from people whose lives have been completely turned upside down after encountering Jesus while reading and listening to our interviews about death and the afterlife.

Don't miss this part, because this is important. These tales of the afterlife that you've been reading—they're basically God's love letter to you. He longs for you to meet His resurrected Son Jesus and to know beyond a shadow of a doubt that Heaven isn't some fairytale dreamland but a real, honest-to-God destination that you can be bound for through His Son. And the best part? You'll be there with Him, in His divine presence, for all of eternity. It's kind of a big deal.

So have you been paying attention? Because God's been reaching out to you in so many ways through these stories. Don't ignore it, don't put it off, don't make excuses. It's time for you to respond to His call, and Ivan Tuttle's prayer from the end of his 2 Christian Dudes interview will help you do just that. Tag, you're it. The ball is in your court. It's time for you to make that next move.

> *Heavenly Father, I ask now that You forgive me of my sins. I know that Jesus died on the cross for me so that all my sins can be forgiven. I accept Jesus as my Lord and Savior, and I know that He came here for a purpose and that one purpose was to die for me. Thank You, Jesus. Thank You, God. And I change my whole life now in Jesus's name. Amen.*

APPENDIX

MEET OUR NDE STORY CONTRIBUTORS

Ian McCormack

New Zealand native Ian McCormack was in his late twenties and living a carefree surfing lifestyle in some of the most beautiful places on the planet. One fateful night in 1982, he was night diving for lobster off the island of Mauritius when he was stung by five box jellyfish, one of the most venomous creatures in the world. A sting from a single box jellyfish can kill a person in under five minutes. Getting stung by five should have been beyond lethal.

Find Out More

If you would like to encounter more of Ian McCormack's story, be sure to check out the 2014 film *The Perfect Wave*, which tells his story, as well as Randy Kay and Shaun Tabatt's book *Stories of Heaven and the Afterlife: Firsthand Accounts of Real Near-Death Experiences* (Destiny Image, 2022). You can also connect with Ian at aglimpseofeternity.org.

Randy Kay

Randy Kay was a successful executive who had worked at several biotech and pharmaceutical companies. His career had been thriving for years, but then he suddenly found himself in a season when he had lost everything, but at least he had his health. A series of quickly compounding medical issues would soon take his health as well and put him in a position to face one of his biggest fears.

Find Out More

If you would like to encounter more of Randy Kay's story, we encourage you to pick up a copy of his book *Revelations from Heaven: A True Account of Death, the Afterlife, and 31 Supernatural Discoveries* (Destiny Image, 2021). You can also connect with Randy at RandyKay.org.

Heidi Barr

At age 16, Heidi Barr experienced a freak accident when the horse she was riding stumbled off a hillside and crushed her underneath. Although she had been raised Jewish, Heidi found herself holding hands with Jesus.

Find Out More

If you would like to read more about Heidi Barr's experiences as a hospice nurse working with people who are close to experiencing the afterlife, we encourage you to pick up a copy of her book *One Foot in Heaven: Journey of a Hospice Nurse* (independently published, 2013). You can also encounter more of Heidi's story in Randy Kay and Shaun Tabatt's book *Stories of Heaven and the Afterlife: Firsthand Accounts of Real Near-Death Experiences* (Destiny Image, 2022).

Rabbi Felix Halpern

Messianic Rabbi Felix Halpern died when his body became toxic after a medical misdiagnosis and the related wrong prescription.

Find Out More

If you would like to encounter more of Rabbi Felix Halpern's story, we encourage you to pick up a copy of his book *A Rabbi's Journey to Heaven: A Miraculous Story of One Man's Journey to Heaven* (It's Supernatural!, 2021) as well as Randy Kay and Shaun Tabatt's book *Stories of Heaven and the Afterlife: Firsthand Accounts of Real Near-Death Experiences* (Destiny Image, 2022). You can also connect with Felix at chofesh.org.

Jim Woodford

A successful airline pilot and businessman, Jim had it all—a loving family, substantial wealth, and all of the good things that come with it. But none of this was enough to satisfy the emptiness he felt in his heart. He always hungered for something more. And then he died.

Jim was never a religious man. When it came to matters of God and faith, he was ambivalent. But as he lay in the hospital bed, clinically dead for more than 11 hours, his consciousness was transported to the wonders of Heaven and the horrors of hell. When he returned to this world, he brought back the missing peace his soul had been longing for.

Find Out More

If you'd like to encounter more of Jim Woodford's story, we encourage you to pick up a copy of his book *Heaven, an Unexpected Journey: One Man's Experience with Heaven, Angels, and the Afterlife* (Destiny Image, 2017) as well as Randy Kay and Shaun Tabatt's book *Real Near Death Experience Stories: True Accounts of Those Who Died and Experienced Immortality* (Destiny Image, 2022). You can also connect with Jim at JimWoodford.com.

Bryan Melvin

Bryan Melvin, a self-described militant atheist, died after contracting cholera from drinking contaminated water at a construction site.

Find Out More

If you would like to encounter more of Bryan Melvin's story, we encourage you to pick up a copy of his book *A Land Unknown: Hell's Dominion* (Xulon Press, 2005) as well as Randy Kay and Shaun Tabatt's book *Stories of Heaven and the Afterlife: Firsthand Accounts of Real Near-Death Experiences* (Destiny Image, 2022). You can also connect with Bryan at AfterHoursMinistries.com.

Fr. Cedric Pisegna

Fr. Cedric Pisegna was in college and on track for a business career, but grief and turmoil over what he describes as a mortal sin led to two spiritual transformative experiences (STEs) that would not only deepen his faith, but also direct him toward life-long service as a Catholic priest, something that had not been part of is life plan.

Find Out More

If you would like to encounter more of Fr. Cedric Pisegna's story, we encourage you to pick up a copy of his book *Death: The Final Surrender* (independently published, 2021). You can also connect with Fr. Cedric at FrCedric.org.

Alwyn Matthews

Alwyn Matthews was pastoring a thriving church, but a series of unfortunate events would lead down a path of despair and depression that ultimately resulted in a life-altering encounter in Heaven.

Find Out More

You can connect with Alwyn at AlwynMatthew.com.

Ed Loughran

Ed Loughran is a lawyer. He was a good athlete, playing competitive sports into his early forties. Right before his 50th birthday, Ed got a new bike. He planned to take it out on a thirty-mile ride, and around ten and a half miles into the ride, he heard the voice of God say, "Turn your bike around now." Ed would make it all the way home but would soon drop dead of a heart attack.

Gabe Poirot

Gabe Poirot is an evangelist with a passion for seeing young people enter into a life-changing relationship with Jesus. Back in 2021, he had a freak accident on his electric skateboard that would put him into a prolonged coma and a journey to the other side of the veil.

Find Out More

You can connect with Gabe at GabePoirot.com.

Ivan Tuttle

In 1978, Ivan Tuttle was living a carefree life, going from one party to the next, from one high to another—when his fun, free life was interrupted by a pain in his leg. Doctors told him he had a dangerous blood clot—but Ivan didn't pay much attention to that. He was 26 and felt fine; blood clots were a problem for his grandfather, not him. Then the clock ran out.

Find Out More

If you'd like to encounter more of Ivan Tuttle's story, we encourage you to pick up a copy of his book *A Journey to Hell, Heaven, and Back* (It's Supernatural!, 2020) as well as Randy Kay and Shaun Tabatt's book *Real Near Death Experience Stories: True Accounts of Those Who Died and Experienced Immortality* (Destiny Image, 2022). You can also connect with Ivan at IvanTuttle.com.

Captain Dale Black

At age 19, Dale Black was the only survivor of an airplane crash. In the aftermath of that fatal crash, Dale suffered extensive life-threatening injuries and was taken into Heaven where he received a deep revelation of God's love and God's ways.

Following the crash, it would take supernatural intervention from the Lord if he was ever going to walk again, use his left arm, or see out of his right eye. His dream of becoming an airline pilot now seemed impossible. As Dale's story unfolds, you'll see how God equipped Dale with the faith to overcome impossible obstacles again and again.

Find Out More

If you'd like to encounter more of Captain Dale Black's story, we encourage you to pick up a copy of his book, *Visiting Heaven: Heavenly Keys to a Life Without Limitations* (Destiny Image, 2023) as well as Randy Kay and Shaun Tabatt's book *Real Near Death Experience Stories: True Accounts of Those Who Died and Experienced Immortality* (Destiny Image, 2022). You can also connect with Dale at DaleBlack.org.

Mike Olsen

Louisville, Kentucky pastor Mike Olsen suffered for several years with idiopathic pulmonary fibrosis, a disease that kills almost as many patients as breast cancer. Mike was relieved when he received a call from the doctor letting him know that they had received a pair of lungs for him.

During his much-needed lung transplant surgery on January 7, 2019, tragedy struck when the last clamp was removed. Mike bled out, flat-lined, and was dead for a period of time.

Mike had many wonderful experiences on the other side of the veil, most notably meeting his organ donor!

Find Out More

If you'd like to encounter more of Mike Olsen's story, we encourage you to pick up a copy of Randy Kay and Shaun Tabatt's book *Real Near Death Experience Stories: True Accounts of Those Who Died and Experienced Immortality* (Destiny Image, 2022). You can also connect with Mike Olsen at www.facebook.com/Mike-Olsen-Project-179664296283994.

Mark McDonough

When Mark McDonough was a teenager, a catastrophic house fire claimed the lives of his mother and younger brother. Mark had burns on over 65 percent of his body. Ten days after the fire Mark experienced a life-altering NDE during surgery.

Find Out More

If you would like to encounter more of Mark McDonough's story, we encourage you to pick up a copy of his book *Forged through Fire: A Reconstructive Surgeon's Story of Survival, Faith, and Healing* (Revell, 2019). You can also connect with Mark at DrMarkMcd.com.

Joe Joe Morris

Joe Joe Morris grew up in a family that bounced around between multiple Mennonite communities. His life was plagued by depression, anger, sleep paralysis, bedwetting, and other challenges. After hearing his neck snap, Joe Joe discovered that he was out of his body and found himself in Heaven's throne room.

Find Out More

You can connect with Joe Joe at xmenno.com.

Karina Ferrigno Martinez

Karina Ferrigno Martinez left the hospital to be with her kids on Mother's Day and died in her backyard.

Retah McPherson and Aldo McPherson

Retah McPherson's son, Aldo, suffered a severe brain injury due to a car accident when he was 12 years old. During his coma, he had a supernatural experience in which he went to Heaven, saw God, angels, Moses, and Abraham. Aldo came back with one message: *Jesus is alive!*

Find Out More

If you would like to encounter more of Reatah and Aldo McPherson's story, we encourage you to pick up a copy of their book *A Message from God: A 12-Year-Old Boy's Experience in Heaven* (Destiny Image, 2008). You can also connect with Retah and Aldo at RetahMcherson.com.